MONICA

WOMEN IN ANTIQUITY

Series Editors: Ronnie Ancona and Sarah B. Pomeroy

This book series provides compact and accessible introductions to the life and historical times of women from the ancient world. Approaching ancient history and culture broadly, the series selects figures from the earliest of times to late antiquity.

Cleopatra
A Biography
Duane W. Roller

Clodia Metelli
The Tribune's Sister
Marilyn B. Skinner

Galla Placidia
The Last Roman Empress
Hagith Sivan

Arsinoë of Egypt and Macedon
A Royal Life
Elizabeth Donnelly Carney

Berenice II and the Golden Age of Ptolemaic Egypt
Dee L. Clayman

Faustina I and II
Imperial Women of the Golden Age
Barbara M. Levick

Turia
A Roman Woman's Civil War
Josiah Osgood

Monica
An Ordinary Saint
Gillian Clark

MONICA

AN ORDINARY SAINT

Gillian Clark

OXFORD
UNIVERSITY PRESS

OXFORD

UNIVERSITY PRESS

Oxford University Press is a department of the University of
Oxford. It furthers the University's objective of excellence in research,
scholarship, and education by publishing worldwide.

Oxford   New York
Auckland   Cape Town   Dar es Salaam   Hong Kong   Karachi
Kuala Lumpur   Madrid   Melbourne   Mexico City   Nairobi
New Delhi   Shanghai   Taipei   Toronto

With offices in
Argentina   Austria   Brazil   Chile   Czech Republic   France   Greece
Guatemala   Hungary   Italy   Japan   Poland   Portugal   Singapore
South Korea   Switzerland   Thailand   Turkey   Ukraine   Vietnam

Oxford is a registered trademark of Oxford University Press
in the UK and certain other countries.

Published in the United States of America by
Oxford University Press
198 Madison Avenue, New York, NY 10016

Library of Congress Cataloging-in-Publication Data

Clark, Gillian (E. Gillian)
Monica : an ordinary saint / Gillian Clark.
pages cm. — (Women in antiquity)
Includes bibliographical references.
ISBN 978–0–19–998838–9 (hardcover : alk. paper) — ISBN 978–0–19–998839–6 (pbk. : alk. Paper)
1. Monica, Saint, –387. 2. Christian saints—Algeria—Biography. I. Title.
BR1720.M66C53 2014
270.2092—dc23
[B]
2013037099

1 3 5 7 9 8 6 4 2
Printed in the United States of America
on acid-free paper

For Austin's mother

Contents

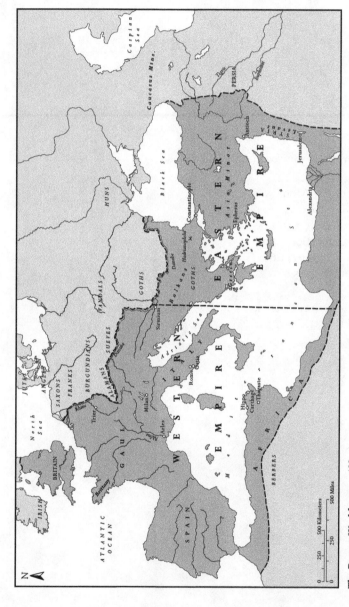

The Roman Worlds ca. AD 400

The World of Monica

Source: Bryan Ward-Perkins, *The Fall of Rome and the End of Civilization* (Oxford and New York: Oxford University Press, 2005).

1

Introduction to Monica

In a scene from a sixteenth-century cycle of paintings, a middle-aged woman in blue sits listening intently as a bishop preaches.[1] Her name is Monica, and she is one of the best known women of classical antiquity. At the time of this imagined scene, in the mid-380s CE, she is a widow in her early fifties. She is listening to Ambrose, a former governor of the North Italian region still known as Emilia, who is now bishop of its capital city of Milan. For her first fifty years Monica led a domestic life in North Africa, known only to her family and friends. For the first forty of those years, she lived in or near the little inland town of Thagaste, where she married a man called Patricius. They had two sons and a daughter, and one of those sons is the reason why she has travelled from Thagaste, first to Carthage, the capital of North Africa, and later across the sea to Italy. Monica is the mother of Augustine, who used the education she helped to finance, his own ability, and some influential contacts, to achieve the publicly funded post of professor of rhetoric at Milan. The city is an imperial capital, and his duties include speeches in praise of the emperor. The painter shows Augustine seated beside Monica, and places them in a church like those of his own time.

At Milan, Monica lives with Augustine, his partner, and their son, who is in his early teenage years. She has brought her other son Navigius and two cousins, and she mothers Augustine's friends and students.

1. www.cassiciaco.it/navigazione/iconografia/cicli/cinquecento/scorel/ambrogio.html, accessed 6 September 2013. Jan Scorel came from the Netherlands; on pilgrimage to Jerusalem, in 1520, he painted for the Church of St Stephen a large picture containing several scenes from the life of Augustine.

FIGURE 1.1. Monica and Augustine listen to sermon by Bishop Ambrose.
Ca. 1520, ascribed to Jan Scorel.

Erich Lessing/Art Resource, NY.

Ambrose praises her piety, and Augustine includes her in philosophical
discussions. Soon Augustine will renounce worldly ambition for a life
of prayer and study, and Monica will travel with him when he decides to
return to Africa. But she will die at Ostia at the age of 55 as they wait for
a passage from Italy. Four years later, her son will become Augustine of
Hippo, priest and then bishop of a North African seaport. In 397 CE, ten
years after her death, Augustine will write about her in his *Confessions*,
which will provide the material for Jan Scorel's painting and for many
other interpretations of Monica. Augustine is one of the most influential theologians in western tradition, and that is why Monica is one of
the best known women of classical antiquity.

We know the name of Monica, wife of Patricius, only from the
prayer which concludes book 9 of the *Confessions*:

> So let her be in peace with her husband, before whom and
> after whom she was married to no one, whom she served

bringing you profit by her patience, so that she could win him also for you. Inspire, my Lord, my God, inspire your slaves, my brothers, your sons, my masters, whom I serve with heart and voice and writings, that all who read this may remember at your altar Monica, your slave, with Patricius, once her spouse, through whose flesh you brought me into this life, how I do not know. (Augustine, *Conf.* 9.13.37)[2]

We do not know whose daughter she was, because Augustine did not say, and his writings are the only source for her life. We have only Augustine's Monica: only what Augustine chose to say about his mother, as a character in the philosophical dialogues he wrote (386 CE) in the year before her death, a decade later as a major presence in the *Confessions*, and in occasional comments in other writings. But Monica is exceptional, both because she is a much more vivid character than other devoted mothers who were praised by their sons, and because she was a moderately prosperous woman who lived in a small provincial town of Roman Africa.

For the lives of women, at all periods of classical antiquity, we depend on men writing about women. There are hardly any texts written by women, because women hardly ever wrote for an audience, and when they wrote letters nobody (including Augustine) kept them.[3] Men did not write about moderately prosperous wives and mothers, unless as characters in comedies. You have only to look at the titles to date in this series: two queens, three empresses, and an aristocrat and another wealthy woman involved in scandals and power plays as the Roman republic fell apart.[4] So Monica is exceptional. She had no political role or influence, and was not a spectacular example of virtue or vice. She was not even rich enough to be locally known as a civic benefactor, commemorated in her hometown by statues and inscriptions, as one Annia Aelia Restituta was at nearby Calama.[5] Nor was she

2. See chapter 3 for the translation 'slave' rather than 'servant'.
3. On texts written by women, including letters, see chapter 4.
4. Duane Roller, *Cleopatra: A Biography* (2010); Marilyn Skinner, *Clodia Metelli: The Tribune's Sister* (2011); Hagith Sivan, *Galla Placidia: The Last Roman Empress* (2011); Elizabeth Carney, *Arsinoë of Egypt and Macedon: A Royal Life* (2013); Barbara Levick, *Faustina I and II: Imperial Women of the Golden Age* (2014); Josiah Osgood, *Turia: A Roman woman's Civil War* (2014).
5. *CIL* (*Corpus Inscriptionum Latinarum*) 8.5366. On women benefactors, see Emily Hemelrijk, 'Public Roles for Women in the Cities of the Latin West', in Sharon James and Sheila Dillon, eds., *A Companion to Women in the Ancient World* (2012), pp. 478–90. Annia Aelia Restituta (p. 483) was a *flaminica* (priestess of the traditional religion) at Calama, and gave a generous donation for a theatre; other examples from Africa pp. 486–7.

a heroine caught up in war or revolution. She was born (331 CE) late in the reign of Constantine, the first Roman emperor to give open support to Christianity, and in her lifetime there were civil wars and uprisings and outbreaks of violent religious and social conflict, but there is no evidence that they affected Monica or her family.[6]

Monica was a dutiful daughter who did what was expected of her. She was married at the appropriate age, probably in her late teenage years, to a moderately prosperous local man, who was probably some years older. She was a faithful and compliant wife; she had three children, and lived to see grandchildren. By Roman standards, this was an admirable life, but men did not write about such women. They were important to family and friends, but what else was there to say? In the first century CE, someone put it bluntly in his funeral oration for his mother Murdia, who is not otherwise known. The oration was inscribed on stone, and part of it survives.[7] Women could choose how to leave their property, and the speaker spent some time on Murdia's fair-minded distribution, which showed her loyalty to two husbands and her love for the children of both marriages. Then he observed:

> The praise of all good women is simple and similar,
> because their natural goodness, safeguarded by their own
> watchfulness, does not require diversity of words. It is
> enough that all have done the same deeds which deserve
> good reputation, and it is difficult to find new forms of praise
> for a woman, as their lives fluctuate with less diversity.
> So their common characteristics must be revered, in case
> something omitted from right teaching should detract from
> the rest. My dearest mother, then, earned greater praise

6. In the early 370s Roman troops fought Firmus, son of King Nubel of Mauretania, but this was far to the west of Monica's region. See this chapter on one encounter with civil war in 387, and see chapter 5 on religious conflict. For the political setting (of Augustine's lifetime, 354–430 CE, rather than Monica's, 331–87 CE), see Christopher Kelly, 'Political History: The Later Roman Empire', in Mark Vessey ed., *A Companion to Augustine* (2012), pp. 11–23; for an introduction to the political and social history of the period, see Averil Cameron, *The Later Roman Empire AD 284–430* (1993); for more detail, Averil Cameron and Peter Garnsey, eds., *The Cambridge Ancient History XII: The Late Empire, AD 337–425* (1997).

7. *ILS* 8394 = *CIL* VI.10230, also translated in Mary Lefkowitz and Maureen Fant, *Women's Life in Greece and Rome*, 3rd ed., n. 43, p. 18 (2005). See further Hugh Lindsay, 'The *laudatio Murdiae*: Its Content And Significance', *Latomus* 63 (2004), pp. 88–97 (reference owed to Josiah Osgood). On women's property, see chapter 3.

than all, because in modesty, integrity, chastity, deference, wool-working, industry, and loyalty she was equal and similar to other women of integrity, nor did she yield to any in the courage, effort and wisdom displayed in danger . . . (*Inscriptiones Latinae Selectae* 8394)[8]

Good women, this speaker says, live similar lives, which offer little variation or excitement, and they show similar good qualities. He praises them for homekeeping virtues, which do not include enterprise. Yet the last fragmentary sentence shows that Murdia lived through danger, perhaps in the civil wars which brought down the Roman republic, and that she, like other women, manifested the courage, effort, and wisdom more often associated with men. Similarly, Augustine praised his mother for deference to her husband, devotion to her son, peacemaking among her neighbours, and firm religious faith. But it is also clear from what he wrote that Monica was an intelligent and enterprising woman, who in widowhood managed the family finances, made the difficult journey from Africa to Italy, and in support of her bishop faced immediate danger from imperial troops.[9]

In the period known as late antiquity (third to sixth centuries CE, more or less), Christian authors became more interested in the lives of women, and more texts have survived because Christians were motivated to copy them and religious communities had the time and skill to do so.[10] These authors found spiritual struggles for eternal life just as interesting as transient political conflicts, and much more important. They wrote about women who died as martyrs, or who maintained their Christian commitment despite temptation and oppression.[11] They were especially interested in the ascetic life (from Greek *askēsis*, "training"), which was sometimes called the "long martyrdom". Ascetics trained the soul for life after death by detachment from bodily desires and from worldly goods and ambitions, and by leading an austere,

---

8. The text is incomplete (Lindsay 2004: 91). On wool-working, unexpected in this list of virtues, see chapter 2.

9. All these aspects of Monica's life are discussed later: finances in chapter 2, Monica's travels in this chapter, and the confrontation with imperial troops in chapter 5.

10. Gillian Clark, *Late Antiquity: A Very Short Introduction* (2011), pp. 1–12 on time-range, pp. 43–44 on survival of texts.

11. Tomas Hägg, *The Art of Biography in Antiquity* (2012) offers perceptive comments, especially pp. 8 and 386; examples in Carolinne White, *Lives of Roman Christian Women* (2010). See further chapter 6.

preferably celibate, life of prayer and study.[12] This was a longstanding philosophical tradition, followed in its more rigorous forms only by a small number of men. But in late antiquity some powerful voices argued that everyone could do it: women as well as men could override human biology and human desire for a spouse and children, and could avoid the constraints of gender roles and of obligations to family and to fellow citizens. In Monica's lifetime, some men began to write about the lives and virtues of holy women known to them, and some women made a spectacular renunciation of wealth and social status. Women travelled to the Holy Land or to visit the monks of Egypt and Syria, funded buildings for monastic communities, and themselves lived in great austerity.[13]

If Monica was even aware of such possibilities, she did not try to emulate them. She did not suffer persecution for her faith, whether from family members, Roman officials, or, except for one temporary threat, Christians who had a different interpretation of Christianity.[14] She was not a martyr or an ascetic. She was a good Christian who showed love of God and love of neighbour. She went regularly to church, heard and read the scriptures, and prayed. She was a peacemaker in her household and among her neighbours, and she was charitable to the poor. In accordance with both Roman and Christian ideals, Monica was the wife of one husband, and in accordance with Christian ideals, her example made her husband Christian: 'women, subjected to your own husbands, so that if any do not believe in the Word, they will be gained without a word by the behaviour of their wives, observing your behaviour [which is] pure in fear [of the Lord]' (1 Peter 3:1–2).[15] All this made her an admirable woman by the standards of the time, but without Augustine, we would never have heard of Monica unless her gravestone had survived by chance, and even then we would know very little. Christians were perhaps more likely than non-Christians to commemorate women as well as men, but the gravestones of women continued to praise their

12. Brief account in Gillian Clark, *Christianity and Roman Society* (2004), pp. 60–77; for changing concepts of asceticism, Peter Brown, *The Body and Society* (1988); and for fourth-century debates, David Hunter, *Marriage, Celibacy and Heresy in Ancient Christianity* (2007). See further chapter 5.

13. For some of the best-known examples, see chapter 6.

14. See chapter 5 on the attempt of the empress Justina to take over a church in Milan.

15. On wives 'subjected' to husbands, see chapter 3.

modesty and fidelity, and many said little more than name, age at death, and a formulaic "rest in peace".[16]

So how did it happen that this ordinary woman is among the best known women of classical antiquity, and that she became a saint? The simple answer is 'because Monica was the mother of Saint Augustine, one of the most influential writers of western tradition, and he wrote about her'. But this is not so simple, for some scholars argue that we know nothing about women in antiquity: all we have is texts constructed by rhetorically trained men, so all we can do is to explore how, and for what purposes, those texts construct women.[17] It is true that there is very little written by women at any period of classical antiquity, and that apart from the writings of Augustine there is no means of access to Monica, who lived in the fourth century CE in Africa and Italy, but it does not follow that we should give up the attempt to understand more about women's lives. Men were taught to use rhetoric to persuade hearers and readers in a particular context, so their purposes and constructions tell us something about what they thought would be persuasive, and therefore about the expectations which helped to shape the lives of women. Moreover, their writings reveal aspects of everyday life which they took for granted. Augustine's writings, an extraordinary range of books and letters and sermons, often give insights into life in Africa and Italy when he deals with a pastoral problem, tells a story, finds an example, or explains an image in the Bible. His early philosophical dialogues and his *Confessions*, the two main sources for Monica, are especially rich in social detail. Other authors provide confirmation or contrast, and material culture helps to illustrate the conditions of life. As the son of the unknown Murdia observed in his funeral oration, it is difficult to say something specific about an individual woman, rather than speaking as if all good women were the same. But in a half-century

16. On gender parity in Christian commemorations of the dead at Rome and in Africa, see Dennis Trout, '*Fecit ad astra viam*: Daughters, Wives, and the Metrical Epitaphs of Late Ancient Rome', *Journal of Early Christian Studies* 21.1 (2013), 1–25, at p. 14; pp. 21–22 for traditional themes. On the content of standard epitaphs, see Brent D. Shaw, 'Latin Funerary Epigraphy and Family Life in the Later Roman Empire', *Historia* 33 (1984), 457–97, at p. 467.

17. Elizabeth Clark, 'The Lady Vanishes: Dilemmas of a Feminist Historian after the "Linguistic Turn"', *Church History* 67.1 (1998), 1–31, has been especially influential. For her discussion of "Monica-functions" in Augustine's texts, see 'Rewriting Early Christian History: Augustine's Representation of Monica', in Jan Drijvers and John Watt, eds., *Portraits of Spiritual Authority* (1999), pp. 3–23.

of research on women in antiquity, it has become possible to be more precise about differences in time and place and social status.

Augustine did not leave a separate '*Life of Monica*', and his longest continuous account of her is not very long. It is a passage of *Confessions* (9.8.17–11.28) in which, he said, he recorded what his soul brought to birth about the woman who gave birth to him. Monica's life story has to be reconstructed from his observations in various writings, supplemented where possible from general information about this time and place. To begin with her name: it was probably spelled Monnica, as it is in the earliest manuscripts of *Confessions* and in some inscriptions from the region where she grew up. Roman Africa was the western range of the Mediterranean coastal region, extending through present-day Tunisia and including parts of Algeria and Libya.[18] Separated from Egypt by a stretch of barren land, the province of Africa belonged to the western, Latin-speaking part of the Roman Empire, and its capital Carthage was a short sea crossing from Italy. Some people feel strongly that 'Monnica' links this woman more closely to her African homeland, whereas the traditional 'Monica' claims her for Roman culture and its later reception.[19]

Augustine said nothing about the social level of his mother's family, but presumably it was close to that of her husband Patricius, who was not very rich, but rich enough to serve on the council of a small town that needed everyone it could get.[20] As was usual for girls, Monica was not formally educated in literature and rhetoric, because women did not have the public roles in which these skills were deployed.[21] Augustine specified her age at marriage only in a phrase from Virgil (*Aeneid* 7.53), *plenis nubilis annis*, literally 'marriageable in full years'. This has no precise meaning. In Roman law marriage was valid at age 12, and it was often said that girls reached a peak of beauty at that age, but doctors knew that it was dangerous for a girl to bear children before she was fully grown.[22] Two Roman aristocrats whose lives overlapped with

18. See map—*The World of Monica*, and for further information William Klingshirn, 'Cultural Geography: Roman North Africa', in Vessey (see n. 6), pp. 24–39. Detailed maps are available on line at www9.georgetown.edu/faculty/jod/augustine/ (accessed 14 June 2013), in 'Research Materials and Essays' under the heading 'Augustine's Africa'.

19. See chapter 5 for the debate on whether, and in what sense, Monnica was Berber. 'Monnica' is increasingly used by specialists, but for this book I have accepted the editors' view that 'Monica' is more widely recognized.

20. For service on the council, see chapter 2.

21. See chapter 4.

22. Gillian Clark, *Women in Late Antiquity* (1993), pp. 80–81.

Monica's are known to have married early; the information survives because both women were of interest to Christian authors as ascetics who renounced their wealth and status. Melania the elder, born some years earlier than Monica, had three children, and had also suffered several miscarriages by the time she was widowed at age 22; Melania the younger, her granddaughter, married at 13, and both her children died in infancy.[23] Wealthy aristocratic families such as these may have preferred early marriage for heiresses, and there is not enough evidence, from literary texts or from funerary inscriptions, to generalize about marriage age across social class and regions. But it is at least a possibility that many women married in their late teens.[24]

Monica was widowed before she was 40, and this suggests that, as was common, her husband was some years older than she was.[25] If she did marry in her late teens, Augustine, born when she was 23, was probably not her eldest child. That guess may be strengthened by his love for Jesus' story of the prodigal son (Luke 15:11–32), in which the younger son (Augustine, *Conf.* 1.18.28) goes off to foreign lands while the older brother dutifully works on the family farm. Monica had another son, Navigius, and a daughter, whose name is not known. Some reference works call her Perpetua, the name of a famous African martyr. This tradition goes back to one of the many works ascribed to Augustine, a letter addressed to his sister Perpetua about the holy life and death of their mother. Monica's daughter was probably named for one of her grandmothers, but there is no evidence for their names or for hers.[26] Augustine had little to say about his brother, and mentioned his sister only in one letter to a community of religious women (*ep.* 211.4), which refers to 'my sister' the former head of the community. His biographer Possidius, a friend and fellow-bishop, confirms (*Vita Aug.* 26.1) that 'my sister' means a family member, Augustine's widowed sister, as well as a sister in Christ. Augustine's silence about his siblings has puzzled commentators, but it is not unique. His contemporaries Basil of Caesarea and Gregory of Nyssa, who like him were bishops and renowned

23. On Melania the elder, Palladius, *Lausiac History* 46.1; on the younger, ibid., 61.3.
24. Brent D. Shaw, 'The Age of Roman Girls at Marriage: Some Reconsiderations', *Journal of Roman Studies* 77 (1987), 30–46.
25. This is a calculation. Augustine was 32 when his mother died at 55 (*Conf.* 9.11.28), so she was 23 when he was born; Patricius died two years before Augustine was 18 (*Conf.* 3.4.7).
26. On naming practices, see chapter 5; on the martyr Perpetua, see chapter 4. The letter of pseudo-Augustine is included in the *Acta Sanctorum 05 Maii* i. 480–1: see further chapter 6.

FIGURE 1.2. The Medjerda River at Souk Ahras (Thagaste).
Wikimedia Commons. http://commons.wikimedia.org/wiki/File:Medjerda.jpg

theologians, were the brothers of four sisters, one of whom was the virgin ascetic Macrina. They do not mention the three who married.[27]

Monica lived to see grandchildren, and we know the names of two. Adeodatus was born when Augustine was a student at Carthage, in the first year of a long-lasting relationship (*Conf.* 4.2.2). Patricius (*ser.* 356.3) was named for his grandfather, and so was probably the son of Navigius who also had two daughters (Possidius, *Vita Aug.* 26.1). There is no mention of children born to Monica's daughter, but this need not mean she was childless; perhaps her children counted as part of her husband's family, or perhaps they did not join her in Augustine's Christian network.

Monica spent most of her life in the small inland town of Thagaste, as a wife and mother among her family and neighbours, and planned to be buried there beside her husband (*Conf.* 9.11.28).[28] In widowhood, she found new possibilities, as her clever son Augustine made good use of the education she helped to fund. In 373/4 CE, when Monica was in her early forties, he became a teacher of rhetoric at the provincial capital, Carthage. She may have spent some time in Carthage with Augustine,

27. For Macrina, see chapters 4 and 5. Opinions differ on whether Basil and Gregory took no interest in the lives of sisters who married and moved away, or simply lacked information: see Raymond Van Dam, *Families and Friends in Late Roman Cappadocia* (2003), p. 94.

28. See chapter 2 for Monica's house and daily life.

his partner, and her grandson Adeodatus. She was there ten years later, when, despite her pleas, Augustine left Carthage for Italy, with the aim of teaching in Rome. He was soon appointed professor of rhetoric at Milan, and Monica crossed the sea and travelled overland to join him. At Milan, she took part in philosophical discussions with Augustine and his friends and students. She was with him when he decided to resign his post, abandon his plans for marriage and career, and lead a life of service to God. She started on the journey home with him when he chose to serve God by living in their family house at Thagaste, in a small community devoted to prayer and study. Their return was delayed because civil war made the sea crossing unsafe, and while they waited at the port of Ostia, Monica died of fever at the age of 55. She told her sons that it did not matter where her body was buried, but asked them to remember her, wherever they were, at the altar of the Lord.[29]

That is a straightforward account of Monica's life and family. This book aims to show how Monica's life raises wider questions about the lives of women, and how we can use texts and archaeology and comparative studies to make a start on answering those questions and on learning more about Monica. Here are some examples, beginning with a seemingly small point: Augustine said, in passing, that two years after his father died, he was a student at Carthage, and his mother paid for his studies (*Conf.* 3.4.7). Patricius and Monica had invested in Augustine's education, sending him away to school at Madauros, a day's journey inland from Thagaste, and accumulating funds for his higher education (*Conf.* 2.3.5).[30] They hoped this would lead to a career in the imperial civil service, from which the whole family would benefit. When Patricius died, Monica continued the investment, with help from a richer neighbour, Romanianus (*c. Acad.* 2.2.3). Did she use her own inherited or acquired property, which was legally separate from her husband's, or did Patricius leave her in control of the family property? Roman law required men to leave their property to their legal heirs, in this case the three children. If (as often happened) the daughter had her share as her dowry on marriage, the remaining property would be divided between Augustine and Navigius, who were old enough not to need legal guardians. But it seems that Monica was in charge, just

29. See chapter 6 on what this meant.
30. On Madauros (now Mdaourouch), see Claude Lepelley, *Les cités de l'Afrique romaine.* Vol. 2. (1978), 126–39. The town was famous as the home of Apuleius, orator, philosopher, and author of the novel *The Golden Ass* (also called *Metamorphoses*).

as in Cappadocia her much wealthier contemporary Emmelia—mother of the ascetic Macrina, of the bishops Basil and Gregory, and of six or seven other children—seems to have been in charge when her husband died soon after the birth of their youngest son.[31]

The official view was that women were not suited to having responsibility for other people. In 295 CE, for example, the emperor Diocletian (or one of his officials in his name) replied to a query 'it is accepted that taking on the protection of another person is a man's job, and beyond the female sex: so if your son is a minor, request a guardian for him' (*CJ* (*Codex Justinianus*) 2.12.18). There are many examples of widows who needed help to protect their children's inheritance in the unfamiliar world of tax demands and lawsuits.[32] Anthousa, mother of Augustine's contemporary John Chrysostom, told her son how difficult it had been for her, as a widow of the age of 20 with two small children, to make the slaves do what she told them and to fend off tax collectors and predatory relatives (John Chrysostom, *On the Priesthood* 1.5, 390/1 CE). But some widows were obviously competent. Roman law came to accept that a mother or grandmother could be the legal guardian of her children or grandchildren, provided she took an oath not to remarry: this avoided any threat to the inheritance from stepfathers and second families. Monica's children did not need a guardian, and her family, like most families, made its own arrangements; unless someone challenged them, there was no need for Roman law to take notice.[33] Chapter 2, 'Monica's House', considers the resources of Augustine's family, and what followed for the domestic life of Monica. Augustine said that he was 'the poor son of poor parents', but what counts as 'poor'? Where in relation to the town of Thagaste was the house and land of Patricius, what was the house like, and how was it managed? Archaeologists now seek to reconstruct how a place felt and sounded and smelled as well as how it looked. We cannot assume that the experience of sights and spaces, sounds and odours, was the same for people who lived in Roman Africa in the fourth century, but we can make some progress in that understanding.

Domestic life had a darker side. Augustine cited Monica's advice to her neighbours on how not to be a battered wife (*Conf.* 9.9.19). She

31. For Emmelia and her family, see chapter 6.
32. Van Dam (see n. 27), pp. 100–1.
33. On women as legal guardians, see A. Arjava, *Women and Law in Late Antiquity* (1996), pp. 89–94.

said that they were to consider the marriage contract as a contract of sale, making them the slaves of their husbands, and to behave accordingly. She said it as a joke, but she meant it, and in sermons Augustine too told wives to regard themselves as slaves. Other wives in Thagaste had visible bruises because they complained about the way of life of their husbands; this meant, in particular, infidelity. But Monica tolerated infidelity and never confronted her husband when he was angry. She waited until he calmed down before explaining that he might have misunderstood. So, in the small town where everyone knew everything, nobody saw her bruised, and the word never went round that the hot-tempered Patricius had beaten his wife. Is this a rare exposure of the general experience of women in antiquity, or was Roman Africa unusually tolerant of wife beating?[34] Chapter 3, 'Monica's Service', considers what men regarded as acceptable behaviour, and why Augustine challenged their infidelity but did not challenge domestic violence.

In Augustine's writings, Monica the widow appears before Monica the wife. The philosophical dialogues he wrote in 386 show Monica in her fifties, on vacation in a country house outside Milan with Augustine, his students, and some other family members. She has much more free time than in her earlier married life, and is able to take part in philosophical discussions. She has had no formal education in the use of language and in techniques of argument, and she is not familiar with classical literature, but Augustine presents her as quick to understand and clear and forceful in expression. She has learned both from hearing her son teach his students and from her own prayerful reading of the scriptures that she has heard expounded in church. Is Augustine's Monica exceptional, or does she show that other women had opportunities to learn? Chapter 4, 'Monica's Education', looks for answers in comparison with three women of Monica's time who were called philosophers: Hypatia of Alexandria, a rare example of a non-Christian woman who chose not to marry;[35] Sosipatra, divinely inspired philosopher, wife, and mother; and Macrina, virgin ascetic.

In *Confessions*, Monica is always and unquestionably a member of the Catholic Church, and her prayers and tears connect Augustine

---

34. Patricia Clark, 'Women, Slaves and the Hierarchy of Domestic Violence', in Sandra Joshel and Sheila Murnaghan, eds., *Women and Slaves in Greco-Roman Culture* (1998), pp. 109–29; Leslie Dossey, 'Wife-Beating and Manliness in Late Antiquity', *Past and Present* 199 (2008), 3–40.

35. A book on Hypatia is expected in this series.

with the church however far he strays. When he joins the Manichaeans, who had a very different interpretation of Christianity, she considers refusing to eat with him or share a house with him (*Conf.* 3.11.19).[36] But was her membership in the Catholic Church always so unquestionable? Chapter 5, 'Monica's Religion', considers alternative paths in a society which was still largely pagan. A rival group called Donatists claimed that theirs was the true Catholic Church, which had not betrayed the faith in time of persecution.[37] Some Christians, known as Arians, claimed that their understanding of Christ the Son and God the Father was the true Christian doctrine.[38] Some Christians argued that the true Christian life required women not to marry, but to live a celibate life of prayer.

Monica has been remembered and interpreted in many ways, and chapter 6, 'Saint Monica', outlines this story. Except for a commemorative inscription at Ostia, where she died, there is almost total silence for eight centuries after her death. Then, as Saint Augustine became increasingly important in medieval theology and church politics, his mother became Saint Monica, patron of devout and anxious mothers, remembered for centuries chiefly as the woman to whom a bishop once said 'the son of such tears cannot be lost' (*Conf.* 3.12.21). Ambrose, bishop of Milan, used to congratulate Augustine on having 'such a mother' (*Conf.* 6.2.2), and much reverent affection has been expended on this theme, in accordance with the ideals of motherhood current at the time of writing. The twentieth century saw new departures, as psychological and feminist theories were used to argue that Monica's tears did not save her son: on the contrary, they controlled him, and her unhealthy devotion helps to explain his unacceptable views on sex, sin, and the subordination of women.[39] Monica's constant weeping could be interpreted as evidence of depression in a woman whose life lacked possibilities, so that she had to live through her son.[40] But tears are understood

36. On Manichaeism, named for its prophet Mani, see chapter 5.
37. On Donatists, named for Donatus, one of their leaders, see chapter 5.
38. On Arians, named for Arius, a priest of Alexandria, see chapter 5.
39. For examples of psychological approaches, see Peter Walcot, 'Plato's Mother and Other Terrible Women', in Ian McAuslan and Peter Walcot, eds., *Women in Antiquity*, 114–33 (1996), pp. 126–30, on Monica. The essays in Judith Chelius Stark, ed., *Feminist Interpretations of Augustine* (2005) bring together the personal and the theological, offering different perspectives on his personal relationships with women and on the connections between his experience and his theological views.
40. Kim Power, *Veiled Desire: Augustine's Writings on Women* (1995), p. 265, n. 121. Power's overall estimate of Monica is much more positive: p. 92.

differently in different cultural contexts. In late antiquity, some ascetics prayed for the 'gift of tears' which would enable them to weep unceasingly for their sins. In the narrative of *Confessions* the purpose of Monica's tears is to maintain the connection between her errant son and the Church, just as in the *Odyssey* Penelope's tears for her absent husband maintain the connection between the wandering Odysseus and his home on Ithaca.[41] Moreover, just as feminist scholars have revalued Penelope as a shrewd tactician and female counterpart of Odysseus, not a helpless woman who sits around weeping and weaving, so Augustine's Monica can be revalued.

The society in which Monica lived did not offer women education or a career. She had no option other than marriage, which made her, in her own interpretation, the slave of her husband. If her husband was abusive, there was little or no support from law or from local culture. In such circumstances a woman might be demoralized or might inflict her bitterness on others, but Monica, according to her son, was respected by her husband, waited for the right time to speak, and never passed on hostile gossip (*Conf.* 9.9.21). Augustine's account also shows, although he does not explicitly say, that Monica was enterprising and adaptable. He praised her as a devoted mother who travelled over land and sea to be with him, and travel was something he did not take lightly. African clergy often found it was 'time to sail' to lobby and gather information in Italy. Augustine's friend Alypius did so four times after he became bishop of inland Thagaste, but Augustine, bishop of a seaport, never went to sea. His two sea journeys from Carthage to Italy (383 CE) and back (387 CE) were enough for him. In his writings, the sea is an image of earthly life: bitter, unstable, and dangerous.[42] Monica, widowed soon after 370 CE, was in her forties or early fifties when she travelled overland from her inland town to Carthage, a journey of about 175 miles. Before that, she had probably never seen the sea. Augustine left it unclear whether she made this journey once, then lived with him, his partner and their son in the years when he taught at Carthage (c. 375–383). If she did live in Carthage, it is surprising that he says nothing about her churchgoing in Carthage, in those years when he was Manichaean, or about any contact with its bishop.[43] In any event she did

41. Tears: see Thorsten Fögen, ed., *Tears in the Graeco-Roman World* (2009); Philip Burton, *Language in the Confessions of Augustine* (2007), pp. 151–64.

42. O. Perler, *Les Voyages de Saint Augustin* (1969), is the classic study. Augustine's travels by land help to date his letters and sermons: for a map of his journeys, see Klingshirn (n. 6), p. 31.

43. See chapter 5.

not lose touch with the family in Thagaste, for when Augustine moved to Milan, Monica followed with his brother Navigius and two cousins.[44] She was in her fifties when she crossed the sea to Italy (384 CE) and adapted to life in Milan, an imperial capital with different church customs.[45] She did not need to go. She could have stayed in the family house with Navigius and his family, just as her own mother-in-law stayed on when Patricius married Monica.

Some readers of this book are interested in the lives of women in different times and places, and in what women expected, or were expected, to do and say and think. Some want to know how this ordinary woman came to be seen as a Christian saint, that is, as a holy person (Latin *sancta*) who is especially close to God. Chapter 6 will try to answer that question, again in comparison with women of Monica's time who were presented as paragons: Emmelia, mother of the bishops Gregory of Nyssa and Basil of Caesarea, and her eldest child Macrina; Nonna, mother of their friend and fellow bishop Gregory of Nazianzus, and his sister Gorgonia; and the Roman aristocrats Marcella and Paula, who were eulogized by Jerome. Augustine did not claim that his mother was a saint, but he did think that the challenges of everyday life require courage and commitment to Christian principle. Monica's life, as he told it, showed both.

Augustine writing about Monica

The two main sources for Monica present her differently because they were written at very different times in Augustine's life. Both were times of crisis. The philosophical dialogues of 386 CE are Augustine's earliest extant writings; we know this from the *Retractationes*, the annotated chronological list of his books, which he compiled late in his life, starting from the time of his commitment to Christianity.[46] Monica, as a participant, is proof that a faithful Christian can attain wisdom without the formal education in language, literature, and rhetoric to which Augustine had devoted his life until that time, first as student and then

44. See chapter 4.
45. On conditions of travel, see Stéphanie Guédon, *Le voyage dans l'Afrique romaine* (2010), pp. 80–99, on transport and places to stay, 167–80 on security risks. The 'journey over land and sea' is discussed later in this chapter.
46. See further chapter 4.

as teacher.[47] In the *Confessions,* begun in 397 CE, Augustine explained how in 386, aged 31, he had decided not to pursue his career as a teacher of rhetoric. Education and contacts had taken him from his hometown Thagaste, where he briefly taught literature (*Conf.* 4.4.7), to Carthage, capital of the province of Africa, where he had been a student and, in 375/6, became a teacher of rhetoric (ibid. 6.7.22). In 383 he crossed the sea to Rome (5.8.14), the traditional capital of empire, in hopes of less disruptive students. Teaching in Rome presented different problems, but he was soon appointed to the publicly funded post of professor of rhetoric at Milan (5.13.23), a capital city with an imperial court in residence. He had hopes of moving into the imperial civil service, as other expert speakers had done, and Monica, who joined him in Milan, helped to negotiate a marriage that would advance his career (6.11.19, 6.13.23). But he chose to resign his professorship, abandon his marriage plans, and give in his name for baptism by Ambrose, bishop of Milan (9.5.13). In Augustine's view, Christian commitment entailed a celibate life of prayer and study, but he had not decided how, in practice, he should lead such a life (9.8.17).[48]

After Augustine's baptism (Easter 387 CE), he and Monica, with other family members and friends, decided to return to Africa. They waited at Ostia, the port of Rome, until it was safe to sail. On this occasion civil war did affect their lives, though Augustine did not mention it. They left Milan shortly before Magnus Maximus moved from Trier to displace Valentinian II, the young emperor for whom Augustine had delivered praise-speeches. Valentinian took refuge with Theodosius I, ruler of the eastern Roman Empire; Theodosius invaded Italy, and fighting continued until 388. In this time of waiting Monica died, perhaps from malaria, when she was 55 and Augustine was 32. They had expected to lead a life of prayer and study in the family house at Thagaste, and for a while Augustine did so. But four years after Monica's death he became Augustine of Hippo, first (in 391 CE) as a Christian priest assisting the bishop of this coastal town, then (in 395 CE) as co-bishop.

According to Augustine, and to his biographer Possidius (*Vita Aug.* 3–4), this major change in Augustine's life was not planned.[49]

---

47. On late antique education, see Robert Kaster, *Guardians of Language: The Grammarian and Society in Late Antiquity* (1988); Raffaella Cribiore, *Gymnastics of the Mind* (2001). See further chapter 4.

48. For Augustine's developing ideas about the 'philosophic life', see Gillian Clark, 'Philosopher: Augustine in Retirement', in Vessey (see n. 6), pp. 257–69.

49. Possidius had his own agenda in writing the life of Augustine: see Erika Hermanowicz, *Possidius of Calama* (2008).

Augustine said (*ser.* 355.2) that he had not wanted to be a bishop, and had avoided towns that were looking for a bishop. But he visited Hippo, which already had a bishop, in an attempt to convert a friend, and the congregation seized upon him. Augustine knew that the responsibilities of a bishop's life, the 'bishop's burden' (*ep.* 86.1) of preaching and pastoral work, arbitration, and correspondence, were not compatible with a life of prayer and study. But he was just the kind of man a congregation would want. He had shown his commitment by renouncing his property and his worldly ambitions, but he was still able to fulfil the important social role of a late antique bishop.[50] Bishops could be asked to act as arbitrators in disputes, and were expected to intervene with local officials to get help for their towns or to plead for mitigation of punishment. Augustine was an expert speaker, debater, and writer, and his worldly career had given him useful contacts and experience. Some present-day scholars, more sceptical than Possidius, suggest that the political situation at Milan was difficult enough to make Augustine resign his chair of rhetoric, hoping for Ambrose as his patron in the church. When that failed he kept his options open at Thagaste, using his *otium* (freedom from business) for study and discussion, as educated men did. It was only when his son Adeodatus died young that he gave up his share of the family property and looked for a place where he could become a bishop.[51] But, as Augustine said to readers of *Confessions*, how do they know what was in his heart? Only God knows that (10.3.3).

Augustine began *Confessions* when he was 43, ten years after Monica's death and six years after he was made a bishop. There are many theories on why he wrote the *Confessions*, and why then, but there are several reasons for saying that 397 CE, like 386, was a time of crisis for him.[52] Being a bishop was still a new experience, and he was challenged by opponents who remembered him as a Manichaean, not as a Catholic Christian. They could raise doubts about his baptism overseas

50. On what was expected of bishops, see Claudia Rapp, *Holy Bishops in Late Antiquity* (2005); on the content of the 'burden', see Neil McLynn, 'Administrator: Augustine in His Diocese', in Vessey (see n. 6), pp. 310–22.

51. James J. O'Donnell, *Augustine: Sinner and Saint* (2005), 58.

52. James J. O'Donnell, *Augustine: Confessions* (1992), 1. xli–li; brief account in Gillian Clark, *Augustine: Confessions 1–4* (1995), pp. 4–8. There is much debate on the relationship of books 1–9, which take the story of Augustine's life to his baptism and Monica's death, with books 10–11 on memory and time and books 12–13 on the creation narrative in Genesis. Some scholars think books 10–13 were added over the next three or four years.

without support from his home church. Why did he not show letters of commendation from the bishop of Milan? Why was he ordained priest without further investigation? They were right to object that Augustine should not have been consecrated as bishop of Hippo in the lifetime of his predecessor Valerius.[53] One purpose of *Confessions* is to set out Augustine's progress to Christian commitment, his recognition of past sins and errors, and his lifelong connection, through Monica, to the Catholic Church. Another purpose is to show how God acts in human lives: reading, reflection, and experience had convinced Augustine that people cannot escape sin without the freely given help of God, which Christians call grace (from Latin *gratia*, 'favour'). Perhaps also, as James O'Donnell (1992) suggests, physical illness once again gave him time to think about his life. In 386 CE it was chest problems (*Conf.* 9.2.4), in 397 it was piles. Augustine wrote to a friend 'in spirit, so far as the Lord pleases, I am well; in body I am in bed. I cannot walk or stand or sit from the pain and swelling of fissures and haemorrhoids' (*ep.* 38.1; he used the technical medical terms).[54] But he could dictate this letter, just as he dictated other works, to the secretaries who took them down in shorthand and had them transcribed. 'The writing of the *Confessions* was an act of therapy', Peter Brown wrote in his classic biography of Augustine, and O'Donnell observes that some projects which had been on hold were resumed or begun after *Confessions*, as if the book freed Augustine from writer's block.[55]

The explicit purpose of *Confessions* was confession in a double sense. Latin *confessio* means "acknowledgement": Augustine wanted to acknowledge the glory of God the Creator and Redeemer, with special reference to the ways in which, as he could now see, God had acted in his own life, and to acknowledge the sins and confusions which had alienated him from God. Monica is a constant presence, taking the child Augustine to church, praying for the young man however far he

53. In *ep.* 213.4, making arrangements for his own successor, Augustine explained 'When my father and bishop of blessed memory, Valerius, was an old man still in the body, I was ordained bishop, and sat [in authority] with him; I did not know that this had been forbidden by the Council of Nicaea, nor did he know.' This council of bishops, summoned by Constantine in 325, was supposed to have worldwide authority, but in practice its rulings were often disregarded or not reliably known.

54. O'Donnell (see n. 52) 1. xli. This experience helps to explain Augustine's deeply sympathetic account, in *civ.Dei* 22.8, of a friend who needed a second operation for anal fistula, but was miraculously healed.

55. Peter Brown, *Augustine of Hippo* (1967, rev. ed. 2000), p. 158; O'Donnell (see n. 52), 1. xliv.

strays, joining the grown man in Milan as he progresses to baptism and changes his way of life, and, at Ostia shortly before her death, sharing with him an experience of God's presence (*Conf.* 9.10.23–25).[56] It is sometimes suggested that Monica represents Mother Church nurturing her children, an image Augustine often used.[57] If so, this is not the Church as a splendid abstract, gendered feminine because in Greek and Latin the word for "church" is a feminine noun and because the New Testament speaks of the church as the bride of Christ (Ephesians 5:25). It is the church made up of imperfect human beings who get things wrong.

In *Confessions*, what Augustine says of Monica exemplifies his understanding of how God works in human life.[58] In his experience of growing up, episodes which others dismissed as trivial showed the fundamental problems of human nature: self-love, arrogance, and attraction to lesser goods. These problems alienate people from love of God and love of neighbour. A crying baby wants to get his own way, now, and to make others do what he wants (1.6.8). Parents urge their children to do well at school because, whatever they say, they want worldly success (1.12.19). A bored teenager with his friends steals pears he does not need or like, for no reason except that he wants to do something bad (2.6.12). Augustine thought that such challenges of everyday life undermine commitment to Christian teaching, and that this commitment is not possible without the grace of God.

Augustine told his congregation not to say 'there is no persecution now, so I can't be a martyr'. Christians, he said, can still bear witness to their faith, for even when persecution stops, temptation does not. The fight of the soul against temptation is not a public event like a martyrdom, but God sees it (*ser.* 328.9.6). Augustine used the dramatic example of someone weak with illness, who is offered spells and charms which promise a cure. This is a good example of his work as a source for social history:

56. On the episode known as the 'vision at Ostia', see chapter 4.

57. Joanne McWilliam, 'The Cassiciacum Autobiography', *Studia Patristica* 18.4 (1990), 14–43. A mosaic in Santa Sabina, Rome, constructed in Augustine's lifetime, shows *Ecclesia Mater* (Mother Church) as a woman swathed in the dark clothing of a widow or a nun, holding a book: see the illustration in F. Van der Meer, *Augustine the Bishop* (1961), opposite p. 200.

58. Garry Wills, *Augustine's Confessions: A Biography* (2011), p. 14, is among those who think that Augustine inserted into *Confessions* book 9 a tribute to Monica he had written at the time of her death. If he did use earlier material, he adapted it to the style and themes of the *Confessions*.

Some people, when their health is endangered, even if they are called Christians, seek out sorcerers, send to astrologers, hang unlawful remedies round their necks. [. . .] But this one says 'I don't do that' when a friend suggests it, and the neighbour or the neighbour's slave-woman whispers, or sometimes even someone on the charity-list.[59] This one says 'I don't do that. I am a Christian. God forbids this. They are hidden mysteries [*sacramenta*] of demons: hear the Apostle [Paul], "I do not want you to be associates of demons".' The one who suggests it replies 'Do it and you will be well. X and Y did it. Aren't they Christians? Aren't they baptized? Don't they go to church? But they did it and they are well. Z did it and was cured immediately. Don't you know he's a Christian, a baptized Christian? He did it and he's well.' [. . .] The fever does not subside; faith goes ahead to God. But here are the neighbour and the friend and the slave-woman, even, as I said, someone on the charity-list, carrying wax or an egg in their hands, and saying 'Do this and you will be well. Why make your illness last longer? Tie this on. I have heard someone who invokes the name of God and the angels over it, and you will be well.[60] Who will take care of your widow and children?' But he says 'I don't do that, because I am a Christian. Let me die in such a way that I do not die forever.' Hear the word of the martyr. See if this is not what the pagan used to say, 'sacrifice and you will live'. But he says 'I don't do that'. (*ser.* 335D 3, 5)

Augustine did not deny that amulets work, but he explained in *Christian Teaching* (*Doc. Chr.*) that they work only by agreement with demons about the meaning of the amulet: such agreements are the 'hidden mysteries of demons' in the sermon. 'It is one thing to say "if you drink this herb ground up, your belly will not hurt", and another thing to say "if you hang this herb round your neck, your belly will not hurt"' (*Doc. Chr.* 2.74–5, 2.111). So there is an explicit comparison between the present-day Christian who will not save his life by accepting the

59. To qualify for the bishop's charity-list (*matricula*), people had to be devout Christians who lacked other support.
60. See for such practices Theo de Bruyn and Jitse Dijkstra, 'Greek Amulets and Formularies from Egypt Containing Christian Elements', *Bulletin of the American Society of Papyrologists* 48 (2011), 163–216.

amulet, and the martyr from the days of persecution who will not save his life by sacrificing to the false gods. Both reply 'I am a Christian' and accept the risk of death. Most temptations are less dramatic, but in Augustine's view, if temptations win they can cause the gradual death of a soul which turns to itself, not to God. When Augustine preached on martyrs, he did not confront his hearers with violent images of torment. His focus is on the grace which enabled martyrs to hold to their faith.[61]

Augustine's Monica encountered challenges, made mistakes, and needed forgiveness (*Conf.* 9.13.35). His own experience showed him that just as everyday life offers dangerous temptations, so apparently chance or trivial events, or a few words spoken for another reason, can bring about moral and spiritual change. In *Confessions*, this is exemplified by the remarkable sequence of memories his 'soul brought to birth' (9.8.17) about Monica. It begins with his only story of Monica's childhood, one that she often told him herself (9.8.18). Classical literature hardly ever offers stories about childhood, unless they foreshadow the future greatness of a boy, so it is exceptional to find a story about a girl.[62] This story is a particularly good illustration of Augustine's purpose in writing about Monica, because he might be expected to keep it quiet. Here, then, is what he wrote immediately after his statement of her death:

> And while we were at Ostia on the Tiber, my mother died.
> I pass over many things, because I am in a great hurry: receive
> my confessions and thanks, my God, for innumerable things,
> even in silence. But I shall not pass over whatever my soul
> brings to birth about that slave [*famula*] of yours, who gave
> me birth both in the flesh, so that I should be born into this
> temporal light, and in the heart, so that I should be born into
> eternal light. I shall speak not of her gifts but of your gifts
> to her, for she did not make herself or bring herself up. You
> created her: her father and mother did not know what kind
> of person would come from them. The rod of your Christ, the

61. On Augustine's preaching about martyrs, see Elena Martin, 'Commemoration, Representation and Interpretation: Augustine of Hippo's Depictions of the Martyrs', in Peter Clarke and Tony Claydon, eds, *Saints and Sanctity* (2011), pp. 29–40.

62. Stories of childhood: Christopher Pelling, 'Childhood and Personality in Greek Biography', in C. Pelling, ed., *Characterization and Individuality in Greek Literature* (1990), pp. 213–44.

rule of your only son, educated her in fear of you, in a faithful house, a good member of your church. She used to praise not so much the devotion of her mother in training her as that of an elderly slave [*famula*], who had carried her father as a baby, in the way that little children are usually carried on the back of a girl who is growing up. For that reason, and because of her old age and excellent character, she was greatly honoured by her masters [*domini*] in that Christian home. So the care even of the masters' daughters was entrusted to her, and she undertook it with devotion, forceful with holy severity in restraining them when it was necessary, and with sober wisdom in teaching them. Except for the times when they were being fed, very moderately, at their parents' table, she would not allow them even to drink water, even though they were burning with thirst, warning them against a bad habit and adding a salutary word: 'Now you drink water, because you do not have wine in your power; but when you come to your husbands and are made mistresses [*dominae*] of store-rooms and cellars, water will pall, but the habit of drinking will be strong.' With reason in giving advice and authority in giving orders, she checked the greed of a tender age, and shaped even the thirst of the girls to a decent limit, so that what was not fitting should not even be pleasant.

But it crept up on her, as your slave [*famula*] used to tell me, her son: drunkenness crept up on her. For when, as the custom is, she was told by her parents, as a sober girl, to take wine from the cask, she dipped in the bowl where the cask is open at the top, and before pouring the wine into the flask, she would take a tiny sip with the edge of her lips, because she could not take more, repelled by the taste. She did not do this from any drunken desire, but from the overflowing excesses of that age, which bubble up in silly impulses and are suppressed in childish souls by the weight of the elders. So, by adding to that measure daily measures ('for one who spurns measures gradually falls' [Eccl. 19:1]), she fell into the habit of eagerly swallowing almost whole cupfuls of neat wine. Where then was the sage old woman and the forceful prohibition? Had she any power against the hidden disease, if your medicine, Lord [*domine*], did not watch over us? Her father, her mother, her nurses were absent: you were present, you who created, you who call, you who even through people who are put in charge do good for the salvation of souls. What did you do then, my God? How did you care for her? How did you heal her? Did you not bring forth from another soul a harsh and piercing reproach, like a surgeon's knife, from your hidden providence, and cut out that rottenness with one stroke? For the slave [*ancilla*] with whom she used to go to the cask, quarrelling, as happens, with a younger mistress [*domina*], when they were alone together, flung this accusation at her, calling her with the most bitter mockery 'little lush' [*meribibula*]. Struck by this goad, she looked at her own foulness, immediately condemned it, and got rid of it. Just so do flattering friends corrupt, and quarrelling enemies often correct; but you repay not what you do through them, but what they meant to do. [The slave] was angry, and sought to distress her young mistress [*domina*], not to heal her, and in secret, either because that was where the time and place of the quarrel found them, or to avoid putting herself at risk because she had been so slow to betray her. (*Conf.* 9.8.17–18)

Monica used to tell her son this story, and it is not surprising that he remembered it. But it is surprising that he repeated it at length at the start of his memories of Monica. The slave's insult—*meribibula*, 'little lush'—means that Monica was a drinker of wine when it was neat, *merum,* before it was diluted with water at the table. Respectable people did not drink wine neat, and Augustine's envisaged audience knew the dangers just as the old nurse did. If the *domina* of a household was addicted to wine, she could not manage the house or maintain the hierarchy of master and slave.

Households were built on three relationships of superior and subordinate: husband and wife, parents and children, masters and slaves.[63] In the Christian household of her parents, Monica too is a slave, *famula*, of the Lord, *dominus*. In human contexts *dominus* means 'master' of a slave, and the slave-master relationship is so important in this passage that it seems best to translate *famula* and *ancilla* as 'slave', rather than the innocuous 'servant' or 'handmaid'.[64] Monica is brought up, in the

63. See chapter 3.
64. See further chapter 3.

fear of the Lord, by the rod which is Christ. This is not meant to evoke a child frightened by beatings into obedience, for Augustine expected his readers to hear 'thy rod and staff my comfort still' (Psalm 23:4), and 'the fear of the Lord is the beginning of wisdom' (Proverbs 9:10). Monica lives in a 'faithful house', that is, a household of baptized Christians, and Augustine uses a familiar metaphor in which the church is Christ's body on earth and Christians are members (limbs) of the body (e.g., Eph. 5:30). Christians were not told that they must free their slaves, who might have fared worse outside the household, but they were told to regard them as fellow Christians who had their own spiritual gifts (e.g., Eph. 6:9).[65] In sermons, Augustine pointed out that master and slave are brothers, because both pray to 'Our Father' (*ser.* 58.2.2, 59.2.2). For Christians and non-Christians alike, it was not a disruption of hierarchy when an old and respected slave had authority over the daughters of the *domini*. The masters recognized the moral standing of the slave, and gave her authority over children which she did not have over adults. Similarly, it was usual for a slave *paedagogus* to have authority over the boy he escorted to and from school. This practice caused anxiety only if parents assigned the task, and other child-care, not to a slave of proven character, but to a slave who was too old or too weak for other work.[66]

But hierarchy was disrupted when Monica started to drink wine. The story is often interpreted as if the *ancilla* was Monica's age and the two girls got into a childish quarrel, but when Augustine says that the *ancilla* quarrelled, 'as happens', with a younger *domina*, he may mean that the *domina* was younger than the slave to whom she gave orders. The custom of sending a daughter to fetch wine did not simply rely on a child's dislike of the taste. It showed that she, as a 'sober girl', was growing up as a *domina* who could be trusted with responsibility for her household. The *domina* kept the keys because it was assumed that slaves would steal what they could, but in this instance it was the *domina* who pilfered wine. There survives a sermon (ascribed to Augustine, but not in his style) on the dangers of drunkenness. The preacher describes a married woman who loses all modesty of appearance and speech. She cannot control her household, because she does not know what is happening and cannot give coherent orders. Her slaves mock her, steal the

---

65. On Christians and slavery, see further chapter 3.
66. Keith Bradley, *Discovering the Roman Family* (1991), pp. 52–5.

keys, and raid the storerooms. She no longer fears her husband, who sees his house neglected and his work gone to waste.[67]

Augustine explained at some length that the girl Monica sampled the wine out of childish silliness. He was also careful to explain what the grown-up Monica did when, in accordance with African tradition, she took offerings of cooked grain, bread, and unmixed wine to the tombs of the dead (*Conf.* 6.2.2). At Milan, she was told that the bishop had forbidden the practice, and she willingly abandoned it, for 'drunkenness did not besiege her spirit, nor did love of wine prompt hatred of truth'. African custom was to taste the offerings, then place them on stone tables (*mensae*) beside the tombs for others to share. Monica never set down more than one small cup, of wine watered to suit her sober taste, and took only one small sip. If there were several tombs to visit, she took round the same small cup, in which the wine was very well watered and only just warm, from which she and her companions took a tiny sip. The implied contrast is with people who drank fresh cups of strong, hot wine at every tomb they visited.

This detailed account may have been intended to show how Christians should honour the dead, rather than to defend Monica's reputation: in 393 CE Augustine began a campaign against riotous celebrations of the dead, especially of martyrs.[68] But he took a risk in using the story from Monica's girlhood.[69] Its purpose in *Confessions* is to show how even a well-brought-up girl succumbs to a temptation which starts as childish naughtiness but might have wrecked her life, and how the grace of God works in unexpected ways to rescue her, so that even at this young age she can see what has happened and stop.[70] Augustine wrote another brief narrative (*Conf.* 6.7.11–10.16) about his friend and fellow townsman Alypius, and included a similar story (6.7.12) of how Alypius was rescued from addiction. Alypius was then a student at Carthage, where Augustine was teaching rhetoric. He was not a student of Augustine, who had a disagreement with his father, but he would

---

67. *Sermo de ebrietate et castitate* (sermon on drunkenness and chastity), *PL* (*Patrologia Latina*) 40. 1110–11; see further chapter 2.

68. On funerary banquets, see Éric Rebillard, *The Care of the Dead in Late Antiquity* (2009), pp. 142–53. On riotous martyr-feasts at Carthage (celebrating St Cyprian) and at Hippo (celebrating the town's patron St Leontius), see Serge Lancel, *St. Augustine* (2002), pp. 156–8.

69. Virginia Burrus phrases it as 'childhood alcoholism framed by class conflict', *The Sex Lives of Saints* (2004), p. 83.

70. See also chapter 6 on the bishop who said words that Monica treasured: he said them because he was tired of her persistence and wanted her to leave.

come to Augustine's lecture-room to offer a formal greeting and listen for a while. Alypius had tried, but failed, to resist his attraction to the bloodlust of 'the games' in which gladiators fought and sometimes died. Augustine had almost forgotten that he meant to talk to Alypius about this problem, but one day, when he was explaining a text to his students, it occurred to him that a comparison with the games would make his point. Just as the slave meant only to hurt Monica, so Augustine meant only to use a comparison his students would enjoy and remember. But Alypius was there, and took Augustine's mordant comments as a rebuke addressed to him.

Alypius later became bishop of Thagaste, and we do not know whether this story of his student days was exploited by his religious opponents. But late in Augustine's life, Julian, bishop of Aeclanum in Italy, exploited the story of Monica's childhood, and the association of wine with sexual desire, in his argument against Augustine's views on the genetic transmission of sin.[71] He picked up the word 'disease' which Augustine had used. Augustine's reply used a standard rhetorical technique of selectively quoting, then rejecting, what Julian said:

> JULIAN: You add that the business of marriage [i.e., sexual inter-
> course] is a disease. That can be heard with indulgence, if you
> say it only about your parents. For perhaps you could be aware
> of some secret disease of your mother, who, you indicated in
> your *Confessions*, was called (to use the exact word) *meribibula*.
> AUGUSTINE: You saw fit to assault with abuse my mother, who
> did you no harm and did not argue against you. You were
> overcome by the lust to speak evil, not fearing what is writ-
> ten: 'Evil speakers shall not possess the kingdom of heaven'.
> But it is not surprising that you show yourself hostile to her,
> when you are hostile to the grace of God, by which I said that
> she was freed from that childish fault. (*c. Jul .imp.* 1.68)[72]

Confessions is concerned with the workings of God's grace in Augustine's life, and in the lives of his mother and his closest friends. Understandably, the focus is on their relationship to Augustine, but

---

71. On "original sin" transmitted at conception, see chapter 6.
72. On the "cut and paste" technique, see Caroline Humfress, 'Controversialist: Augustine in Combat', in M. Vessey (see n. 6), pp. 323–35, and at pp. 329–30.

Augustine himself shows that there were other relationships in their lives. A passage from a work written much later in his life (*De cura* 421/2) prompts one more question about Augustine's Monica: just how single-minded was she in her devotion to him? This short work, *On Care for the Dead*, responds to a question from Paulinus, bishop of Nola, who had been asked by a mother to have her son buried as close as possible to the tomb of St. Felix. Augustine respected the tradition of praying for the dead at the altar, that is, at the Eucharist, when Christians share bread and wine in commemoration of Christ.[73] But he did not think that the actions of the living could benefit the dead, or that the dead appeared to the living:

> If the souls of the dead took part in the concerns of the living, and themselves spoke to us in dreams when we see them: to say nothing of others, my devoted mother would not desert me on any night, she who followed over land and sea to live with me. Heaven forbid that she should become cruel in the happier life, to the point that when something grieves my heart she would not console even her sad son, whom she loved *unice*, whom she was never willing to see unhappy.
> (*De cura* 13.16)

Does *unice*, "uniquely", mean that Monica loved him more than she loved her other children, or more than other mothers love their children, or with a love which was exceptional in this life? Monica followed Augustine 'over land and sea', a tag from Virgil which Paulinus and other readers would recognize: the mother of Euryalus laments the death in battle of her son, whom she followed over land and sea (*Aeneid* 9. 492). Other women among the refugees from the sack of Troy had given up on the difficult journey to Italy, but she had stayed with her son. (She is another unnamed mother; Virgil did not give her a name, and Augustine observed that people thought teachers of literature ought to know what it was (*ord.* (*de ordine*) 2.12.37).) In *Confessions*, Augustine wrote that his friend Nebridius 'left his homeland near Carthage, and Carthage itself where he spent much time, left the excellent country estate of his father, left his home and his mother who was not to follow him' (6.10.17). When Nebridius returned from Italy to Africa, his

73. See further chapter 6.

mother could not bear him to be away (*Ep.* 10.1), but in *Confessions* she is not as devoted as Monica. Augustine described Monica's impassioned attempts to hold him back, or to go with him, as he left for Rome:

> You knew, God, why I was leaving [Carthage] and going to [Rome], but you did not tell me or my mother, who lamented grievously as I set out and followed me all the way to the sea. But I deceived her, as she held me violently, to call me back or to go with me. I pretended that I did not want to leave a friend until the wind rose and he sailed; I lied to my mother, to that mother. And I got away, because this too you permitted to me, in your mercy preserving me safe from the waters of the sea, full as I was of accursed filth, until I reached the water of your grace; when I was washed in that, the streams that flowed from my mother's eyes could dry up, those streams with which every day, praying to you for my sake, she drenched the ground below her face. And yet I could scarcely persuade her, as she refused to go back without me, to stay that night at a place very near our ship, the shrine of blessed Cyprian. But that night I set out in secret, and she did not; she stayed, praying and weeping. And what did she ask of you, my God, with all those tears, but that you should not allow me to sail? But you, in your deep wisdom, hearing the central point of her longing, did not bring about what she asked then, in order to make me what she always asked. The wind blew and filled our sails and took from our sight the shore on which, in the morning, she was wild with grief, and filled your ears with complaints and groans; but you did not take notice of them, because through my desires you were snatching me away in order to end those desires, and you were justly chastising her fleshly longing with the scourge of grief. She loved my presence with her, as mothers do, but much more than many, and she did not know what joys you would bring her from my absence. She did not know, and so she wept and wailed, and those torments showed the remnants of Eve in her: she sought with groans what she had borne with groans (Gen. 3:16). And yet, after accusing me of deception and cruelty, she turned back to pray to you for me, and left for her accustomed life, and I came to Rome. (5.8.15)

FIGURE 1.3. Monica on the shore of Carthage as Augustine sails for Rome.
Basilio Pacheco. http://www.cassiciaco.it/

As so often in *Confessions*, Augustine expected his readers to hear both classical and Biblical allusions. Every schoolboy read at least some of the *Aeneid*, Virgil's great epic poem on the foundation of Rome. In his own schooldays Augustine was especially moved by the story of Dido, queen of Carthage, who killed herself for love of Aeneas (*Conf.* 1.13.20). She wanted Aeneas to stay with her in Carthage, but he said that he must obey the command of Jupiter, king of the gods, to leave for Italy. He set sail secretly, and Dido in despair invoked the gods of the underworld and took her own life. Monica too clung to a loved one whom God was sending to Italy. She was too much attached to his physical presence, and she was still affected by the punishment of Eve: 'I will multiply your sorrows and your groaning, and in sorrow you shall bring forth children' (Genesis 3:16). Monica was distraught, like Dido, but she had a different relation to her God, who did not hear her immediate prayers. She did not despair, but prayed at the shrine of Cyprian, the martyred bishop of Carthage, and returned to her usual life.[74]

What Augustine did not say in *Confessions*, although it is evident in the philosophical dialogues, is that when his devoted mother crossed land and sea to join him in Milan, she brought the family: Augustine's

74. On Augustine and Virgil, see further Sabine MacCormack, *The Shadows of Poetry* (1998), especially pp. 97–9 on Dido.

brother Navigius, two cousins, and presumably some slave attendants. All the family could benefit from Augustine's career, and those who came to Milan could hope for contacts and business opportunities.[75] But in *Confessions* the focus is on Augustine. Navigius appears just once, unnamed, at the deathbed of Monica, encouraging her to think that she will not die abroad. Monica looks at him reproachfully, then looks at Augustine and says 'see what he says' (*Conf.* 9.11.27). She knows that it does not matter where her body is buried. Augustine acknowledges (9.11.28) that he knew Monica had always been 'in a fever of concern' about the burial-place she had prepared beside her husband's.[76] She had wanted it to be remembered that after her travels overseas, the same earth had covered the dust of both: this sounds like a phrase from an epitaph. Navigius, the son who had stayed in their home town, would be responsible for the burial and the epitaph, but it is Augustine, not Navigius, who is expected to understand that she has changed.[77]

Augustine wrote that a little before her death, after he and she had shared an experience in which the world and its delights became insignificant,[78] Monica said:

> 'My son, as far as I am concerned, I no longer delight in anything in this life. What I am doing here now, and why I am here, I do not know, now that hope in this world is used up. There was one thing for which I wanted to remain a little in this life: to see you a Catholic Christian before I died. God has given me this in heaping measure, so that I see you his slave, earthly happiness disregarded. What am I doing here?' I do not properly remember what I replied, for within five days, or not much longer, she took to her bed with fever.
> (*Conf.* 9.10.26–11.27)

Did Monica really not delight in her other children and her grandchildren, or acknowledge that other people needed her? In the same house was her teenage grandson Adeodatus, whose mother had been sent away in preparation for the marriage Augustine had planned.

---

75. See chapter 4.

76. *Noveram quanta cura semper aestuasset.*

77. On the burial of husband and wife together, see also the poem of Ausonius on his mother, quoted in chapter 6.

78. See chapter 4.

Augustine remembered his own anguish at that separation, but said nothing about his son's, though he did record the grief of Adeodatus when Monica died (9.12.29). From Augustine's perspective, what mattered was that Monica had come to understand the difference between love of God and physical ('carnal') concern for family:[79]

> I did not know when that pointless concern [for burial beside
> her husband] had begun, in the fullness of your goodness,
> not to be in her heart, and I was glad, marvelling that she had
> shown herself to me thus; though in that conversation we had
> by the window, when she said 'What am I still doing here?',
> she did not show herself as longing to die in her fatherland.
> I heard later that already when we were at Ostia, she was
> talking one day, with maternal confidence, to some friends of
> mine about disregard for this life and about the good of death;
> I was not there. They were amazed at the courage of a woman
> (for you had given it to her) and asked whether she was not
> afraid to leave her body so far from her own city. 'Nothing is
> far from God', she said, 'and there is no need to fear that he
> will not see where to raise me up at the end of the world.' So
> on the ninth day of her illness, in the 56th year of her age and
> the 33rd of mine, that devout and pious soul was released from
> the body. (9.11.28)

There is an obvious difficulty in asking such questions as 'did Monica really not delight in her other children and grandchildren?' How can we tell? Augustine was not the only man in the late fourth century to praise a mother who wept for her son in grief and anxiety and who was distraught when he left home. But he made Monica much more alive and forceful than the devoted mothers of the orator Libanius and of the bishop John Chrysostom, and much less of a paragon than the mothers of two other bishops, Gregory of Nyssa and Gregory of Nazianzus.[80] So readers are likely to feel that they know Monica. Teachers of classical literature warn their students against writing 'Penelope (or Medea, or Dido) must have felt . . .' Penelope, teachers say, was invented by Homer, Medea by Euripides, Dido by Virgil. Unless Homer or Euripides or Virgil shows us what these characters felt, we do not know. Once there

79. See further chapter 6 on mothers whose devotion is misguided.
80. See chapter 6.

was a real live woman called Monica, wife of Patricius: 'the real Monica', some would say, but Augustine would say that the real Monica, like the real Augustine and everyone else, is known only to God. We do not know what Monica felt unless Augustine, for his own reasons, tells us. Nor, of course, do we know what Augustine felt unless he tells us, and even then we may not know.[81]

It is also unwise to assume that we know what Monica felt because any mother, in any time and place, would feel the same. Monica was anxious and afraid when her son was dangerously ill in childhood (*Conf.* 1.11.17), and when in his student days he joined a religious sect which she thought dangerously wrong (3.11.19). That seems immediately recognizable, and her story remained a comfort for mothers whose children lapsed from their faith.[82] But many people do not share Monica's beliefs about the soul of a child who dies unbaptized, or Roman beliefs about the deference owed by a son to his mother and the combination of love and moral strictness she should show to him.[83] The study of women in antiquity teaches us about conditions of life for Monica and for other dutiful wives and mothers unknown to history. It also teaches us to be aware of present-day assumptions about the lives of women.

81. O'Donnell (n. 51) gives a salutary warning against thinking we know Augustine: what we know is Augustine's books.

82. See chapter 6.

83. On mothers and children: see Suzanne Dixon, *The Roman Mother* (1988); Gillian Clark, 'The Fathers and the Children', in Diana Wood, ed., *The Church and Childhood: Papers Read at the 1993 Summer Meeting and the 1994 Winter Meeting of the Ecclesiastical History Society* (1994), pp. 1–27.

2

Monica's House

Most of Monica's life was spent in a house: first with her parents, then with her husband and children, then with her son and his partner and son, and always with slaves. At all periods of classical antiquity, respectable women lived at home, then married and managed a house, then, if they were widowed, lived with family. This does not mean that they were confined to the house and saw no one but family. In Thagaste, Monica met her women neighbours (*Conf.* 9.9.19). Wherever she was, she went to church, twice daily in widowhood (*Conf.* 5.9.17); women and men stood in church separately (*civ. Dei* 2.28) but in sight of each other, and were likely to meet on their way to or from church. She did "good works" of charity (*Conf.* 5.5.17, 6.2.2), but this may mean that she gave alms to be distributed through the bishop, not that she visited the poor.

Unless her house had a private bath suite, Monica went to the town baths, for health as well as for cleanliness. This need not mean that she bathed in the company of men: customs varied in different times and places, but public baths often had times reserved for women, either by regulation or by local tradition.[1] Even in his advice for monastic communities, whether of women or of men, Augustine assumed that there would be visits to the baths, and specified only that people must not go alone.[2] He told nuns that they should not always be going to the baths,

1. Garrett Fagan, *Bathing in Public in the Roman World* (1999), pp. 26–9, on conflicting evidence for mixed bathing; Yvon Thébert, *Thermes romains de l'Afrique du Nord* (2003), on the archaeological evidence for public baths.

2. *Reg. (regula)* 5.7. The masculine and feminine versions of this "rule" differ only in grammatical gender and in references to "brothers" or "sisters," not in the advice given. It is difficult to decide who compiled the documents and when: on the complexities of the texts, see George Lawless, *Augustine of Hippo and his Monastic Rule* (1987).

FIGURE 2.1. Women going to the baths: Mosaic from Piazza Armerina, Sicily, fourth century.

Wikimedia Commons.

but should have the customary bath once a month, or more often (even if they did not want to) if a doctor advised it (*ep.* 211.13). It would be sensible to have a slave attendant at the baths, to look after clothes and belongings. Was there also a slave with Monica in church, or whenever else she went out? Augustine did not say whether that was expected. Perhaps she could move freely in her own town, where everyone knew who she was and where she was going; and at Carthage and Milan she may have had greater freedom of movement as a widow, dressed in the dark cloth which signalled her status.

Monica may also have gone to market. Augustine did not mention this, but much of the information about Roman markets comes from Africa; in particular, information on the occasional markets which were held on estates outside towns.[3] There was such an estate outside Thagaste. It was part of the immense landholdings of the younger Melania, who spent some years there after the Goths attacked Rome in 410.[4] According to Melania's biographer, the estate was bigger than the town, with its own baths and two churches, one for Catholics and one

---

3. Luuk de Ligt, *Fairs and Markets in the Roman Empire* (1993), pp. 155–98.

4. A priest called Gerontius wrote a *Life* of Melania: *The Life of Melania the Younger* (1984), annotated translation by Elizabeth A. Clark. On lives of holy women, see chapter 6.

for the Donatists who claimed to be the true Catholic Church,[5] and its workers included craftsmen in precious metals. It is likely that this estate had occasional markets, and that in Thagaste itself people regularly sold local produce, wood for fuel, and craft work such as textiles, footwear, and pottery. From the second century on, Roman Africa saw a great increase in local production of fine pottery and glass.[6] Perhaps more exotic goods were sometimes available, if traders found it worth their while to use the road from Carthage to the upland grain-producing areas, bringing spices and silverware, or silks and damasks.[7] Whenever possible, Monica's household supplies came from the land Patricius owned, and slaves could be sent to buy anything else which was needed, but she might want to make her own choice from the products of craft workers. Like the good wife in the book of Proverbs, she may herself have engaged in small-scale trading, using a slave to sell home-produced goods or surplus produce, and she could have made deals on property she owned or inherited; such economic activities of women leave traces in papyrus documents and in late Roman law.[8]

Women were not confined to the house, but running the house was the main duty of a *materfamilias*, the married woman who was the "mother of the household" of which her husband was the *paterfamilias*. What was Monica's house like? This question is difficult to answer, because Augustine is vague about his family's social and economic status in Thagaste, and there is no local archaeological record to offer a range of possibilities. In the early nineteenth century the French colonial town of Souk Ahras was built over the site of Thagaste. There was little excavation, and drawings of the site show only that Thagaste was not a planned town on a grid pattern like the veteran settlement inland at Timgad, and that it was indeed a small town, *civitas parva*, just as the priest who wrote the life of Melania said.[9] Very few inscriptions were found, and none survived from the forum to document benefactors and civic buildings. There are a few inscriptions in Libyan, a local language, but these are from the first and second centuries.[10] One

5. On Donatists, see chapter 5.
6. Leslie Dossey, *Peasant and Empire in Christian North Africa* (2010), pp. 62–77.
7. Route of the road: S. Lancel, *St. Augustine* (2002), p. 23. Augustine mentions the Street of the Silversmiths at Carthage, *Conf.* 6.9.14.
8. The praise of the Good Wife is quoted in chapter 3. For some examples of the economic activity of women, see Gillian Clark, *Women in Late Antiquity* (1993), p. 94.
9. See Lancel (n. 7), p. 4, with some suggestions on how the Roman town might have looked.
10. On Libyan and other local languages, see chapter 5.

stone slab carries the name '[COR]NELIUS ROMANIANUS', perhaps the same local great man who was Augustine's patron (*c. Acad.* 2.2.3), perhaps another of his family. Otherwise, the evidence for the town of Thagaste comes from Augustine.[11]

So we must look to the many other examples of late antique housing. There are remains of about a thousand houses dating from the third to the sixth century, some of them in Africa, and other projects of survey and excavation are in progress.[12] The best known of these houses are too grand to be relevant for Augustine's modest family: imperial palaces, immense country villas on tenant-farmed estates, aristocratic town houses which were also centres of political activity. But there is a wider range of houses that show that their owners had, or aspired to, social status, and Kim Bowes surveys a deliberately broad category of such houses in town and country.[13] The signs of status include mosaic floors, painted or sculpted decoration, and coloured marble cladding, all of which vary in quality; separate reception spaces, such as apsed dining rooms; and private bath houses. Augustine asked how anyone would try to convince Romanianus that he was not really happy if he were a benefactor praised and honored by all, and 'lived in the choicest of buildings, in the splendour of baths' (*c. Acad.* 1.2.2). Their part of Africa prospered in the third and fourth centuries, especially from the export of grain and olive oil to Rome, and many villas were built or rebuilt at that time.[14] But we do not know whether Augustine's family house was among them, and what signs of status it had.

We do not even know whether the family house was a town house, fitted in where there was space and closely connected to others, or a villa in its own grounds on the outskirts of the town.[15] Augustine,

11. The evidence is collected in C. Lepelley, *Les Cités de l'Afrique romaine au bas-empire*. Vol. 2 (1978), 175–84.

12. Kim Bowes, *Houses and Society in the Later Roman Empire* (2010), p. 11. Margherita Carucci, *The Romano-African Domus* (2007), includes a catalogue of African peristyle houses—that is, houses with a central courtyard surrounded by a colonnade. My thanks to Jo Quinn for advice.

13. Bowes (n. 12), pp. 17–18.

14. Kim Bowes, *Private Worship, Public Values, and Religious Change in Late Antiquity* (2008) p. 128, and pp. 162–9 on the complex landscape of settlement in Africa. She notes (p. 163) that there are not many elite houses, and Lisa Nevett, *Domestic Space in Classical Antiquity* (2010), p. 138, confirms that an archaeological survey has found farms, sometimes fortified, rather than elite villas.

15. Yvon Thébert, in Paul Veyne, ed., *A History of Private Life* 1 (1987), pp. 319–409, offers town plans, house plans, and useful comment on the management of space within houses. He is concerned with 'the urban homes of the ruling class' (p. 319), a category not closely defined.

FIGURE 2.2. Villa with fruit trees: Mosaic from Tabarka, North Africa.
© Bardo Museum.

telling how he and his teenage friends stole pears they did not need or even like, says that the tree was near 'our vineyard' (*Conf.* 2.4.9), but does not say how big the vineyard was or where it was in relation to the house and the town. Monica's regular churchgoing suggests that the house was not far from the church, but we do not know where the church was in relation to the town, or whether Monica walked or had transport such as a mule, a carrying-chair, or even a carriage.[16] It is often assumed that the house was outside the town, because on his return from Italy Augustine lived there with friends in a philosophical community. But such communities were not always in the peace of the country like the villa Augustine borrowed at Cassiciacum, or outside the city walls like the monastery Ambrose established at Milan (*Conf.* 8.6.15).[17] The communities Augustine established at Hippo were not isolated. As Richard Finn observes, his form of monastic life was not solitary, but apostolic: that is, it was designed to send Christian teaching into the world.[18] When Augustine was ordained priest, his bishop gave

16. Transport for shorter or longer distances: Stéphanie Guédon, *Le voyage dans l'Afrique romaine* (2010), pp. 80–2. A friend of Augustine advised a *basterna* as comfortable wheeled transport for the ailing Nebridius (*ep.* 10.1).
17. See chapter 4 on the villa at Cassiciacum.
18. Richard Finn, *Asceticism in the Graeco-Roman World* (2009), p. 148.

him a *hortus*, a garden, where he could live in community (*ser.* 355.2). Possidius (*v. Aug.* 5.1) says it was 'inside the church' (*intra ecclesiam*), and this must mean that it was within the block of land which belonged to the church.[19] When Augustine became bishop himself, he needed to show hospitality to visitors, so he lived in the bishop's house, but still in community and without possessions (*ser.* 355.2). His advice to men and women monastics does not mention seclusion behind walls, and does assume that the monastics will meet people. They are told always to go out in groups of at least two or three, not to let their eyes linger on people of the opposite sex, and to behave modestly in places where men and women are together, as they are in church.[20]

So we do not know about the size and location of the house in which Monica was "mother of the household" of husband, children, slaves, and perhaps other relatives. What was it like to manage a house?[21] Very few male authors had anything to say about it, except for some ascetic Christian authors who argued that women would do better to escape to celibacy from the demands of domestic life, and that men can meet their needs for food and clothes without having to share their lives with women.[22] There are no writings by women on housework, except perhaps for some sayings ascribed to Amma (Mother) Syncletica, who led the ascetic life in the Egyptian desert. She used everyday domestic tasks to illustrate spiritual effort: it is compared to lighting a fire, which smokes before it gives warmth, and to treading the dirt out of clothes as they are washed.[23] But nothing survives to say how women felt about their houses, or whether they felt the houses to be theirs. This silence is interesting. Male authors blame women for too much attention to their clothes and jewels, makeup and hairstyles, or in some cases praise them for their lack of concern. They do not blame women for expenditure on marble cladding, floor mosaics, wall paintings, sculptures, furniture, and textiles and dinner services. It is rich men who surround them-selves with silverware and tapestries and citronwood tables and family

19. For a plan and discussion of this area, see Lancel (n. 7), pp. 240–4.
20. *Reg.* 4.2, 4.5–6: see n. 2 for the difficulties.
21. Alexandra Croom, *Running the Roman Home* (2011), uses texts, archaeological evidence, comparison with other cultures, and experiment.
22. Clark (n. 8), pp. 98–105.
23. Ps-Athanasius, 'Life of Syncletica', paragraphs 30 and 60. See the translation by Elizabeth Castelli in Vincent Wimbush and Richard Valantasis, eds., *Ascetic Behavior in Greco-Roman Antiquity* (1990), pp. 265–311.

portraits. Houses advertised status, and public status was especially the concern of men.

Status could be advertised by building a new villa, or by upgrading an older house, and women could take part in that major financial decision. But there may have been little scope for a woman to change the look of the house she entered on marriage. Floor mosaics, in particular, can survive for centuries, reflecting the taste of a much earlier generation. Monica's Christian household may have lacked any Christian imagery; she and her children and slaves may have walked over mosaics and past wall paintings, if there were any, hardly noticing standard mythological motifs.[24] Augustine remarked in a sermon (*ser.* 17.7) that even glass, fragile as it is, lasts if kept carefully, so that people drink from glasses once owned by their grandfathers or great-grandfathers. Woven door-curtains and wall hangings, coverings for beds and couches and cushions, and wooden furniture, could also last for many years, and perhaps signs of old wealth also advertised status.[25] But archaeology can tell us little about changing styles of furniture and textiles, because in most environments wood and fabrics are likely to rot, and portable goods are likely to be removed. So, for example, the material evidence for a new kind of dining couch, the curved *stibadium*, does not come from surviving couches. It comes from couch-bases, or from floor mosaics that surround a couch base or leave space for couches, or from dining or reception rooms with an apse suited to a curved couch. Walls could be repainted with new colours and designs more easily than floor mosaics could be installed or replaced, but, again, we know little about decorative fashions in late antiquity. It is very unusual, for any period of classical antiquity, to have the combination of texts and material evidence that makes it possible to discuss changing tastes,[26] and textual evidence must be used with awareness of its author's purpose. For

24. Thébert (n. 15), pp. 392–405, considers decoration, and notes (p. 397) the absence of Christian motifs in mosaics. On the general question of mosaics and changing tastes, see Birte Poulsen, 'Patrons and Viewers: Reading Mosaics in Late Antiquity', in Stine Birk and Birte Poulsen, eds, *Patrons and Viewers in Late Antiquity* (2012), pp. 167–87.

25. On the importance of textiles, see Henry Maguire, 'The Good Life', in G. Bowersock, P. Brown, O. Grabar, eds, *Late Antiquity: A Guide to the Postclassical World* (1999), pp. 238–57, at pp. 239–40.

26. As in *Arethusa* 45.3 (Fall 2012), a special issue on *Collectors and the Eclectic: New Approaches to Roman Domestic Decoration*, guest editor Francesca C. Tronchin. The papers focus on the exceptional case of Pompeii in the context of first-century Italy.

example, there is a list of furniture in a poem of Augustine's contemporary Prudentius, who came from Spain:

> In the house of the rich man, there is much furniture in every
> corner. The golden goblet gleams, and the polished bronze
> basin is not lacking; there is a pot made of clay and a broad
> and heavy silver tray; there are ivories, and vessels hollowed
> out from oak and elm. (*Epilogus* 13–20)

Perhaps all these things were indeed found in the houses of the rich, but Prudentius names them when comparing himself and his poetry to a humble clay vessel, and his list is influenced by Christian scripture: 'in a great house there are not only gold and silver vessels, but also those made of wood and clay' (2 Tim. 2:20).

Did Monica's house have any signs of status, such as a private bathhouse? Augustine remembered (*Conf.* 2.3.6) his father's satisfaction on realizing, at the baths, that his son had reached puberty, and his mother's anxiety when she was told.[27] The town baths, a general amenity and meeting place maintained by the town council, are a more likely setting than a domestic bathhouse, which would require large supplies of water and wood as well as slaves to stoke the furnace. There are African examples of private bathhouses in villas and even in farmhouses away from towns, and a mosaic from a house near the centre of Carthage appears to show a bathhouse among other signs of the status of its owner, who is named as Dominus Iulius, "Lord Julius." But water was always a problem. Perhaps supplies were easier at Thagaste because it was in the valley of the Medjerda, a perennial river which could be used for irrigation. Wells were used wherever possible, houses had cisterns to collect seasonal rain and run-off from the roof, and towns had reservoirs and aqueducts.[28] At Cassiciacum, the country villa of Augustine's friend Verecundus had its own bathhouse, and a place outside for the 'necessities of nature': that is, a lavatory, which could be flushed by the water supply for the baths.[29] But Cassiciacum was some distance from the baths of Milan, and it was in the country, presumably with easy

27. On this episode, see chapter 6.
28. On the management of water in the towns of Africa, see G. Charles-Picard, *La civilisation de l'Afrique romaine*, 2nd ed., (1990), pp. 178–82. For more bathhouses being built see Dossey (n. 6), pp. 81–2; a possible bathhouse in the 'Dominus Iulius' mosaic, Nevett (n. 14), p. 122.
29. See further Barry Hobson, *Latrinae et foricae: Toilets in the Roman world* (2009), and chapter 4 for the house at Cassiciacum.

FIGURE 2.3. The house of Dominus Iulius: Mosaic from Carthage.
© Bardo Museum.

access to wood and water. How were the 'necessities of nature' managed at Thagaste? Perhaps there were public lavatories near the baths. Houses could have their own rubbish tips, depending on their location, or slaves could take human and other waste to recognised places outside the town. Dung (*stercus*) was used as fertiliser; Augustine observed that sadness is like *stercus*, which is filth when it is in the wrong place, but in the right place makes the field fertile (*ser.* 254. 2). A dungheap saved the life of a victim of sectarian violence in another North African town: he was badly beaten, but survived being thrown from a tower because he landed in a dungheap, and was found by a poor man who had left the road to relieve himself there (*Cresc.* (*contra Cresconium*) 3.43.47).

Space for receiving visitors is another indicator of status. Where did Monica have the friendly conversations in which her neighbours complained about the behaviour of their husbands (*Conf.* 9.9.19)? Perhaps in a reception room, or in a central courtyard with a roofed colonnade to give shelter from rain and sun, a pool to collect rainwater, and plants which were both decorative and useful. Did Patricius entertain fellow councillors in a reception room at home, and if so, were wives invited? Or did he meet his friends at the baths, where there were private rooms for dining and conversation, or even at a local temple which had dining rooms? Many temples were also civic buildings, used as treasuries and as places for formal meetings, so even when pagan cult was banned, temples could lawfully be maintained as part of a town's heritage, and members of the town council might meet there to celebrate a traditional festival. Augustine, as a bishop, was concerned that Christians who accepted invitations to dine in a temple might appear sympathetic to paganism; but Patricius, for most of his life, was not a Christian, and he died twenty years before Theodosius I made a serious attempt to ban pagan cult.[30]

The shape and use of domestic space could be changed temporarily with curtains or permanently with dividing walls.[31] Archaeology supplies a range of possibilities for the arrangement of reception rooms and of domestic space in general, and Roman Africa has impressive visible remains, but archaeological evidence does not answer all the questions.[32] Usually what survives is the ground plan of a house, with nothing left of the walls. Sometimes there are remains of a staircase leading to an upper storey, as shown, for example, in the Dominus Iulius mosaic. But a ground plan does not show how the house might look from the outside, or how rooms were lit by windows. In towns especially, the ground plan may be incomplete because the site has been built over. Ground plans and wall bases rarely show where one house ends and another begins, and they cannot show how many people lived in a house, how they allocated space, and how much of the house was accessible to visitors who were not part of the family.

Floor mosaics often show how a particular space was used. More elaborate designs were suitable for reception rooms: presumably visitors did not look at the floor as they advanced, but they could be given a general impression of richness. Simpler geometric or floral patterns were suitable for less formal rooms. Sometimes a floor mosaic leaves space for a bed or couch, and sometimes there are traces of a platform

30. On invitations to dinner in a temple, see chapter 5.
31. Thébert (n. 15) comments on frequent adaptation in African houses.
32. On late antique housing, with several examples from Africa, see Leslie Dossey, 'Sleeping Arrangements and Private Space', in David Brakke, Deborah Deliyannis and Edward Watts, eds., *Shifting Cultural Frontiers in Late Antiquity* (2012), pp. 181–97. Nevett (n. 14) pp. 119–41 uses African floor mosaics as a case study of houses expressing the values of their owners.

for a bed, which might be placed in an alcove or under a barrel vault. But it does not follow that a particular room was always, or only, used for sleeping or eating, and we cannot tell how many people used a room.[33] Augustine's philosophical dialogue *Order* (*de ordine*), set in the country villa at Cassiciacum, begins with Augustine and his two students lying awake in the dark (*ord.* 1.3.6). It is not clear whether Navigius and Alypius, who are away at the time of this conversation, also have beds in this room (*conclave*). In bad weather, the group retires to the bathhouse for discussion, perhaps because the bathhouse retained warmth from the furnace which heated the water, perhaps also because the slaves were doing housework in the main house. But it seems that Augustine did not expect a separate teaching space, for he wrote that Monica had already heard readings from the books he discussed with students and friends.[34] He did not suggest that some parts of a house were women's territory and some were men's; probably the use of space varied with the time of day and with the number and kind of visitors.

There is some evidence that late antiquity saw a growing wish for privacy, both in terms of personal modesty and in terms of separating family from visitors. Privacy, or guarded access, was also a sign of status: 'the more honorable someone is, the more curtains (*vela*) hang in his house', said Augustine (*ser.* 51.4.5). In bigger houses, small rooms that had once opened directly on to a central space could be made to open instead onto a corridor or antechamber. Ground plans show the change, but do not show how the closed-off rooms would be lit. North Africa and Italy have several examples of adaptation in houses where rooms, perhaps screened only by a curtain, opened off a central peristyle courtyard, that is, a courtyard surrounded by pillars which supported a roof to give shade. The spaces between the pillars could be walled in, and the rooms could be subdivided into apartments with protected space. This seems to have become common practice in the west, but the evidence is later than Monica's lifetime. For example, in the late fifth century the peristyle House of the Frescoes at Tipasa (Mauretania) was subdivided into four apartments, and in one of these there is further subdivision of interior space. Nearby is the country villa of Nador, built in the early fourth century around a central courtyard, and subdivided

33. On the uses of the *cubiculum*, see Carucci (n. 12) pp. 73–82.
34. See chapter 4, and for discussion of the gendered use of space, see Lin Foxhall, *Studying Gender in Classical Antiquity* (2013).

into apartments also in the late fifth century.[35] But privacy is not the only possible explanation. Houses may have been subdivided in difficult economic times, because more family members had to be sheltered, or because there was not enough money and part of the space had to be sold or rented out as shops or apartments. We still do not know how big Monica's house was, how the space was divided, and whether she had or expected to have any space of her own.

It is also difficult to say how rich the family was in relation to others in Thagaste. Augustine wanted to show that he and his parents were not rich. He discussed in a sermon (*ser.* 356) the property of the men who lived in his clergy house at Hippo. All but two of them had given up their property, as Augustine had. He observed:

> Suppose, for example, I am given an expensive cloak [*birrus*, such as he always wore]. Perhaps it is suitable for a bishop, although it is not suitable for Augustine—that is, for a poor man born of poor parents. People will soon say that I wear expensive clothes which I could not have either in my father's house, or in my worldly profession. (*ser.* 356.13)[36]

Pauper, the word here translated "poor", does not signify poverty. It means someone who is not rich, and in some contexts it means specifically someone who is not rich enough to be liable for civic duties.[37] But Patricius was rich enough to be a member of the local *curia*, the city council whose members were responsible for tax collection and for maintaining public amenities, such as the water supply and the baths and the public buildings in the forum.

Taxes, in money and kind, were chiefly used to fund military and civil services: the army and the administration. The imperial government assigned to each province the amount of tax to be collected for a period of years, in kind or in money, according to a calculation of landholdings and the number of people and animals who worked them. The provincial governor then allocated amounts to local landowners and

---

35. Dossey (n. 32) pp. 188–91, with house-plans.

36. *Offertur mihi, verbi gratia, birrus pretiosus: forte decet episcopum, quamvis non deceat Augustinum, id est, hominem pauperem, de pauperibus natum. Modo dicturi sunt homines, quia induo pretiosas vestes, quas non possem habere vel in domo patris mei, vel in illa saeculari professione mea.*

37. Caroline Humfress, 'Poverty and Roman Law', in Margaret Atkins and Robin Osborne, eds., *Poverty in the Roman World* (2006), pp. 183–203, at pp. 198–200.

cities. This system meant that taxes were collected by people with local knowledge. It also meant that *curiales* came under personal pressure to help out or let off their fellow citizens, or to appeal for reduction of the amount in a bad year, in the knowledge that they had to make up any shortfall. Understandably, many people tried to avoid this honour. The property qualification for the *curia* was, almost always, land, but the minimum must have varied from one town to another. In larger towns there were differences of status among *curiales*, and in small towns there were not many candidates.[38] Augustine told a story about a *curialis pauper* (*de cura* 12.15), a poor man who served on a council even though he was a *rusticanus*, a peasant farmer.

Augustine did not suggest that Patricius married a rich wife, and said nothing about the dowry Monica brought to the marriage. He said something about his own inheritance in a letter to Albina, mother of the heiress Melania who, with her husband Pinianus, wanted to dispose of her wealth.[39] Displaced from Rome when the Goths attacked in 410, the three crossed to Africa, where Melania's holdings included the great estate outside Thagaste. They visited Hippo, where the congregation tried to force the ordination of Pinianus as a priest, just as it had once forced the ordination of Augustine. Albina thought that what they wanted was the wealth of Pinianus, and Augustine tried to convince her that they admired his renunciation of wealth:

> For if they loved it in me that, as they had heard, I had
> disregarded the few little fields inherited from my father
> and had turned to the free service of God, and they did not
> in this envy the church of Thagaste, which is my homeland
> according to the flesh, but, since that church had not imposed
> clerical status on me, they seized upon me when they could . . .
> (*ep.* 126.7)

If they loved Augustine for giving up a modest inheritance at Thagaste, he argued, how much more did they love Pinianus for his far more spectacular disregard of wealth! Augustine wrote that the 'few little fields', *agelluli*, were equivalent to one twentieth of the property of the church

---

38. Variations in different places: A. H. M. Jones, *The Later Roman Empire.* 3 vols. (1964), 737–57.

39. On Melania, see n. 4.

at Hippo which he now managed as bishop (*ep.* 126.7), and many people thought he had gone from poor to rich, not vice versa.

These *agelluli* were not the complete family inheritance, as all three children of Patricius and Monica were entitled to their shares. Augustine gave up his share at some time after his return to Africa. His letter to Albina implies that it was given to the church at Thagaste, but he must also have made some arrangement with the *curia*. People who held publicly funded teaching posts were exempt from curial service, because their work was itself a contribution to the city where they taught, but Augustine had given up his post. His brother Navigius must have served on the *curia* from the time of their father's death; even if Monica was in charge of the family property, she was not a member of the *curia*, because women did not hold public office.[40] 'Little fields' reappear when Augustine explains to his congregation why his nephew Patricius, who has joined him in the clergy house at Hippo, is one of two people there who have yet to carry out their intention to give up their property:

> Since my nephew was converted and began to be with me,
> he too was hindered from doing something with his little
> fields [*agelli*] by the life of his mother, who had the usufruct.
> [That is, she did not own the land, but had the use of it and
> was entitled to the profits.] She died this year. There are some
> questions between him and his sisters which, with Christ's
> help, will be quickly settled, so that he too can do what befits a
> servant of God. (*ser.* 356.3)

So, according to Augustine, his family was far from rich. The best known indicator of its economic status is the investment of Augustine's parents in his education:

> In that year my studies were interrupted. I was brought
> back from Madauros, the neighbouring town in which I had
> already begun to be away from home for the sake of acquiring
> literature and rhetoric. Funds were being gathered for a
> more distant absence from home at Carthage. For this my
> father had enthusiasm rather than wealth: he was a citizen
> of Thagaste with modest resources [*admodum tenuis*]. [. . .]

40. Jones (n. 38) on curial status and exemptions.

Everybody praised my father to the skies, because his son was far away from home to get an education, and he expended on him whatever was needed, beyond the means of the family property. Many far wealthier citizens took no such trouble for their children. (*Conf.* 2.3.5)

In the next book of *Confessions* Augustine remarked, in passing, that in his nineteenth year his father had died two years earlier, and his studies at Carthage were financed *maternis mercedibus* (3.4.7): that is, Monica paid the fees.[41] If the family property was not enough to fund Augustine's time at Carthage before Patricius died, it was certainly not enough when the inheritance was divided among the three children; but if Monica could pay from her own property, she could have done so earlier. Perhaps Patricius gave Monica the usufruct of the estate, as her son Navigius later arranged for his own widow, so that she could continue to live in her house and benefit from the produce.[42]

The local great man Romanianus, who was much richer, helped to fund Augustine (*c.Acad.* 2.2.3). There is no suggestion that Romanianus also had to help his relative Alypius (*ep.* 27.5), Augustine's friend, who came from leading citizens (*primatibus municipalibus*) of Thagaste (*Conf.* 6.7.11), and whose parents hoped he would have a career in law (*Conf.* 6.8.13, 6.10.16). We do not know what this education cost. Augustine said that teachers' fees were regulated and were displayed in the forum (*Conf.* 1.16.26), but teachers may also have expected presents, and living away from home brought expenses. Perhaps Augustine lived in the house of his teacher, as his own two students do in the early dialogues. But these students may be a special case, because Licentius is the son of Romanianus, he and Trygetius are both from Thagaste, and neither has a partner and child as Augustine did when he lived in Carthage. In the end, the *curia* of Thagaste lost the contributions of Augustine, Alypius, and Licentius, because Augustine and (presumably) Alypius gave up their property, and Licentius achieved a post in the imperial civil service.[43]

41. Readers often note the difference between this brief mention of the death of Patricius and the long account of Augustine's grief at the death of Monica; see chapter 6.

42. See chapter 1 on Monica's control of family finances, and chapter 3 on the separate property of wives.

43. Lepelley (n. 11) 2, pp. 181–2.

The financial status of the family makes a difference in the next question: what did Monica do all day? That question is very easy to answer in relation to any woman who did not have slaves to look after children, to bring in supplies of food and water and fuel, to prepare meals and to clean cooking pots and dishes, to make and mend and wash clothes and bedding, to clean floors and surfaces, and to dispose of rubbish. Rooms did not have fires to be laid and maintained or chimneys to be kept clear, but heating and lighting still required work and caused dirt. Charcoal braziers gave out some warmth, and light from oil lamps could be improved by hanging one or more lamps from a lampstand, a *candelabrum*, which might have metal parts to reflect the light, but braziers and oil lamps produced oily soot stains.[44] Augustine noticed that in Italy, even the well-off had to put up with darkness at night (*ord.* 1.3.6). He did not say why, but further north there were longer hours of darkness, and olive oil, the most widely used fuel, was probably more expensive in Italy than it was in Africa, which was a major producer of oil.

Monica had slaves, but we do not know how many; Augustine mentions only the nurses who fed and cared for him (*Conf.* 1.6.7). He was familiar with households in which slaves had specialized duties, as no doubt they did in the grand house of Romanianus, where he was made welcome as a student and as a young teacher (*c.Acad.* 2.2.3). He used the example of household staff to illustrate how customs vary to fit a particular time and place. When people object that, according to the scriptures, Abraham and Isaac and Jacob and Moses and David behaved in ways which are not permitted to Christians:

> It is as if they saw, in one house, something handled by one
> slave that is not allowed to the one who brings the drinks, or
> something done behind the stables which is forbidden in front
> of the dinner table, and they were angry because, in the same
> dwelling-place and the same household, the same actions were
> not allowed to every person in every place. (*Conf.* 3.7.13)

Unless Monica had a housekeeper, and even if she did, she probably had to order meals, check and distribute household supplies, settle arguments, go through the household accounts, and oversee the quality of

---

44. On all these tasks, see Croom (n. 21).

work. She spent time with the children. She was attentive to the mother-in-law who was in residence when she married (*Conf.* 9.9.20), and presumably she visited, and was visited by, other family members. She talked to her neighbours. In later centuries, housekeeping books and journals, and novels written by women, show days routinely occupied by these responsibilities, and in some cases also by charitable activities and spiritual reading. Augustine's contemporary Jerome, arguing that celibate asceticism was superior to marriage, thought that the spiritual reading was crowded out by the domestic duties:

> The babies are prattling, the slaves are shouting, the children
> want attention and kisses, the expenditure is added up
> and the payment got ready. On one side a posse of cooks,
> girded for action, is pounding meat; on the other a crowd of
> weaving-women is chattering. Meanwhile, the arrival of her
> husband and his friends is announced. She ranges through the
> rooms like a swallow. Is the couch smooth? Have they swept the
> floors? Are the wine cups set out? Is the dinner ready? Answer
> me, please: where in all this is the thought of God? (*adv.Helv.* 20)

Augustine recognised that his mother had much more leisure as an older woman, at the time when he wrote his early dialogues (*ord.* 2.1.1). She was then a widow, living away from her family house, and her children were grown up. She still mothered Augustine, his students and his friends (*Conf.* 9.9.22), and still took charge of the borrowed house at Cassiciacum and its slaves.

One kind of work in particular was traditionally "women's work". A Latin epitaph of the second century BCE (*CIL* 6.15346) includes the line 'she kept house, she worked wool', and this has been taken to summarize the domestic life of a good woman. In the western world, until the twentieth century, "women's work" was always something to do with textiles: spinning and weaving, sewing and knitting, tapestry and embroidery, making and mending. In classical antiquity it was spinning and weaving wool, *lanificium*. Other kinds of fabric were in use, but linen is suitable only for warm weather; silk, worn by the rich, was expensive to buy and to care for; and wool holds colour better than either. *Lanificium* (like home cooking in more recent years) was the sign of the good wife who stayed home and cared for her household.[45]

45. Lena Larsson Lovén, 'Wool Work as a Gender Symbol in Ancient Rome', in C. Gillis and

That is why, in the funeral oration for Murdia, it appears, disconcertingly, in the list of virtues shared by good women.[46] That oration was spoken in the late first century BCE, near the time when Livy began his history of Rome, in which wool-work as domestic virtue is exemplified in the story of Lucretia. She was raped by a prince of the royal family, told her husband and father, and despite their support, committed suicide; this outrage led to the overthrow of the monarchy and the foundation of the Roman republic. The story begins (*Ab urbe condita* 1.57.4–5) with three aristocratic young men, on campaign outside Rome, getting drunk and arguing about whose wife is the most virtuous. They decide to settle the question by an unexpected visit home. Reaching Rome as night falls, they find two of the wives having parties with others of their age group. It is late when they arrive at the third house, but Lucretia and her women slaves are still sitting in the atrium, the central space of the house, working wool by lamplight.

Did women in Monica's lifetime actually do wool work, or did they buy clothes and textiles for the household, or have some of the work done outside the house? Augustine made a passing comment in a sermon:

> You are told to keep the Sabbath spiritually, not in carnal
> leisure as the Jews observe the Sabbath. They want to be free
> to enjoy their trivialities and luxuries. A Jew would be better
> doing something useful on his farm than causing trouble
> in the theatre. And their women would be better doing
> wool-work on the Sabbath than dancing immodestly all day
> on their balconies. (*ser.* 9.3)

This, evidently, is stereotypical thinking. Not all men had farm work to do; did all women have wool work? Augustine often used images and metaphors from farming, especially from harvesting grain and pressing olives, and took it for granted that his urban congregation in Hippo understood them. He did not use images from spinning and weaving, and did not show understanding of the processes, the work and the time required to make even one woollen garment. Fortunately, there is recent practical research.[47]

M.-L. Nosch, eds., *Ancient Textiles. Production, Craft and Society* (2007), pp. 229–36, taking the story to the time of Augustus in the first century CE.

46. Cited and discussed in chapter 1.

47. For the range of imagery Augustine used in preaching, see Suzanne Poque, *Le langage*

First, fleece had to be cleaned of grease and dirt, dyed if colour was wanted, and carded (combed) so that it was ready to be spun into woollen thread. The spinning wheel had not yet been invented, so spinning required only a handful of carded wool placed on a rod (a distaff), and another rod (a spindle), weighted at the end, which is turned to draw down and twist a woollen thread. Spinning of this kind can easily be picked up and put down, and in many cultures women, and sometimes men, spin thread whenever their hands are not otherwise occupied. Roman men did not spin, but some were employed as weavers.[48] When there is enough thread, the next task is to set up a loom of the appropriate size. Fabric was not yet produced as lengths of cloth which were cut and sewn as required, presumably because hand-woven fabric is likely to fray when it is cut. Instead, garments and textiles were woven to shape. It takes time and skill to set up a loom with the right number of warp (vertical) threads, weighted to produce the right tension, and to weave even a simple rectangle of plain fabric with firm edges. Further skill is needed if the plan is to keep the body narrow but to widen the fabric for the sleeves of the garment. Advanced workers could add borders and stripes, and experts could produce tapestry panels in high-status garments.

It is not surprising that wool-work was seen as an occupation that kept women busy, at home and out of trouble, in any time they had to spare from other domestic tasks. An anonymous sermon on drunkenness makes the point strongly:

> So, through drunkenness [*vinulentia*], the mistress's keys are
> stolen away; the well-stocked store rooms are emptied by the
> daily thefts of the slaves; attempts are made on everything;
> the whole house echoes to the shouts of a household out
> of control. Attention to *lanificium* becomes careless, or
> nonexistent, or hateful. To such a mistress, the slave woman
> who hands her a bigger wine cup is dearer than the slave

symbolique dans la prédication d'Augustin d'Hippone (1984). My thanks to Mary Harlow for advice on recent work at the Textile Research Centre, Copenhagen. For techniques of weaving and clothes-making, see also Alexandra Croom, *Roman Clothing and Fashion*, 2, ed. (2010), pp. 16–30.

48. Lovén (n. 45), p. 232. The Stoic philosopher Hierocles, writing in the second century CE, saw no reason why men should not share some household tasks, including wool-work, provided there were no concerns about their masculinity: Stobaeus 4.85.21, in Ilaria Ramelli, *Hierocles the Stoic* (2009), p. 95.

woman who has finished all her allocation of wool before evening. [. . .] She looks for the measure of wine brought in, not the measure of clothes to be made. She does not set up warp-threads for weaving as a guard for chastity: she has long since, through drunkenness [*ebrietas*], lost the use of the loom from the house, and the warps she withdrew from her idle slave women she gave to spiders to weave. (*de sobrietate et castitate*, PL 40.1110–11)[49]

Perhaps there was always spinning and weaving for Monica and her slave women, just as, within living memory, there was always sewing and knitting and the mending basket. Possibly Monica's good works included making clothes and blankets for the poor, following the Bible example of the widow Dorcas (Acts 9: 39); but that is more likely for widows, or for women religious, than for women with a household to manage. Jerome suggested it to Demetrias, who chose the path of virginity (*ep.* 130.15), and he also recommended spinning for the little granddaughter of his ascetic friend Paula (*ep.* 107.10). But it may not have made economic sense to produce clothing and textiles at home, or to do all the stages of the process at home. Cloth itself rarely survives well for excavation, but there is evidence for textile workers and for production in workshops, some of which were small-scale, some exporting large quantities. In the late third century the emperor Diocletian, in his Edict on Prices, fixed the maximum price of many kinds of fabric and clothing that were available for sale.[50] The veteran settlement at Timgad, inland from Thagaste, had two clothes markets. It also had a complex of workshops for fulling and dyeing cloth; these are messy, smelly tasks that would be better done away from home.[51] Fulling involves removing any grease and dirt which was left in the cloth, then finishing the cloth by felting or by raising or smoothing the nap. Fullers also cleaned clothes. In his advice for monastic communities, Augustine wrote that clothes could be washed at home or by the fullers, whichever the superior decided, and that people should not expect to have clean clothes

49. On the danger of wives getting drunk, see chapter 1.

50. J.-M. Carrié, 'Vitalité de l'industrie textile à la fin de l'antiquité', in *Antiquité Tardive* 12 (2004), pp. 13–43, is a valuable introductory survey for a special issue on *Tissus et vêtements dans l' Antiquité tardive*.

51. Andrew Wilson, 'Timgad and Textile Production', in D. Mattingly and J. Salmon, eds. (2001), *Economies beyond Agriculture in the Classical World*, pp. 271–96.

too often (*reg.* (*regula*) 5.4). He did not say who would do the home washing. He expected monks and nuns not to have slaves, or other personal possessions, but his careful account of the community at Hippo shows that some members had brought slaves with them (*ser.* 356. 6–7).

So Monica had options. She could have chosen to buy textiles or to make them at home, to send out some unpleasant tasks to fullers, to assign the spinning and weaving to slaves, or to work with them when she had time. Perhaps she made special items for which she could select the weave, design, and colours. One of Augustine's letters (*ep.* 263) seeks to console a nun, Sapida, whose brother had died before he could wear the tunic she had woven for him; she sent it to Augustine. A different family gift appears in a letter from Symmachus, the man who as Prefect of Rome appointed Augustine professor of rhetoric at Milan. He thanks his daughter for a birthday present she had woven or overseen in person:

> My lady daughter, I rejoice to be honoured with the rich
> memento of your wool-working: it displays both your love for
> your father and your industry as a married woman. Women in
> the old days are said to have led their life like this. Their times,
> barren of enjoyments, made them attend to the distaff and the
> weaving-frame, because when there are no allurements people
> live as things are. But for you even Baiae [a seaside resort] on
> the doorstep cannot distract your concern for this sober work.
> You leave the water to those who row on it, and sitting or
> walking among the wool weighed out for your slave girls and
> the threads which mark their daily weaving, you think that
> these are the sole delights of your sex. (*ep.* 6.67)

Symmachus knows that wool-work is the traditional activity of the home-loving daughter and wife; he knows the words for the daily allocation of wool to be spun and for the threads that were used to mark off the weaving done in a day.[52] It is not clear whether his daughter was "sitting and walking" to supervise, or herself worked a loom.

A final question: what were Monica's own clothes like? Here at least there is some visual evidence. It must be interpreted with caution, because the images were not intended to show how an individual woman actually looked, but the study of dress is now recognized as a

---

52. This translation expands *pensa et foragines.* The lexicon of Festus explains that *forago* is the thread with which women weavers mark off a day's work.

FIGURE 2.4. Tomb image of Victoria: From Tabarka, North Africa, late fourth or early fifth century.

© Bardo Museum.

valuable contribution to cultural history.[53] In some regions of the Roman empire there were distinctive local styles, but this is not apparent in late antique Africa.[54] Women might wear an undertunic, with close-fitting sleeves. The main tunic was floor-length and wide-shouldered, and its sleeves, if any, were also wide. It could be tied in under the bust or at

53. Clark (n. 8), pp. 105–6, on the limitations of the visual evidence; Mary Harlow, 'Introduction', in M. Harlow, ed., *Dress and Identity* (2012), pp. 1–5.
    54. Croom (n. 47), p. 161.

the waist. The tunic was woven to the right length and width for the wearer, then sewn at the sides; or it could be made from two lengths of fabric fastened at the shoulders. It often had one or two vertical stripes in a contrasting colour, which could be repeated in bands at the end of the sleeves. The neckline was high, and was filled in by the most important item of jewellery, a heavy necklace. A mantle, a simple rectangle of fabric, could be draped in many different ways over the tunic. Probably a woman outside her house would draw a fold of the mantle, or a scarf, over her hair. Then as now, different places had different expectations about head covering, but Augustine advised nuns that their head covering should not be so thin that their hairnets showed through (*ep.* 211.10). He did not suggest that they should veil their faces, and one comment shows that women's faces could be seen: some of Monica's neighbours had the marks of blows even on their disfigured faces (*Conf.* 9.9.19). [55]

What exactly Monica wore, or how she did her hair, we do not know. Augustine once advised a married woman that there is a happy medium between seductive dress and looking like a widow before you are one, but he did not say how it was to be achieved (*ep.* 262.9). He avoided detailed advice on clothing, and in a hurried reply to his friend and fellow bishop Possidius he recommended caution:

> I don't want you to make too quick a decision about
> forbidding adornments of gold or of clothing, except for those
> who are neither married nor wish to marry, and should think
> how to please God. Married people think about the things of
> this world, how husbands can please their wives or wives their
> husbands. Except that women should not uncover their hair
> even if they are married, for the Apostle tells them to veil their
> heads. As for colouring with makeup to appear more rosy
> or more fair-skinned, that is adulterous deception, and I do
> not doubt that even husbands would not want to be deceived;
> and it is only for husbands that women are allowed to adorn
> themselves, as a concession not as an instruction. For the
> true adornment of Christian men and women is not only no
> lying colour, and no display of gold and clothing, but good
> behaviour. (*Ep.* 245.1)

55. On domestic violence, see chapter 3.

Widows generally wore dark clothing: not black, which was expensive because it needed so much dye, but the colour of dark undyed wool. Seductive dress probably involved thin clinging fabrics in eye-catching colours, jewellery, and makeup, and hair imperfectly covered, perhaps revealing a jewelled hairnet. It seems unlikely that Monica dressed seductively, even in the years when she had a husband to please.

3

Monica's Service

The word "served" echoes through Augustine's writing about Monica.
She was given to a husband and served him as her master (*Conf.* 9.9.19).
She served her parents and her son's friends: 'she cared for us as if she
had given birth to all, and served us as if she had been born from all'
(*Conf.* 9.9.22). Service to others is often admirable, but *servire* is what
slaves did, and Latin words which are often translated "servant" or
"handmaid" actually mean "slave": *serva, famula, ancilla*. Similarly,
dominus is often translated "lord" rather than "master". In *Confessions*
Monica is repeatedly shown among slaves. In her parents' house, her
upbringing is entrusted to an elderly slave nurse, and a quarrel with a
woman slave saves her from drunkenness (9.8.17–18).[1] In her husband's
house, women slaves tell her mother-in-law malicious stories about her
(9.9.20), and slave nurses share the breastfeeding and care of her children (1.6.7). All this shows the close relationship of slaves and owners
who share a house. But Monica tells her women neighbours that they
too should think of themselves as slaves, *ancillae*, of their husbands
(9.9.19), and Augustine's account of Monica's marriage is likely to shock
present day readers, both by his approval of Monica's service and by his
acceptance of domestic violence:

> So, brought up modestly and soberly, and subjected by you
> to her parents rather than by her parents to you, when she
> was 'of full years marriageable' she was given to a husband,
> whom she served as if a master, and strove to gain him for

1. On this episode, see chapter 1.

you, speaking of you to him by her behaviour, by which
you made her beautiful to her husband, as one to be loved,
revered and admired.[2] Moreover, she bore with wrongs of the
bed in such a way that she never had any quarrel with her
spouse on this matter. She waited for your mercy upon him,
so that, believing in you, he would be made chaste. He was
as hot-tempered in anger as he was outstanding in kindness.
But she knew not to resist her husband when he was angry,
by action or even by a word. When she saw him calmed down
and quiet, and the time was right, she would explain what she
had done, if he had been roused to anger without sufficient
reflection. Many married women, whose husbands were
milder, bore the traces of blows even on their disfigured faces.
In friendly conversation they blamed the way of life [*vita*] of
their spouses, but she blamed their tongues. She advised them
in all seriousness, though apparently in jest, that from the
time when they heard the documents called 'marriage lines'
[*tabulae matrimoniales*] read out, they should have thought
of them as contracts [*instrumenta*] by which they were made
slaves [*ancillae*]; and so, mindful of their status [*condicio*],
they ought not to be arrogant towards their masters. The
other women were amazed, knowing how fierce a spouse she
endured, that it had never been heard, or had become clear
by some indication, that Patricius had beaten his wife, or that
they had disagreed for even one day in some domestic dispute.
They asked in friendship why that was, and she told them her
practice, which I have mentioned above. Those who followed
it were thankful from experience; those who did not follow it
were subjected and harassed. (*Conf.* 9.9.19)

Was Monica a slave? There were very few legal limits on how slaves
could be treated, but beating was the usual punishment for insubordi-
nation or for any other behaviour to which their owner objected. It was
not appropriate for free people, but it was used to punish children and
people of low social status, so the visible bruises of Monica's neighbours
were degrading as well as painful.[3] In law, Monica was certainly not a

2. Augustine draws on 1 Peter 3:1, quoted in these notes.
3. See Peter Garnsey, *Social Status and Legal Privilege in the Roman Empire* (1970), on the
increasing use of physical punishment for the freeborn poor.

slave: she spoke 'apparently in jest' because a contract of marriage was plainly not a contract of sale. Two centuries after Monica's lifetime, the emperor Justinian made it explicit that Roman law did not recognise bride-price, because it allowed a woman to be bought by her husband as if she were a slave (*Nov. J. (Novellae Justiniani)* 21, 536 CE).[4] A wife was a free woman who could not be bought or sold by her husband; marriage with a slave was not possible, because a slave was the property of her or his owner. A slave owned nothing, because he or she was owned; a wife was expected (though not required) to have a dowry, which her husband could use, but which had to be returned if the marriage ended.[5] A wife could also own property acquired by inheritance, investment, or trading. Her property was legally separate from her husband's, and she could choose how to leave it, whereas he had to leave his property to his legal heirs.[6]

When Monica heard her marriage contract (*tabulae matrimoniales*) read out, most of what she heard was about property. A written contract was not required to make a marriage valid, but it was sensible to have a record of this major financial transaction. Moreover, the ceremony of reading the contract, and having it signed by family members and distinguished guests, ensured that the marriage was generally known in the community, and could also display the wealth and connections of the contracting families. There are no extant *tabulae* from the time of Monica's marriage in the mid-fourth century, but where marriage contracts do survive from late antiquity, they are chiefly concerned to specify the property which the woman brought as dowry and the arrangements for returning it if the marriage ended in divorce.[7]

According to the law, a wife remained in the *potestas* of her father (or nearest male relative) and did not enter the *potestas* of her husband. *Potestas* means "power", and in this context it means the power to take actions which had an effect in law. So a wife's birth-family could

4. On the difference between "nuptial gifts" and bride-price, see Antti Arjava, *Women and Law in Late Antiquity* (1996), pp. 52–62.

5. Owners could recognise the partnership, *contubernium*, of a slave couple, but they could nevertheless sell the couple, and their children, separately. They could allow a slave to make use of assets, called *peculium*, in order to build up resources and eventually buy freedom, but in principle the *peculium* was owned by the master.

6. See Arjava (n. 4) pp. 62–73 on inheritance by women, 133–46 on separation of property.

7. Judith Evans Grubbs, *Law and Family in Late Antiquity* (1995), pp. 140–7. Most of the evidence comes from Egypt in the sixth and seventh centuries: Joelle Beaucamp, *Le statut de la femme à Byzance 4e-7e siècles.* 2 vols (1990), 2.128–9.

demand the end of a marriage if the husband misused the dowry or mistreated his wife. Augustine said nothing about Monica's parents, except that they were Christian, and did not suggest that his grand-parents, maternal or paternal, were a presence in his childhood. What would Monica's parents (or other close kin) have counted as mistreat-ment which required intervention, rather than as treatment wives should expect and should learn to manage? Roman divorce law changed several times in the course of the fourth century, but Constantine, in the year of Monica's birth, probably expressed a widely held view in saying that a husband's drinking, gambling, and womanizing were 'far-fetched reasons' which could not be cited by his wife as grounds for unilateral divorce (CT 3.16.1, 331 CE).[8] In law, a woman could herself send a notice of divorce, but in practice, few women had the confidence to do this, even if they had the resources to investigate the law and some-where to go when they left the marriage. Presumably a woman would not herself send the notice if she had the support of a birth family, and almost certainly divorce would mean that her children stayed with the man she had chosen to leave, and perhaps acquired a stepmother who would at best favour her own children.[9] Constantine's law assumed that, unless the husband was guilty of major crimes, the wife wanted divorce because of her 'depraved desires': in other words, she wanted to live with someone else. These social attitudes could trap a woman in an abusive marriage.

Monica escaped the common experience of domestic violence, according to Augustine, because of her tact in managing her husband's anger, and in particular because she 'bore with wrongs of the bed', whereas the battered wives of Thagaste blamed the 'way of life' (*vita*) of their spouses. The polite phrase 'wrongs of the bed' (*cubilis iniurias*) means that Patricius was unfaithful, and some of Augustine's sermons show the most likely kind of infidelity: not affairs with married women, or visits to the local brothel, but relationships with women who, because of their social status, could not expect to marry. Actresses, for example, and (according to Constantine) barmaids, could not marry, because they were on public view and so were assimilated to prostitutes.[10] If a man's

8. Context of Constantine's law: Evans Grubbs (n. 7), pp. 225–60. Changes to divorce law: Gillian Clark, *Women in Late Antiquity* (1993), pp. 17–27; fuller discussion in Arjava (n. 4), pp. 177–89.

9. Sometimes, but not usually, children remained with their mother after divorce: Arjava (n. 4), pp. 86–7.

10. Barmaids: *C.Th.* 9.7.1, 326 CE. Landladies, who were less exposed, could marry.

sexual partner was one of his own slaves, nobody else had a right to object. Augustine challenged the men in his congregation:

> Someone will say 'But she's not a prostitute, she's my
> concubine.' You who say this, do you have a wife? 'I have.'
> Then whatever you think, she's a prostitute. Go and say that
> the bishop does you wrong, if you have a wife and another
> woman sleeps with you. Whoever she is, she's a prostitute. But
> perhaps she's faithful to you, she knows no other man except
> you, she has no plans to know one. If she is chaste, why do you
> fornicate? If she has one man, why do you have two women?
> It's not allowed, not allowed, not allowed. (*ser.* 224.3)

Wife, concubine, and prostitute name three kinds of sexual relationship. When Monica heard her marriage contract read, it specified that she was given to her husband 'for the procreation of children'. A wife was the woman whose children would be the legal heirs of the man who was her husband. This fact distinguished a wife from a concubine, whose children were known to be the children of a particular man because she was known not to have other sexual relationships. Nobody doubted, for example, that Monica's grandson Adeodatus was the son of Augustine, whose faithful partner vowed, when she was sent away, that she would never go with another man (*Conf.* 6.15.25). Living with a concubine was socially acceptable when a man was not yet married, or when a widower or divorced man did not want to marry again and produce more heirs. Augustine took responsibility for his son, but he did not regard his partner as a wife, and she had to leave when his marriage was arranged.[11]

The men who said "she's not a prostitute, she's my concubine" were wrong in terms of Roman law, which ruled that a man could not have a concubine, an acknowledged partner whose children were known to be his, at the same time as a wife, whose children were his legal heirs. The children of a prostitute might have been fathered by any of her clients, so had no claim on any of them. In another sermon (9.15) Augustine imagined a man saying "if I kill, or steal, or do not honour my parents, or if I commit adultery, or covet my neighbour's wife or property, I do what I do not want done to me; but if I go to a prostitute [*meretrix,*

11. See further chapter 5.

literally 'female earner'], to whom do I do something that I do not want done to me?" This is revealing. The obvious answer is "you do it to the prostitute, unless you want someone to pay you for sex", but the imagined speaker thinks "no one is injured if I pay a prostitute for sex, because she does not belong to another man."

For the men in Augustine's congregation, "having a concubine" meant having a stable relationship with a woman who was neither a wife (actual or potential) nor a prostitute with other clients. In Roman law, a married woman committed adultery if she had a sexual relationship with any man other than her husband. A man, whether married or unmarried, committed adultery only if he had a sexual relationship with another man's wife. Adultery was a serious offence, not only because it was an insult to the husband, but because it disrupted inheritance: an adulterous wife might bear a child who would wrongly inherit from her husband, and her infidelity cast doubt on the legitimacy of her other children. Similarly, a sexual relationship with a freeborn woman who could marry raised the question whether she would be faithful when she did marry.[12] So the men Augustine challenged thought their behaviour was acceptable, because they were not adulterous, or promiscuous, but had a decent extramarital arrangement with one woman who (in many cases) belonged to them anyway. Patricius probably shared this view, and though Monica hoped he would eventually be faithful, she did not complain.

Such arrangements had a practical use which Augustine did not acknowledge, but which Monica may well have recognized. As a bishop, Augustine argued forcefully for the single standard of sexual morality. But he wanted more of men than fidelity to their wives: he wanted them to have intercourse only with their wives and only in the hope of children. He invoked the wording of their marriage contracts:

> A man who desires the flesh of his wife more than is permitted by the limit 'for the procreation of children' acts against the contract by which he married her. The contract is read out, it is read out before all who witness it, and there is read out 'for the procreation of children', and the contract is called a marriage contract. Unless wives are given and received for this purpose, who in his right mind gives his daughter to another's lust? But

12. Adultery: see Evans Grubbs (n. 7), pp. 203–25.

the contract is read out so that the parents do not blush when they give her, so that they are parents-in-law not pimps. What, then, is read out from the contract? 'For the procreation of children'. (*ser.* 51.13.22)

A wife was the woman given for the procreation of children; she was not given for the satisfaction of sexual desires. Augustine ignored the problem that marital desires could result in more pregnancies than were good for the wife's health and more children than the property could support. Monica and Patricius were able to support their three children, but their investment in Augustine's education strained the family finances. Was it just by self-control and good fortune that they had the optimum number of children for their circumstances?

Augustine did not suggest that Monica suffered miscarriages or stillbirths, or that other children died in infancy. Respectable women were not supposed to know about contraceptive methods or drugs; that knowledge was for prostitutes, not for wives. Medical texts were more concerned with achieving fertility than with preventing it. Even so, women probably did know something, from "friendly conversations". Herbal medicines had a wide range of uses, so women could claim to have taken a medicine without any intention of denying their husbands another child; but traditional methods and herbal remedies were not reliable.[13] Augustine deplored the fact that some men did not 'spare' their wives even in pregnancy. He also said that a woman who used or agreed to contraceptive practices was treating her husband as if he were her adulterous lover, and her husband was treating her as a prostitute (*nupt.et conc.* 1.15.17)—that is, as if their relationship was of a kind in which pregnancy was a threat rather than a hope.[14] In a more realistic mode, he asked whether any married man was ever heard saying, in friendly conversation, that he had sex with his wife only in the hope of children (*b.conjug.* 13.15). (These "friendly conversations" must have been the masculine equivalent of those in which the women of Thagaste complained about the behaviour of their husbands.) But he continued

13. Clark (n. 8), pp. 84–8.
14. Augustine and his partner had no children except Adeodatus, born in the first year of their thirteen-year relationship. For most of this time Augustine was a Manichaean, and presumably shared the belief that procreation should be avoided because it traps souls in bodies (see chapter 5). It is often suggested that he used contraceptive techniques learned from Manichaeans, but he never confesses this, and it is also possible that his partner became infertile after a difficult birth.

to argue that for baptized Christians, the answer was male self-control. Patience and prayer, according to Augustine, helped Monica to tolerate the infidelity of a husband who was not yet Christian. Monica could also have welcomed time to recover from pregnancy and childbirth, and could have reflected that the children (if any) of a slave "concubine" would add to the domestic workforce without inheriting a share of the property.

Monica, the daughter of baptized Christians, did not exchange promises at a church wedding; this was not because her husband was not a Christian, but because Christian marriage ceremonies were a later development.[15] Perhaps her parents invited their bishop to be one of the guests who witnessed the contract. But even without a church wedding, she could hear and read the scriptures on the submissive behaviour and willing service of a good wife. A letter to the church at Ephesus, ascribed to Paul of Tarsus, uses a comparison with Christ and the Church to instruct Christians on marriage:

> Being subject to one another in the fear of Christ, wives are
> to be subject to their own husbands as to the Master, because
> the man is the head of the woman just as Christ is the head
> of the church, and he [i.e., Christ] is the saviour of the body.
> But as the church is subject to Christ, so wives are subject to
> their husbands in everything. Husbands, love your wives as
> Christ too loved the church and gave himself for her, so that
> he might cleanse her by water and the word and sanctify her,
> and present to himself the church glorious, without blemish
> or wrinkle or anything of the kind, but so that she should be
> holy and blameless. That is how husbands should love their
> wives, like their own bodies. For no one ever hates his own
> flesh, but nurtures and cherishes it, as Christ does the church,
> because we are members of his body. 'For this reason a man
> shall leave his father and mother and be joined to his wife,
> and the two shall be one flesh.'[16] This is a great mystery; I say it
> with reference to Christ and the church. Except that you also,

15. David Hunter, 'Augustine and the Making of Marriage in Roman North Africa', *Journal of Early Christian Studies* 11.1 (2003), 63–85, shows that Augustine provides no evidence for a Christian marriage ceremony, but regards the *tabulae* as central.
16. Genesis 2:24, quoted by Jesus in Mt 19:5.

as individuals, must each love his wife as himself, and the wife must fear her husband. (Eph. 5:21–33)

Husband and wife, parent and child, master and slave, are the three basic household relationships of superior to subordinate. The letter to the church at Ephesus advises the superior as well as the subordinate on the right way to behave; it goes on to say that children must obey their parents, and fathers must not make their children angry; slaves must obey their masters as they obey Christ; and masters must not threaten slaves. Augustine drew on another passage, from the first letter of Peter, in his account of Monica's marriage:

> Be subject to your own husbands, so that if any of them
> disbelieve the word [that is, the Christian gospel] they will
> be won over without a word by the behaviour of their wives,
> observing your respectful and chaste behaviour. Your beauty
> should not be external, in braiding hair and putting on
> jewellery and wearing fine clothes, but should be the hidden
> self of the heart, in the imperishable quality of a gentle and
> quiet spirit, which is precious in the sight of God. This is
> how in former times holy women who put their hope in God
> adorned themselves, being subject to their own husbands, as
> Sarah obeyed Abraham and called him master.[17]

Monica won her husband for God by her behaviour, which made her beautiful to him (*Conf.* 9.9.19, quoted above). He became a catechumen, under instruction in the church, not long before Augustine was fifteen (2.3.6). At the end of his life, perhaps a year later, he was baptized, and his infidelities ended as Monica had hoped: 'She did not lament in her husband, once baptized [*fidelis*], what she had tolerated in one not yet baptized' (9.9.22). But, as James O'Donnell points out, Augustine avoids saying that Monica was subject to her husband: when he cites in relation to Monica passages of the New Testament which tell wives to be subject (*subditae*) to their husbands, he changes the word to 'serve', but in sermons he keeps *subditae* (e.g. *ser.* 392.4).[18] As a faithful Christian, trying to do God's will, Monica is superior to her husband,

---

17. I Peter 3:1–2. The book of Genesis, which tells the story of Abraham and Sarah, does not say that she obeyed him and called him master.

18. James J. O'Donnell, *Augustine: Confessions* III. 412–13, on *Conf.* 13.32.47.

the only member of the household who is not Christian: '. . . for she worked to make you my father, my God, rather than he, and in this you helped her to overcome her husband, whom she, the better, served [*cui melior serviebat*], because in this she served you who gave this order' (*Conf.* 1.11.17).

Augustine also avoided saying that Monica overcame her husband in other respects. He presents her as entirely serious in saying that wives should think of themselves as their husband's slaves, and behave accordingly. That is what, as a bishop, he told wives to do. One example is especially striking, because he was preaching on the praise of the good wife which concludes the Book of Proverbs. In this passage of scripture the good wife is praised, not for service and submission, but for her contribution to the household and provident care of her family:

(10) Who can find a good wife? Her worth is far beyond red coral.
(11) Her husband's whole trust is in her, and children are not lacking.
(12) She works to bring him good, not evil, all the days of her life.
(13) She chooses wool and flax, and with a will she sets about her work.
(14) Like a ship laden with merchandise, she brings home food from far off.
(15) She rises while it is still dark, and apportions food for her household, with a due share for her servants.
(16) After careful thought she buys a field, and plants a vineyard out of her earnings.
(17) She sets about her duties resolutely and tackles her work with vigour.
(18) She sees that her business goes well, and all night long her lamp does not go out.
(19) She holds the distaff in her hand, and her fingers grasp the spindle.
(20) She is open-handed to the wretched and extends help to the poor.
(21) When it snows she has no fear for her household, for they are wrapped in double cloaks.
(22) She makes her own bed coverings, and clothing of fine linen and purple.
(23) Her husband is well known in the assembly, where he takes his seat with the elders of the region.
(24) She weaves linen and sells it, and supplies merchants with sashes.
(25) She is clothed in strength and dignity, and can afford to laugh at tomorrow.

(26) When she opens her mouth, it is to speak wisely; her teaching is sound.

(27) She keeps her eye on the conduct of her household and does not eat the bread of idleness.

(28) Her sons with one accord extol her virtues; her husband too is loud in her praise.

(29) Many a woman shows how gifted she is; but you excel them all.

(30) Charm is deceptive and beauty fleeting; but the woman who fears the Lord is honoured.

(31) Praise her for all she has accomplished; let her achievements bring her honour at the city gates.[19]

Augustine did not in *Confessions* link this passage to Monica, though she may well have deserved such praise for her management of family resources. When he preached on it, in the same year that he began *Confessions,* he focussed on the first verse, which in his Latin translation was 'Who shall find a strong woman?' He explained at once that the "strong woman" (*mulier fortis*) is the Church, mother of the faithful; it would not be proper to speak of another woman (*ser.* 37.1). He expounded the praise of the strong woman, always in relation to the Church, not suggesting even in general terms that he or his hearers knew strong women who worked with their hands making clothes, and who got up while it was still dark to provide food for the household and make allocations to many slaves. Then he asked:

> Are these slaves [*ancillae*] hers, or her husband's? Are they
> hers because they are her husband's? Is she herself the
> many slaves? Although she is the mistress of the household
> [*materfamilias*], she does not disdain to be a slave. Let her
> wait for her price, let her love her Master. Let her recognize,
> I say, that she is a slave, and let her not fear her condition. For
> he does not disdain to make her his wife whom he bought for
> so much. Every good wife calls her husband master. She does
> not only call him so, she thinks it, she speaks it, she carries
> it in her heart, she utters it with her mouth, she regards the
> marriage contract as the instrument of her purchase. So she

19. Proverbs 10:10–31. Translations vary: this one is from the Revised English Bible. It was chosen for clarity, much as I regret the loss of 'her price is above rubies'. The book of Proverbs brings together several collections of sayings, which are difficult to date.

> is a slave giving tasks to slaves. She is a slave, so he is her son
> who says 'I am your slave and the son of your slave'. (*ser.* 37.7)

Augustine was speaking of the Church, the spouse of Christ who bought her with his own death (Eph. 5:25, quoted above). Christ buys the Church out of slavery to sin and makes this freed slave his wife; but clearly the Church is not yet free from sin, so, as Augustine puts it, she must wait for her purchase price. He seems not to notice that a slave who is freed and made a wife is the reverse of what he says next, when he expects his congregation to agree that every good wife calls her husband "master" and thinks of her marriage contract as a contract of purchase: that is, a wife who was free is made a slave. Perhaps he had not, in Milan, heard Ambrose discuss the punishment of Eve for disobeying God's command in the Garden of Eden: she was told that she would bear children in pain and that 'your husband shall be your master', but Ambrose reminded his hearers 'You are not a master, but a husband. You have not acquired a slave, but a wife.'[20] Or perhaps Ambrose, an Italian aristocrat who did not marry, did not share the perspective of men in Thagaste and Hippo.

'She regards the marriage contract as the instrument of her purchase', repeats Monica's advice to her neighbours. Did Monica, like Augustine, also make the most of the custom that 'every good wife calls her husband master'? *Domine*, "master", was indeed the way slaves addressed their owners, but *domine* for men and *domina* for women was also a widely used form of address, polite or affectionate, within and beyond the family.[21] Patricius may well have called Monica *domina*, without any implication that he was her slave. What then did it mean, to Monica and her friends, to think of oneself as a husband's *ancilla*? This is difficult to assess. For example, the response of Mary mother of Jesus to the angel Gabriel, *ecce ancilla Domini* (Luke 1:38), is conventionally translated 'behold the handmaid of the Lord'. Would "I am the master's slave" be more accurate, or would it be misleading, because "slave" had a different resonance in classical antiquity, or because "I am

---

20. Genesis 3:16; Ambrose, *Hexaemeron* 5.7.19. The contrast with Augustine is made by Kim Power, *Veiled Desire* (1995), p. 124.

21. Eleanor Dickey, *Latin Forms of Address: from Plautus to Apuleius* (2002), pp. 77–109 (summarized pp. 321–2), discusses the complexities of *domine* from the earliest surviving Latin texts to Apuleius (second century CE).

the master's slave" was perhaps a conventionally respectful response, like "I am at your service"?

The problem for translators is that slavery is now seen as obviously wrong.[22] How can it be right to buy and sell human beings who must do what their owner requires? But in classical antiquity, the relationship of master and slave was fundamental to households and thus to society. Domestic service was done by slaves, because free people by definition did not serve others. Hired workers were temporary employees, and the responsibility of their employer ended there. Slaves, for preference, were born in the household, and were part of it for all their lives, like the nurse who as a girl had carried Monica's father on her back. Only a bad owner would be brutal to slaves or would sell a slave who was too old and frail to be useful. So slavery did not in itself prompt outrage.

Augustine saw slavery as a consequence of human sin.[23] He wrote that it is not a natural subordination, like that of female to male, but a just punishment, in that all humans are sinful (*civ. Dei* 19.15). Individual slavery may result from the sin of that individual, or from the sin of others. Augustine thought that the human urge to dominate others is a fundamental problem, but that did not mean he tried to change patterns of domination in human society. He expected the members of his monastic community to free any slaves they still had (*ser.* 356.6–7), not because he thought slavery was wrong, but because the members of the community were not to have possessions. Unlawful slavery was another matter. Augustine's congregation at Hippo intervened to rescue one-hundred-and-twenty people who said they had been kidnapped by slave traders and brought to this coastal town to be shipped abroad. Far from their homes, they could not bring witnesses to their free status. Augustine sought advice on the law and help in enforcing it (*ep.* 10*). But the people who intervened to rescue these victims took it for granted that they themselves, and anyone else who could afford it, owned slaves to work in the house, on the land, and on business.

So if Monica thought of herself as her husband's slave, she probably meant that she was a subordinate member of his household, and

22. This is not to say that "servant" solves the problem, both because of changing attitudes to domestic service, and because slaves in classical antiquity did a much wider range of tasks, from manual labourer to confidential secretary and business manager. A slave in the imperial household might be a rich and influential civil servant.

23. The most important passages are quoted and discussed by Peter Garnsey, *Ideas of Slavery from Aristotle to Augustine* (1997), pp. 206–19.

should defer to his wishes (unless, of course, he had misunderstood the situation). She may also have meant that women should hear their marriage contract as if it were a contract of sale, because the power balance of husband and wife was like that of master and slave. Marriage was not a relationship of equals. Even when women managed to get some education, they were not trained as men were to construct and present a reasoned and persuasive argument, because they had no place in public life where these skills were needed.[24] So husbands were usually better educated than their wives and had more experience of the world, even if they were not also (as they often were) some years older. Patricius died before Monica was 40, which suggests, but does not prove, that he was older than she was. Augustine, in his early thirties, expected to marry in two years time a girl who would then be 12: she would have been more than twenty years younger than her husband (*Conf.* 6.13.23).

These social conventions reinforced the widespread belief that women are weaker in reason than men, just as they are weaker in body; so women need care and protection from the men who are responsible for them, and may sometimes need discipline.[25] Augustine, discussing in his *Questions on the Heptateuch* (the first seven books of the Bible) the rule of superior over inferior, argued that people have dominion over animals because it is right that reason has dominion over nonrational life. Slavery, by contrast, results from human wickedness or misfortune. 'And there is a natural order among people such that women serve their husbands, and children their parents, because here too it is justice that the weaker reason serves the stronger.' He acknowledged that the one who dominates is not always stronger in reason, because of human wickedness or because of diversity among humans. When this happens, good people endure it, and will achieve full happiness in heaven.[26] Augustine did not suggest that the relationship should change so that the stronger reason was in charge. In the case of his parents, this would have been Monica.

Augustine thought that the domination of men over women was part of the punishment of Eve, the first woman, for disobedience to God: 'you will give birth to your children in pain; your yearning will be for your husband, and he will dominate you.'[27] He also thought that

---

24. See chapter 4.
25. See chapter 4 for philosophers who argued that women are not weaker in reason.
26. *qu.Gen.* 1.153, on Genesis 46:32–34.
27. Genesis 3:16, Jerusalem Bible translation.

FIGURE 3.1. Monica and Patricius take Augustine to school. Benozzo
Gozzoli, 1464–1465.

Wikimedia Commons.

women were naturally subordinate to men, in the God-given order of
creation.[28] He asked in a sermon 'What is worse than a house in which
the woman gives orders to the man? A house is right when the man
gives orders and the woman obeys' (*Jo. ev. tr.* 2.14). In another sermon
(*ser.* 152.4) he put it more bluntly: 'If in one house man and wife have
a disagreement, the husband must work to tame [*domare*] the wife.
A wife tamed is subjugated to her husband; when the wife is subjugated
to the husband, let there be peace in the house.' This is an image of
spirit controlling flesh, but he expected his congregation to agree with
the general principle. Monica and Patricius did not have disagreements,
according to Augustine, but how were other women to be tamed?

28. Carol Harrison, *Augustine: Christian Truth and Fractured Humanity* (2000), pp. 169–77,
offers a concise and perceptive account of Augustine on women. For a survey of feminist critique, see E. Ann Matter, 'Christ, God and Woman in the Thought of St Augustine', in Robert
Dodaro and George Lawless, eds., *Augustine and His Critics* (2000), 164–75.

In *City of God* (19.16) Augustine affirmed the responsibility of the head of household to punish, by rebuke or beating or any other lawful punishment, those who oppose the domestic peace which in turn contributes to the peace of the city. *Confessions* provides an example from Monica's life:

> Her mother-in-law was at first provoked against her by the whispers of bad slave women. [Monica] won her over by deference, persevering in tolerance and meekness, so that she of her own accord reported to her son the interfering tongues of the slaves, by which domestic peace between her and her daughter-in-law was disrupted, and demanded punishment. So he, in obedience to his mother and attention to the good order of his household and concern for the harmony of his family, restrained by beatings those who were reported, as she who reported them wished; and she then promised that anyone who told her anything bad about her daughter-in-law, to win favour, should hope for the same reward from her. No one dared, and they lived in memorably pleasant good will towards each other. (9.9.20)

Augustine made it clear that these beatings were not routine violence, or the result of an outburst of anger: they were formally ordered by the master of the house, at the request of his mother, to ensure the peace and discipline of the household. [29] But he also acknowledged (9.9.19, quoted above) that his father was hot-tempered, and that his mother knew not to confront him until his anger subsided. Anger, as many philosophers pointed out, showed that the man who claimed to be master of his household was in fact the slave of his passions.[30] Had Monica learned the hard way to evade rather than confront? Augustine claimed that no one saw his mother bruised, or heard that there had been a quarrel, and presumably 'no one' includes her children. He said that Monica had wanted to be buried with her husband 'because they had lived in great harmony', *valde concorditer vixerant* (*Conf.* 9.11.28). He

29. Augustine's contemporary John Chrysostom deplores women who frequently asked their husbands to beat their slaves: Joy Schroeder, 'John Chrysostom's Critique of Spousal Violence', *Journal of Early Christian Studies* 12 (2004): 413–12, at pp. 422–3.

30. W.V. Harris, *Restraining Rage* (2004), especially pp. 307–16 on anger and violence in the Roman family. He notes that philosophers have little to say about being angry with a wife or child.

followed his praise of Monica's peacemaking with a denunciation of the damage done by angry words (9.9.21); it was this kind of anger, rather than anger discharged in physical violence, which distressed him.[31] Perhaps he saw what he wanted to see in his parents' marriage; perhaps Monica led him to believe that battered wives had only themselves to blame for their failure of deference and tact.

Augustine provides evidence that many men thought wife-beating was acceptable, not only if the wife behaved so as to disgrace her husband, but also if the wife resisted her husband's wishes or objected to his behaviour. He did not challenge this assumption, as his contemporary John Chrysostom did when preaching in Antioch and in Constantinople.[32] John emphasized that a wife, although subject to her husband, is a free woman who should not be beaten or otherwise abused. He expected wives to obey their husbands, but he also recognized their contribution to the household. A wife, he said, is good at making cloth, managing the household, raising children, and keeping a watchful eye on the women slaves. Her husband is relieved of concern about the house and the storerooms, wool-work, meals, and clothes.[33] But even this more positive attitude did not make the church a refuge or a source of support for battered wives. The bishop had perhaps signed the marriage contract, and he certainly knew that wives were not slaves, but Christian preachers urged battered wives to remain with their husbands, patiently enduring and hoping to win them by gentleness.[34]

In one respect Augustine offered wives the support of the church, even against the wishes of their husbands: insistence on the single standard of sexual morality. In sermons urging married men to be faithful to their wives, he cited the contract which made the husband master and the wife his slave, and juxtaposed it with the teaching of Paul that the wife's body is not her own but belongs to her husband, and the husband's body is not his own but belongs to his wife:

31. Gertrude Gillette, 'Anger and Community in the *Rule* of Augustine', *Studia Patristica* 70 (2013), 591–600.

32. Schroeder (n. 29), p. 426 sets out his argument that men should not beat women, especially not their wives; Leslie Dossey, 'Wife-Beating and Manliness in Late Antiquity', *Past & Present* 199 (2008), 3–40, discusses the difference in attitude between the western and eastern Roman empires.

33. Wolf Liebeschuetz, *Ambrose and John Chrysostom* (2011), p. 179.

34. Schroeder (n. 29).

Let your wives be enough for you, because you want to be
enough for your wives. You don't want something to happen
to her without you; don't you do something without her.
You are the master, she is the slave, God made both. Sarah,
Scripture says, deferred to Abraham, calling him master.
[1 Peter 3:6, quoted above.] It is true; the bishop signed that
contract: your wives are your slaves, you are the masters
of your wives. But when it comes to the business which
distinguishes the sexes, and each sex mixes with the other,
'The wife does not have power over her own body, but the
husband does.' You were happy, you stood tall, you showed off.
Well said, apostle; very well said, chosen vessel! 'The wife does
not have power over her own body, but the husband does.'
'Yes, because I am the master.' You praised that: hear what
follows, hear what you don't want to hear, will you please?
'What's that?' Listen: 'and likewise the husband', that's the
master, 'and likewise the husband does not have power over
his own body, but the woman does.' Listen willingly to that. It
is vice that is taken from you, not mastery: your adulteries are
being forbidden, women are not being raised up. (*ser.* 332.4)

Everyone in the congregation knew what Augustine meant by
this careful language. A wife must comply with her husband's sexual
demands, and must not have sex with anyone else. But a Christian wife
could require the same of her Christian husband. Augustine claimed
that 'women are not being raised up' by this teaching, that is, wives
were not being made insubordinate; but this sermon brilliantly depicts
men who liked to think of themselves as masters, and he knew from
Monica how they might react. Another sermon (*ser.* 392.2) shows how
strongly Augustine argued that, in everything but this demand for the
single standard, wives should be slaves, submissive to their husbands
and ready to give up their property. But in this respect, he says, everyone must listen: those seeking baptism (*competentes*) must not forni-
cate and must not have a concubine during or before marriage; those
already baptized (*fideles*) must do public penance for relationships
'after or besides' wives:

I entrust you to your wives to be guarded. They are my
daughters, as you are my sons. Let them hear me: let them

be jealous [*zelent*] for their husbands; let them not keep the empty glory of married women who are praised by unchaste husbands because they calmly bear the unchastity of their husbands. I do not want Christian women to have such patience: no, let them be jealous for their husbands, not for their own flesh but for the souls of their husbands. I most strongly advise this, I teach it, I order it; the bishop orders it; Christ orders it in me. [Women should appeal against their husbands, not to the civil authorities, but to the Church and to Christ.] In all other matters be the slaves [*ancillae*] of your husbands, subject to them and respectful [*subditae ad obsequium*]. Let there be no boldness in you, no arrogance, no stiff neck, no disobedience of any kind: serve like slaves. But when it comes to the business in which the blessed Apostle made you equal, saying 'Let the husband give his wife her due, and likewise the wife her husband', he added 'The wife does not have power over her body, but the husband does.' Why exalt yourself? Hear what follows, 'Likewise the husband does not have power over his own body, but the wife does.' When it comes to this, cry out for your property. Your husband sells your gold for his needs: bear it, woman; bear it, slave; do not litigate, do not argue against it. Disregard of your gold is love of your husband. If he sells your *villa*, which is yours too, for his needs (it cannot be his if it is not yours, if there is in you the love which ought to be in a wife), bear it patiently, and if he hesitates, offer it yourself: disregard everything for love of your husband. But want him to be chaste, litigate for him to be chaste. Let your house perish, patiently; do not let his soul perish while you are patient. I do not tell men to be jealous for their wives in this matter. I know they are. Who could bear an adulterous wife? Yet a woman is told to bear an adulterous husband! What justice! Why, I ask you, why? 'Because I am a man.' (Aug. *ser.* 392.4–5)

Augustine then uses a favourite argument: if you are a man, be a man. The man is supposed to be the head of the woman, guiding her where she should go.

Augustine knew how much men disliked his attacks on the double standard, which women had come to accept (*ser.* 9.4). People heard that a woman caught with a slave was dragged to the forum, where she could be accused and disgraced; they never heard that about a man caught with a slave woman. But the sin is the same:

> And if perhaps today someone has suffered from a wife who
> is more bitter and complains more freely, because she thought
> it was allowed for a man, and has heard in church that it is
> not allowed for a man; well, if he has suffered from his wife
> complaining more freely, as I said, and saying 'What you are
> doing is not allowed. We heard it together. We are Christians.
> Give me what you demand of me. I owe you fidelity, you owe
> me fidelity, we both owe Christ fidelity. And if you deceive
> me, you do not deceive him to whom we belong, you do not
> deceive him who bought us'; hearing such things which he
> is not used to hearing, he does not want to become sane in
> himself, so he is insane against me. He is angry, he curses.
> Perhaps he says 'How does it happen that this man comes
> here, or on this very day comes up to my wife in church?'
> I think he says this in his own thoughts, because he does not
> dare break out and say it aloud, not even before his wife on her
> own. For perhaps if he did break out and say it, she could reply
> 'Why are you cursing the man you applauded a little earlier?
> We are married: if your tongue is discordant, how can you live
> in concord with me?' (ser. 9.4)

Monica, presumably, was one of the married women who were 'praised by unchaste husbands because they calmly bear the unchastity of their husbands' (ibid. ser. 9.4). She could have argued that she did not challenge her husband because Patricius was not a Christian, whereas Augustine's sermons addressed men who were Christians, or who were at least interested enough to be in church listening to him. He did not tell them how shocking it would be if the protests of their wives were met with anger and violence. He did at least distinguish the discipline of wives from the discipline of slaves:

> If you try to ensure that nothing wrong happens in your
> house, then if you see something wrong in the house of God,
> where there is salvation and eternal rest, should you put up
> with it as best you can? For example, do you see your brother
> rushing off to the theatre? Stop him, warn him, grieve, if

zeal for the house of God consumes you. Do you see others rushing off to get drunk, even in holy places, where it is quite unfitting? Stop those you can, hold back those you can, frighten those you can, speak gently to those you can, but don't keep quiet. Is it a friend? Let him be mildly admonished. Is it your wife? Let her be sharply reined in. Is it your slave woman? Let her be checked, even by beating. (*Jo.Ev.Tr.* 10.9)[35]

But the master of the house was responsible for maintaining domestic peace by whatever method was necessary and was permitted by the laws (*civ. Dei* 19.16). In another sermon, Augustine mocked the astrologer who tells people that the stars determine their lives, but does not act on his beliefs. His wife may say "it wasn't me, it was Venus", but:

If that astrologer sees his wife flirting, or improperly waiting around for men from outside the household, or constantly going to the window, doesn't he seize her, beat her, and impose discipline in his house? (*En.Ps.* (*Enarrationes in Psalmos*) 140.9)

The expected response is "of course he does".

Many epitaphs record a marriage with never a disagreement (*sine ulla querela*), and a favourite word of praise for a wife is *morigera*, "compliant" or "obliging" to her husband. Monica was a good wife by traditional Roman and by Christian standards.[36] 'She had been the wife of one husband, she had repaid the care of her parents, she had dutifully managed her household, her good works bore witness to her, she had brought up her children' (*Conf.* 9.9.22). These phrases are taken from the description of a good widow in Paul's first letter to Timothy (5:4,9,10).[37] Tact, patience, peacemaking, are all admirable, but the risk

35. On Augustine's view of correction as an expression of love, see Brent Shaw, 'The Family in Late Antiquity: The Experience of Augustine', *Past & Present* 115 (1987), 3–51; Peter Garnsey, 'Sons, Slaves—and Christians', in Beryl Rawson and Paul Weaver, eds., *The Roman Family in Italy* (1997), pp. 101–21, especially pp. 112–19 on Augustine; Theodore De Bruyn, 'Flogging a Son: The Emergence of the *pater flagellans* in Latin Christian Discourse', *Journal of Early Christian Studies* 7.2 (1999), 264–73.

36. On marriage ideals, see further Evans Grubbs (n. 7), pp. 54–102.

37. Paul was concerned to distinguish a true *vidua*, that is, a truly 'bereft' woman who depended on the church for support, from a widow who had continuing duties to her family. Augustine borrowed part of the description of a widow who qualified for enrolment on the list of those supported by the church.

is that such service allows or even encourages violence against women. It is sometimes suggested that violence against slaves discharged anger which might otherwise have been directed at wives and children, but that is not what Greek and Roman philosophers thought: they warned against indulgence of anger because it reinforces the habit.[38] Service and submission is an ideal still held up to many women and embraced by some. In Monica's hometown, where domestic violence was endemic and, it seems, unchallenged by family or neighbours, deference was a way of managing, for wives as it was for slaves.

Monica's advice to her friends was that they had only themselves to blame for the bruises which resulted from complaints about a husband's way of life. Abusive men say the same: it was all her fault, she made me angry, I had to teach her a lesson. There are still cultures and subcultures in which men are allowed, or encouraged, to think in this way, and one factor in such abuse is the way women teach their daughters and their sons how they should behave. Victims stay in abusive relationships, sometimes because the culture gives them no other resource and their families would suffer if they complained, but also because they believe it is all their fault, that they deserve it. Patricia Clark, in a perceptive study of women and slavery, observes that in *Conf.* 9.9.19 Augustine reflects 'a traditional discourse which suggests, among other things, that women are responsible for men's behavior and for changing it: by altering their own behavior, they can stop their husbands from beating them; they must placate; they should keep quiet about domestic violence and avoid making it public; and if all else fails, they must endure.'[39] Augustine's Monica is not a battered wife, weeping because she is a victim of abuse in a culture which prevents her from using her abilities, so that she subordinates her own wishes to the service of others and invests too much hope in her son.[40] She is respected as wife, mother, and neighbour, and though Augustine does not explicitly call her competent and enterprising, he shows that she was. But perhaps Augustine imagined Monica's marriage in accordance with his own views; or perhaps Monica's success contributed to his acceptance of domestic violence.

38. Harris (n. 30), pp. 88–128.

39. Patricia Clark, 'Women, Slaves and the Hierarchy of Domestic Violence', in Sandra Joshel and Sheila Murnaghan, eds., *Women and Slaves in Greco-Roman Culture* (1998), pp. 109–29, at p. 115. Schroeder (n. 9) also makes effective use of recent comparative material on domestic violence.

40. See chapter 1.

4

Monica's Education

In the early autumn of 386, in a borrowed villa at Cassiciacum outside Milan, Augustine, two students, and his son, are engaged in philosophical argument:

> Then I noticed that the others, who knew nothing of all this
> and wanted to know what was being discussed so enjoyably
> among just us, were watching us without a smile. They looked
> just like people who, when dining (as often happens) among
> greedy companions who grab food, refrain from grabbing
> because of their dignity, or are afraid to grab because of
> their modesty. [Augustine did not want unfair shares at the
> intellectual feast for which he was the host.] I smiled at my
> mother. And she with great liberality, as if ordering what they
> lacked to be brought out from her storeroom, said 'Come on,
> then, tell us who these Academics are and what they are all
> about.' When I had explained to her, briefly and so plainly
> that none of them would go away uninformed, she said 'Those
> people are fallovers [*caducarii*]' (for that is the common name
> in our part of the world for those who are made to fall by
> epilepsy), and got up to leave. That put an end to it, and we all
> left cheerful and laughing.
>
> *The Happy Life (De beata vita) 2.16*

This passage comes from one of Augustine's earliest works, the philosophical dialogues he wrote after he had decided to resign his post as professor of rhetoric at Milan (summer 386 CE) and before his baptism

(Easter 387). These dialogues are a major source for Monica, second only to the *Confessions*. But her part in them is unexpected: as she says, 'have I ever heard, in those books you read, of women brought in to this kind of discussion?' (*Ord.* 1.11.31, discussed below). She had not heard of it because the techniques of philosophical argument belonged to higher education, which was almost always the preserve of men. So the dialogues raise questions about Augustine's Monica and about opportunities for women to learn. Why did Augustine make his mother a presence in these dialogues, and what is her role?[1]

The Cassiciacum dialogues are *Against the Academics* (*contra Academicos*), *The Happy Life* (*de beata vita*), and *Order* (*de ordine*). Monica makes only a brief appearance in *Against the Academics*, where she says nothing, but ends a discussion by pushing the participants in to lunch. In *The Happy Life*, and in *Order*, she takes part in the discussion. *Against the Academics*, the most technical of the dialogues, asks whether it is possible to know the truth. *The Happy Life* is concerned with the right way to live so as to achieve happiness: not a subjective feeling of happiness (which in Latin makes one *laetus/a*) but objective happiness or blessedness (which makes one *beatus/a*). *Order* is concerned with the order of the universe, and asks whether everything, including evil, is within God's order.

In the passage quoted above, Monica saves others from embarrassment by asking 'Who are these Academics?' It is a reasonable question. The name comes from Plato's Academy: the place where Plato taught philosophy, outside Athens, was named Akadēmeia because there was a shrine of the (little known) hero Akadēmos. Today, scholars engaged in higher education call themselves "academics" because they continue Plato's tradition of following the argument where it leads and questioning received ideas, including their own. In classical antiquity, Academics were a philosophical school. The philosophers of the "New Academy" (third century BCE) argued that we can never securely know truth, and must judge and act in accordance with probability. Augustine learned about them from Cicero's philosophical dialogue *Academica*, and wrote that they were an important influence as he moved on from the religious beliefs of Manichaeism: 'I began to think that the philosophers they call Academics were wiser than the rest, because they held

1. On Monica's role, see especially Catherine Conybeare, *The Irrational Augustine* (2006), pp. 63–138; references to other interpretations pp. 64–6.

that everything must be doubted and declared that nothing of the truth can be grasped by human beings' (*Conf.* 5.10.19).[2]

Monica's response to Augustine's explanation sounds like common sense dismissing the tangles of philosophy. She also gives that impression when one of her interventions begins "Clearly" (*plane*) and two others begin "Certainly" (*prorsus*). Augustine suggests that this was characteristic: in *The Happy Life* he begins some lavish praise with 'Certainly, mother', and in *Order* his two students begin statements with 'Certainly'. Monica is not overawed by her son the professor. She dislikes complicated phrasing, and what she says is crisp and concise.[3] Monica's confidence expresses her faith, but Augustine does not use the dialogues to contrast simple faith with complex philosophy.[4] He praises Monica's intelligence (*ingenium*) and the understanding she achieves through her devotion to God and her grasp of scripture. She is not trained in literature and philosophy, but, as Augustine put it (*Conf.* 9.9.21), God is the inner teacher in the *schola* of her heart. A *schola* is a group of students with their teacher, and the heart, for Augustine, is the centre of thought as well as feeling. Monica listened to Bible readings and to preachers expounding them. We do not know what preaching was like at Thagaste before Augustine's well-educated friend Alypius became its bishop, but at Milan Monica heard the sermons of Ambrose, who was an expert speaker and well informed about theological debate. She could follow up Bible readings at home; she thought about them, and prayed. This does not mean that she had a one-volume Bible, as is usual now, containing all the canonical scriptures. Such a volume would have been difficult and expensive to produce, so the Bible (in Greek *ta biblia*, "the books") was a collection of books. As priest and bishop in Hippo, Augustine assumed that his congregation could easily get the books they wanted.

In one of his own sermons, Augustine borrowed from the book of Proverbs (6:6–7) the image of the industrious ant who stores up grain for the winter:

---

2. On Manichaeism, see chapter 5.

3. The same characteristic appears in *Confessions*: see chapter 5 on Monica's dream of Augustine standing beside her on a wooden rule.

4. This was a favourite Christian tactic, used (for example) in the life of Antony of Egypt: see further Samuel Rubenson, 'Philosophy and Simplicity', in Tomas Hägg and Philip Rousseau, eds., *Greek Biography and Panegyric in Late Antiquity* (2000), pp. 110–39.

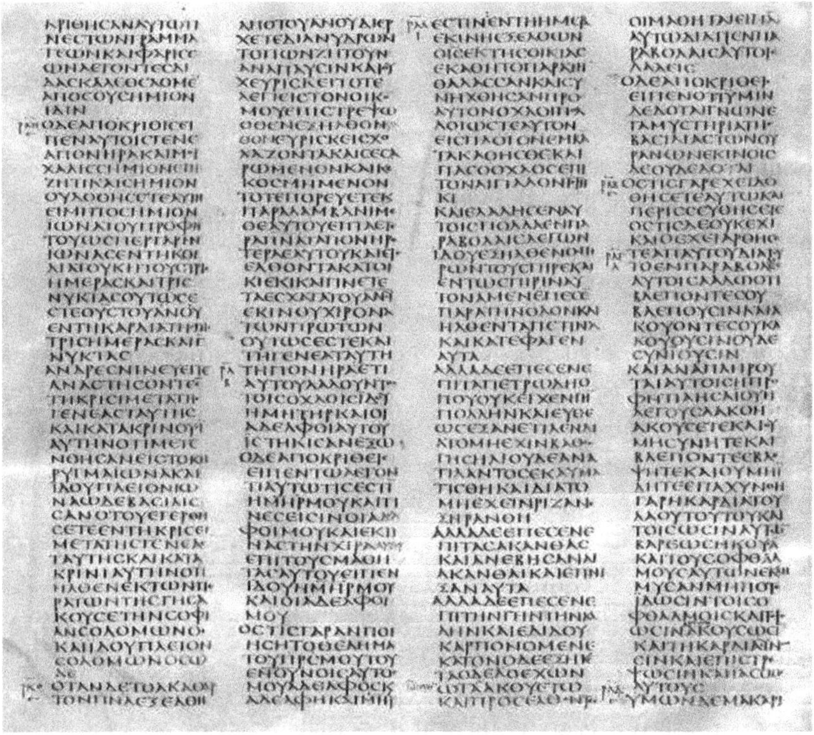

FIGURE 4.1. A page of Codex Sinaiticus, an expensive fourth-century Bible.
© British Library.

See the ant of God: every day she gets up, runs to God's church, prays, hears the reading, sings a hymn, mulls over what she heard, thinks about it, stores within the grain collected from the threshing-floor. This is what people do who listen wisely: everyone sees them go to church and come back from church, hear the sermon, hear the reading, find the book, open it and read. (*En.Ps.* 66.3)[5]

Monica is just such an ant of God, and though she has not been taught the formal use of language (grammar) and the techniques of argument (dialectic) and of public speaking (rhetoric), she is clear and quick-witted in discussion. She exemplifies Augustine's later argument,

5. See further Gillian Clark, 'The Ant of God: Augustine, Scripture, and Cultural Frontiers', in David Brakke, Deborah Deliyannis, Edward Watts, eds., *Shifting Cultural Frontiers in Late Antiquity* (2012), pp. 151–63.

in *Christian Teaching*, that people of ability can learn correct speech and eloquence without training in the rules of grammar and rhetoric, simply by listening to good speakers; that the scriptures themselves demonstrate rhetorical technique; and that people who have greater understanding of scripture speak with greater wisdom.[6] But, as always, we have no way of knowing whether Monica in fact contributed to the discussion, and, if she did, how Augustine reworked her contribution. He said in *Confessions* (9.6.14) that his son Adeodatus, aged sixteen, really did put forward the views (*sensa*) ascribed to him in the dialogue *The Teacher* (*de magistro*), but he did not say that Adeodatus put them forward in those words. He did not say anything about Monica's part in the early dialogues.

Does Augustine's Monica speak like a woman? He could have reported feminine speech, or he could have written in an appropriate style; but there are few, if any, examples of women's speech or writing for comparison. One of the very few female-authored texts from classical antiquity is the prison diary of Perpetua, a married woman from a respectable family, who was martyred at Carthage in 202/3 CE.[7] This short text forms part of a narrative about the arrest and death of several Christians, and it is sometimes argued that the diary, as well as the introduction and the account of the deaths, was written or edited by a male author.[8] Perpetua is described as *liberaliter educata*: this means that she had been educated as befits a freeborn (*libera*) woman, rather than being trained for a trade. It does not mean that she had been trained in the "liberal arts", which included literature and rhetoric. There are differences of opinion on whether she uses the prose rhythms

6. The text of *De doctrina Christiana* has two numbering systems: one book and paragraph, the other book, chapter and paragraph. Augustine discusses the acquisition of eloquence and correct speech in 4.6–13 (4.3.4–5), and gives examples of rhetorical technique in the letters of Paul and in the prophets in 4. 31–58 (4.7.11–20); wisdom proportionate to understanding of scripture 4.19 (4.5.7).

7. On the questions raised by the diary, see Walter Ameling, '*Femina liberaliter instituta*: Some Thoughts on a Martyr's Liberal Education', in Jan Bremmer and Marco Formisano, eds., *Perpetua's Passions: Interdisciplinary Approaches to the Passio Perpetuae et Felicitatis* (2012), pp. 78–102. The volume includes a translation. For other texts which may have been written by women, see Mark Vessey, 'Response to Catherine Conybeare: Women Of Letters?', in Linda Olson and Kathryn Kerby-Fulton, eds., *Voices in Dialogue: Reading Women in the Middle Ages* (2005), pp. 73–96. On the special case of the *cento* composed by Proba from the poems of Virgil, see Roger Green, 'Proba's Cento: Its Date, Purpose and Reception', *Classical Quarterly* 45 (1995), 551–63, and Karla Pollmann, 'Sex and Salvation in the Virgilian Cento of the Fourth Century', in Roger Rees, ed., *Romane Memento: Virgil in the Fourth Century* (2004), pp. 79–96.

8. Ameling (n. 7), p. 80, n. 12, gives recent bibliography.

and cadences (*clausulae*) of formal speech; if she did, she could have acquired them by hearing them in public speeches or sermons. Unlike trained speakers, she repeats words, uses words from "common" Latin (that is, Latin as it was generally spoken) rather than classical Latin, and joins clauses with "and" rather than subordinating one clause to another. Her style may be characteristic of oral, rather than written, communication.[9]

That has also been said of Egeria, a contemporary of Monica, who, in the early 380s, wrote for her "lady sisters" (*dominae sorores*) an account of the sites she visited in the Holy Land and the religious practices she witnessed, especially the liturgy of the church at Jerusalem.[10] She wrote in a more formal style than Perpetua, but by the standards of classical training, she made some mistakes in grammar and syntax. She also repeats words, especially when she wants the sisters to understand exactly where she is and what is there to be shown and seen; she does not quote classical authors, and she does evoke Latin versions of the Bible. But her modestly classical style does not itself show that the author is a woman. Here, for example, she decides to stay over at the shrine of St Thecla at Seleuceia:

> For I found there someone who was the greatest friend to
> me, and for whom all in the east bore witness to her life, a
> holy deaconess called Marthana, whom I knew at Jerusalem,
> where she had gone up to pray [John 5:1; Mt.14:23]; she ruled
> over the monasteries of *apotactici* [hermits: the word is
> explained earlier] or virgins. When she had seen me, what joy
> of hers or mine there could be, can I even write? (*Itinerarium
> Egeriae* 23)[11]

Augustine's Monica can be imagined writing from Italy with just such an alert interest in what she saw and how things were done there; but if she wrote letters home, or to Augustine when they were apart, they

9. Brent Shaw, 'Perpetua's Passion', *Past & Present* 139 (1993), 3–45, at p. 300.

10. John Wilkinson, *Egeria's Travels* (1971) discusses the name of the author (pp. 235–6) and the date of the text (pp. 237–9), and briefly characterizes her style (p. 5).

11. *Nam inveni ibi aliquam amicissimam mihi, et cui omnes in oriente testimonium ferebant vitae ipsius, sancta diaconissa nomine Marthana, quam ego apud Ierosolymam noveram, ubi illa gratia orationis ascenderat; haec autem monasteria aputacticum seu virginum regebat. Quae me cum vidisset, quod gaudium illius vel meum esse potuerit, numquid vel scribere possum?* On the setting, see Stephen Davis, *The Cult of St Thecla* (2001), pp. 55–57, 64–9.

are lost. Letters from women generally did not survive. Augustine kept copies of his replies to letters from women; he did not talk down to women, and he encouraged some to write back, but he did not keep their letters.[12] He provided one small example of a woman's writing when he quoted from her letter to him:

> That is why our admonition was so warmly received by you
> that you replied 'Your Reverence exhorts me not to lend my
> ears to these people who often corrupt our venerable faith
> with corrupt treatises, and I give abundant thanks for this
> pious admonition.' But you add 'But Your Priesthood should
> know that I and my little house are widely separated from
> people of this kind, and our whole household follows the
> catholic faith so closely that it has never gone astray into any
> heresy, nor has it ever fallen—I do not say into those ways of
> thinking which can scarcely be expiated: not even into those
> which appear to make small mistakes.' That is what forces me
> more and more not to remain silent in your hearing about
> those who try to damage even that which is sound. We regard
> your house as no small church of Christ. (*ep.* 188.2–3)

These may indeed be the words of Juliana, politely conveying that Augustine had no need to warn her, rather than Augustine's summary or paraphrase of what she wrote, or a secretary's version of what she wanted to say.[13] If so, nothing in the style shows that the words were written by a woman.

Augustine made it clear in the dialogues that Monica's speech differed from that of the educated male, but this does not mean that it is uneducated in the sense of being unclear or incorrect or rambling. It is more like *sermo humilis*, the consciously simple "low style" Augustine deployed in sermons addressed to both genders, all ages, and varying levels of education, as distinct from the formal style he used when he needed to impress an audience.[14] But *sermo humilis* was also used

12. See Catherine Conybeare, 'Spaces between Letters: Augustine's Correspondence with Women', in Olson and Kerby-Fulton (n. 8), pp. 57–72.

13. Raffaella Cribiore, *Gymnastics of the Mind* (2001), p. 90, notes that in the letters of women that survive in papyri from Egypt, it is difficult to characterize gendered style; but scribes may have used standard phrases.

14. Augustine preached to urban congregations; on the difference from surviving sermons addressed to "rustics", see Leslie Dossey, *Peasant and Empire in Christian North Africa* (2010), pp. 150–72.

by Cicero, and was taught to rhetoric students.[15] In the dialogues, Augustine did not cite the speech of the two uneducated cousins who were also present, but used indirect speech to report their reactions.

Augustine presents the dialogues as records of conversations which take place in private in a country house. The participants are all, in a way, family: Monica; Augustine's brother, Navigius; his son, Adeodatus; two cousins, Lartidianus and Rusticus; and Augustine's two students, Licentius and Trygetius, and his close friend Alypius, all of whom come from Thagaste. Nothing further is known of Trygetius, but Licentius was the son of Romanianus, who helped to finance Augustine's education, and Alypius was a relative of Romanianus. Some of these conversations are said to be recorded by "the pen", that is, by a shorthand writer (*notarius*). The record includes arrivals and departures, and notes of reactions which are not expressed in words: silence, hesitation, laughter, agreement. Augustine remarked (*ord.* 1.2.5) that the notes made it easy for him to write up (that is, to dictate) what he wanted, without an effort to recall what was said or to put it differently. He sent the written versions to dedicatees who could be expected to circulate them more widely: *Against the Academics* to Romanianus, who was in Milan on legal business; *The Happy Life* to Theodorus, a former provincial governor who retired to Milan to study philosophy;[16] and *Order* to Zenobius, a friend who taught literature and studied philosophy. So discussion among family and friends resulted in texts which others could read. Were the recipients surprised, or disconcerted, by the inclusion of Augustine's Monica?

Plato established the literary form of the philosophical dialogue: conversation, and sometimes speeches, in an informal setting.[17] In his dialogues all the participants are men or older boys. Sometimes they meet in the all-male setting of the gymnasium, the place for physical training. In *Symposium*, 'The Dinner Party', all the guests are men, in accordance with Athenian convention. They send away the flute-girl, and the only (reported) female contribution to the discussion

---

15. On *sermo humilis,* see Philip Burton, *Language in the Confessions of Augustine* (2007), pp. 112–16.

16. On Theodorus, see James J. O'Donnell, *Augustine: Confessions* (1992) 2: 419–20. He returned to public life in 397; in *retr.*1.2 Augustine commented that he had said more than he ought in praise of Theodorus.

17. Alex Long, 'Plato's Dialogues and a Common Rationale for Dialogue Form', in Simon Goldhill, ed., *The End of Dialogue in Antiquity* (2008), pp. 45–59.

of love is an account by Socrates of what he was told as a young man by Diotima, priestess and seer.[18] In *Phaedo* (60a) Socrates sends away his wife and baby, before his execution, so that he can talk to his male friends. Augustine had probably not read Plato's dialogues. At Milan he was given some 'books of the Platonists' in Latin translation, but it is not clear that they included the dialogues, or indeed anything by Plato rather than by later Platonist philosophers.[19] In any event, for philosophical dialogues in Latin, the model was provided not by Plato but by Cicero.[20] His participants are men who have a leading role in Roman public life, so here too there was no need to comment on the absence of women. They are excluded, not by Roman social convention, but by lack of relevant experience.

Women did not take part in philosophical discussions because they were not educated to do so. They had no public role, so they were not trained to speak in public or to debate. In late antiquity, boys whose families expected, or hoped, they would have civic duties were sent to a *grammaticus*, a teacher of language and literature. With him they studied classic authors; for Latin speakers, the favoured authors were Cicero and Virgil, and Terence and Sallust. Cicero supplied prose appropriate for different kinds of public speaking, to different audiences, on politics and law and the merits of individuals and cities. Virgil provided a vision of Roman history, empire, and culture; the *grammaticus* explained references to Roman tradition and cult with the help of works by the learned Varro, Cicero's contemporary. The dramatist Terence, a century earlier than the others, offered lucid and quotable observation of human nature. Sallust combined epigrammatic style and luridly memorable history. Through these authors boys absorbed the accepted version of Roman history and culture, and stored up quotations and examples for use in public speaking. Remarkably, they were trained to speak and to write in the style of Cicero, who lived four hundred years earlier.[21] This formal style was of course different from the everyday Latin spoken in their homes and towns, but because the works that

18. 'Why is Diotima A Woman?' is a much-debated question. It is the title of a classic paper by David Halperin, *One Hundred Years of Homosexuality* (1990), pp. 113–51.

19. In *City of God* Augustine cites Cicero's translation of Plato *Timaeus* 27d–47b—see Gerard O'Daly, *Augustine's City of God: A Reader's Guide* (1999), pp. 255–7. On the *libri Platonicorum* ('books of the Platonists'), see O'Donnell, n. 16, 2. 421–4, on *Conf.* 7.9.13.

20. Malcolm Schofield, 'Ciceronian Dialogue', in Goldhill, ed., (n. 17), pp. 63–84.

21. On late antique education, see Robert Kaster, *Guardians of Language* (1988).

were copied and thus survived were in the formal style, there are only a few examples of "common" Latin (*vulgaris*, which is sometimes unhelpfully translated "vulgar").

One example occurs in the passage quoted at the start of this chapter. Monica uses the word *caducarius*, and Augustine explains to his readers that this is the word used in his homeland for people who fall down because of *comitialis morbus*. This illness (*morbus*) is epilepsy. In Greek it was called the "sacred disease" because its sudden and unpredictable onset suggested that it was sent by the gods; a famous treatise in the Hippocratic Corpus argues against that view. In Latin it was called *comitialis* because the *comitium* (assembly) could not be held if there were warning signs from the gods. That had not been relevant for centuries, and was clearly inappropriate in Christian times. Nevertheless, later in the dialogue (3.20), Navigius observes that the word *caducarius* is common speech and bad Latin. It seems that correct Latin required the use of an outdated name. Boys taught by a *grammaticus* learned to be sensitive in this way to the choice of words. They were trained to construct arguments, to present them persuasively, and to prompt an emotional response. Training included arguing both sides of a case (often an invented sensational case), and speaking in character. Augustine won a prize, as a schoolboy, for a prose version of a speech made by the angry goddess Juno in the *Aeneid* of Virgil (*Conf.* 1.17.27). But the skills taught were practical, for even if young men did not leave their hometown in search of a career, they might need to argue a case for themselves or for a dependant, persuade an imperial official to help in a crisis or to reduce the tax bill, or make a speech in praise of the town and its benefactors. Their use of classical language, literary references, and familiar examples showed their hearers that they shared the culture of the social elite.[22]

Girls did not need these skills. They were not deliberately kept in ignorance, and were not illiterate unless they came from a poor and illiterate family, but there is very little to show how Monica and other girls were educated. They could learn to read and write at home, or at primary school with the boys. When Augustine urged his congregation to follow up at home the readings they had heard in church, he did not suggest that this would be more difficult for women; and his rule for monastic communities assumes that women, as well as men, will have

22. Peter Brown, *Power and Persuasion in Late Antiquity* (1992).

someone in charge of books.[23] Presumably girls also learned arithmetic, if only to keep track of the household accounts. What else they learned depended on their families.[24] John Chrysostom's mother told him that daughters might cause anxiety, but they did not cause the expense of a son's education (*On the Priesthood* 1.5). Girls might have tutors, including household slaves who worked as secretaries or as readers; it was usual to have texts read aloud, for discussion or for entertainment. Girls could also be taught by an educated mother, and could learn from a sympathetic father or brother, especially if there were books in the house.[25] Gregory of Nyssa wrote that his elder sister Macrina was taught by their mother, not from the usual tragedy, comedy, and poetry, but from scripture suitable for a child, especially the Wisdom of Solomon and the Psalms (*Life of Macrina* 3). In later life, according to Gregory, Macrina could engage in fluent philosophical discourse.

According to Jerome, his women correspondents, who came from elite Roman families, asked for scholarly commentaries on scripture and wanted to learn Hebrew for themselves.[26] Perhaps they already knew Greek, which would give them access to a wide range of literature and to recent theology. For Latin speakers, Greek was a sign of culture. Augustine struggled to learn it at school (*Conf.* 1.13.20), and in Roman Africa, where there were Greek speakers in coastal towns, some epitaphs record 'educated in both languages'. (Most Greek speakers, in contrast, saw Latin as an inferior dialect of Greek, lacking in literature and not worth studying except for those who wanted a career in the imperial service and would have to cope with official Latin documents.) Among Augustine's contemporaries, both the elder and the younger Melania are said to have read extensively in Greek theology,[27] and the poet Claudian enthused about a bride who was not thinking about marriage, but was reading Latin and Greek texts with her mother. Specifically, she was reading Homer, Orpheus, and Sappho, which seems an unlikely

23. Following up the reading: *En.Ps.* 66.3, quoted above. Books in the monastic community: *Regula* 5.10.

24. See Cribiore (n. 13), pp. 74–5.

25. For comparison: the mathematician Mary Somerville (1780-1872) listened while her brother was tutored in mathematics; finding that she could answer when her brother could not, the tutor gave her unofficial teaching. She learned Latin from an uncle, and began geometry in the art lessons that were acceptable for a young lady.

26. Fannie LeMoine, 'Jerome's Gift to Women Readers', in Ralph Mathisen and Hagith Sivan, eds., *Shifting Frontiers in Late Antiquity* (1996), pp. 230–41.

27. Palladius *HL* 55; *vita Mel.* 23.

syllabus: probably Claudian named three revered poets.[28] But these women were of much higher social status than Monica.

Education could also come from a philosophically minded husband. Augustine imagined Reason asking whether he had really given up the idea of a wife: pretty, modest, obliging, educated, or easily teachable by him.[29] Or girls and women could simply listen while slaves read aloud and men talked. Monica is unlikely to have learned from Patricius, but she knew something about the books she had heard Augustine reading with his students (*ord*. 1.11.31). She was a special case in that her son was a teacher, who expected to read texts aloud, or to have them read, for discussion with friends and students, and who did not expect this always to take place in a lecture room outside the house or in a separate room within it. Silent reading was not unknown in antiquity, but it was often easier to read aloud a text which had no word division or punctuation, especially when the teacher had the only copy (this is the origin of lectures, literally "readings"). Augustine remembered his visits to Ambrose, bishop of Milan. Anyone could go in, but no one was formally announced, and if Ambrose was not already engaged in conversation, he was absorbed in silent reading. Augustine wondered why, and concluded that Ambrose wanted a break, did not want to spend time on discussion and explanation when some difficult point came up, and perhaps was resting his voice (*Conf.* 6.3.3).

So women could achieve some education, from tutors, from members of their household, from their own reading, and, if they were Christian, from Bible study and listening to preaching. Augustine's Monica learned from scripture, from prayer, and from her son. Women could also be philosophers, in that philosophy is literally the love of wisdom, and women too can love wisdom (a point Augustine made in *Order*). Moral education does not require formal training in language, literature, and techniques of argument, and in late antiquity educated men accepted that moral education was not beyond the reach of women. Aristotle had argued that women were not only physically weaker than men, they were less able to use reason to control their desires; it was simply a matter of biology that in women reason did not fully develop, so that the virtues of a good woman, modest and able to carry out orders, were different from the virtues of a good man. But the

28. Claudian, *Epithalamium for Honorius and Maria*, 10.229–34.
29. *Sol.* 1.10.17: *pulchra, pudica, morigera, litterata, vel quae ab te facile possit erudiri.*

FIGURE 4.2. Augustine with a book.

Public Domain.

Stoics argued that virtue is the same for men and for women, and that women can overcome female weakness to manifest virtue, even the manly virtue of courage. (In both Greek and Latin, the same word means "manliness" and "courage".) So women can be philosophers, not in the sense that they engage in philosophical discussion, but in the sense that they understand moral principles and try to live in accordance with them, as Monica did.

Philosophers thought that philosophic women made better wives: thus Plutarch, in the late first century, wrote on the virtues of women, praised his wife Timoxena for the courage and self-control she showed when their little daughter died, and in his *Advice to Bride and Groom* assumed that both wished to live in accordance with philosophy. Porphyry, in the late third century, married Marcella, the widow of a fellow student, and assured her that she was capable of living by philosophical principle, even in the midst of domestic demands, and even when he was not there to advise her.[30] Christian writers shared the belief that women are spiritually equal to men and can overcome their natural feminine weakness. But even the first-century Stoic philosopher Musonius Rufus, who put the strongest case for educating girls as well as boys to use their reason, said that of course this did not mean women would be taught to argue.[31] Very few writers represented women actually discussing philosophy. In the late third century, Methodius wrote a *Symposium* in answer to Plato: where Plato has men making speeches in praise of erotic love, Methodius has virgins making speeches in praise of virginity. A century later, Augustine's contemporary Gregory of Nyssa wrote a dialogue, *On the Soul and Resurrection*, in which his sister Macrina takes the leading role. She is one of the very few women in late antiquity who are said to have taught philosophy. The examples which follow show how exceptional they were. Each was the daughter of a philosopher or a teacher, and each led a life which was most unusual for a woman.

Hypatia of Alexandria, a near contemporary of Augustine,[32] was the daughter of Theon, philosopher and mathematician, and grew up among philosophers in a city full of teachers and students. Her father educated her and made it possible for her to teach.[33] She is a rare example of a non-Christian woman who could have married, but chose not to. In general, philosophically minded women did their duty to family and city by marrying philosophically minded men and bearing children. These couples were likely to agree on a simple lifestyle and on celibacy when their family was complete; their shared aim was moral and intellectual progress, and the husband undertook his civic duties without ambition or display. Such marriages linked the families of philosophers, and there would surely have been a suitable spouse in Alexandria. Nobody wrote a life of Hypatia, and we do not know why she did not import a philosophical son-in-law to her father's school. Perhaps she thought that a philosopher should be concerned with the

30. See further Gillian Clark, 'Do Try This At Home: The Domestic Philosopher In Late Antiquity', in Hagit Amirav and Bas ter Haar Romeny, eds., *From Rome to Constantinople* (2007), pp. 153–72.

31. On women and philosophy, see Barbara Levick, 'Women, Power and Philosophy at Rome and Beyond', in Gillian Clark and Tessa Rajak, eds., *Philosophy and Power in the Graeco-Roman World* (2002), pp. 133–55.

32. Augustine was born in 354 CE, Hypatia around 355.

33. See Cribiore (n. 13), pp. 78–83 for other examples of women who taught, at a lower educational level. She notes that there is often a family connection.

immortal and unchanging world, not with the transient world of "generation and corruption", where new life comes into being and old life dies. Her students included Christians, one of whom, Synesius, became bishop of Cyrene. He kept in touch after he had left Alexandria, and in one letter called her "mother, sister, teacher, benefactor in all these" (*ep.* 16). Hypatia could be a benefactor to her students because she was a public figure on good terms with local officials. This contributed to her appalling death at the hands of a Christian lynch mob, who blamed her for turning the city prefect against their bishop Cyril. She is credited with commentaries on mathematics and astronomy, but inevitably, there are claims that she did no more than edit her father's work, and little survives.[34]

Sosipatra, the second example, is a very different kind of philosopher. She appears in a collection of biographies by Eunapius, who wrote in the late fourth century about networks of philosophers in the eastern Mediterranean; too early, unfortunately, to include Hypatia.[35] He was especially interested in the supernatural abilities of philosophers, and he defends his inclusion of a woman by showing that Sosipatra is divinely inspired. She is wiser even than her husband Eustathius, also a philosopher, the only man worthy to marry her. She tells him that they will have three sons, that he will die in five years' time, and that his soul will then return to an exalted level; she is not permitted to tell him about the return of her own, even more exalted, soul. Sosipatra, born into a prosperous family near Ephesus, is taken away at the age of 5, with her father's consent, by two men who are later revealed as initiates in "Chaldaean wisdom": the ancient wisdom of Babylon, which was thought to inspire the text known as the Chaldaean Oracles. These men tell her father 'your daughter shall not be only like a woman and a human being' (Eunapius 467). When she returns at age 10, she too has been initiated into Chaldaean wisdom, and she is entrusted with special clothing and a sealed chest of books (ibid. 468). She has no other teachers, but 'she had on her lips the books of poets, philosophers and orators, and what others with painful effort came dimly to understand, she explained with ease, making it clear swiftly and without trouble' (469).

34. On Hypatia in the context of doctrinal and intellectual tensions in Alexandria, see Edward Watts, *City and School in Late Antique Athens and Alexandria* (2006), pp. 187–203.

35. Eunapius discusses Sosipatra in *Lives of the Sophists*, pp. 466–71. See on these lives Patricia Cox Miller, 'Strategies of Representation in Collective Biography: Constructing the Subject as Holy', in Hägg and Rousseau (n. 4), pp. 209–54, especially pp. 235–49.

In widowhood Sosipatra returns to her family estate at Pergamum, where her sons are taught by the philosopher Aedesius; she experiences, but withstands, love-magic used against her by her cousin Philometor. Philosophers, like other persons in authority, sat in a special chair, a *cathedra*, which had a back and sometimes also arm rests. Sosipatra sets up her chair in her house, and the students of Aedesius come to hear her after his class: 'they devotedly admired the precision of Aedesius, but they revered her inspiration.' In a discussion about the soul, 'Sosipatra began to speak, and gradually, with her demonstrations, dealt with the views that were put forward. Then she fell to discussing the descent of the soul, and what part of it undergoes punishment [by being imprisoned in the body] and what part is immortal. In the midst of her divinely possessed utterance she fell silent': she has a vision, later proved to be correct, of Philometor injured in a carriage accident. Eunapius says nothing about writings by Sosipatra, and none survive.

Macrina is the third example. Her brother Gregory of Nyssa, who called her 'The Teacher', wrote a *Life of Macrina*, and she is the principal speaker in his philosophical dialogue *On the Soul and Resurrection*. She challenges Gregory's distress at the death of their brother Basil, and deploys both scripture and technical philosophy in response to his doubts about the immortality of the soul and about resurrection. For Gregory, "philosophy" is the ascetic life of prayer which perfects the soul.[36] Macrina reaches the heights of human virtue (*Life* 1) and progresses to the angelic life in which, liberated from damaging emotions and from concern for worldly matters and for the body, she wants only to be united with Christ. She is a teacher, adviser and guide for her mother, her brothers, and the members of her religious community. Sheltered from worldly education and debate, she nevertheless shows how Christian truth surpasses pagan philosophy.[37] Debate continues on whether *The Soul and Resurrection* reports Macrina's arguments, or whether Gregory used her to give spiritual authority to his own;[38] her style does not differ from that of her rhetorically trained brother.

36. Pierre Maraval discusses the meaning of "philosophy" in *Grégoire de Nysse: Vie de Sainte Macrine* (1971), pp. 90–103.

37. Samuel Rubenson (n. 4) at pp. 126–7, 134.

38. For the debate on whether Macrina is a woman, see Morwenna Ludlow, *Gregory of Nyssa* (2007), pp. 202–19; and for scepticism about Macrina as philosopher, Elizabeth Clark, 'Holy Women, Holy Words', *Journal of Early Christian Studies* 6 (1998), 413–30, pp. 422–30. See chapter 6 for the 'saint's life' of Macrina.

Augustine's Monica, unlike these three women, came from an undistinguished family and was not given a formal education. Her contributions to discussion are correct in style, but different in manner from those of the men; Augustine made it possible for readers to believe that his mother said these things. It is time to consider them in detail.

Augustine's philosophical dialogues are set in the villa outside Milan which he borrowed from his friend Verecundus (*ord.* 1.2.5) when the vintage vacation began in late August. He read Virgil with his students, and once spent much of a beautiful day in 'domestic business' writing letters (*c.Acad.* 2.4.10, 2.11.25), but he did not need to prepare classes or public speeches, or to visit important people, as he had to do all the time in Milan (*Conf.* 6.11.18). To that extent the setting parallels Cicero's dialogues, written four centuries earlier, in which the participants enjoy their leisure in someone's pleasant house. "Leisure" translates *otium*, the opposite of *negotium*, "non-*otium*"—that is, business. In Cicero's dialogues, his brother Quintus, his friend Atticus, and other speakers are highly educated men for whom *otium* is an opportunity to cultivate their minds, as they will do when they retire from public duties. They exchange literary and philosophical banter in the intervals of discussing law and society, ethics and politics.

Augustine too could have composed a dialogue among highly educated people, but his introduction to *The Happy Life* makes it clear that he did not choose to do so. The dialogue is addressed to Theodorus, the retired provincial governor who used his *otium* to discuss Platonist philosophy with others who were interested, including Augustine (*b.vita* 1.4). Theodorus was learned and Christian (*Retr.* 1.2), and he knew Bishop Ambrose, like him a former provincial governor, whom Augustine calls "our priest" (*b.vita* 1.4). Augustine could have set the dialogue in the circle of Theodorus; or, if he saw a risk of offending people in Milan, he could have followed Cicero's example of using participants from the heroic past. Instead, he chose people whom Theodorus could not be expected to know. On Augustine's birthday, 13 November, the group ate a light lunch, then went to sit in the bathhouse. (This may be a deliberate contrast with philosophical dialogues set at a dinner party, if Augustine had read any examples of those.[39]):

---

39. On dinner-party dialogues, see Jason König, 'Sympotic Dialogue in the First to Fifth Centuries CE', in S. Goldhill, ed. (n. 17), pp. 85–113, especially pp. 96–7 on *de beata vita*.

There were present, for I am not afraid to make them known
by name to your exceptional kindness, first of all my mother,
to whom, I believe, my whole life is owed, my brother
Navigius, and my fellow citizens and students Trygetius
and Licentius. I did not want my cousins Lartidianus and
Rusticus to be left out, although they had not even suffered
under a *grammaticus*, and I thought their common sense was
necessary for the matter I had in hand. Also with us was the
youngest of all, but one whose intelligence, if love does not
deceive me, promises much, my son Adeodatus. (*b.vita* 1.6)

Augustine's mother is not in fact made known by name, here or anywhere else except in the conclusion to Book 9 of *Confessions*, where
Augustine had to name her so that his readers could pray for her. The
same applies to other women praised by their sons: evidently it was
not proper to name them in public.[40] Theodorus, reading these sen-
tences about people he did not know, could assume that Navigius was
educated, like his brother and unlike his cousins, and that Augustine's
mother, like other women, had no more than primary education.
Augustine's point was that no one should be left out for lack of formal education, because everyone needs to think about the right way
to live. He had renounced his worldly career; did he already envisage
serving the Church, perhaps with the patronage of Bishop Ambrose,
explaining scripture and Christian doctrine to anyone who came to
hear? It is often argued that the people who came to church were part
of the social elite, at least in the sense that they were not poor and ignorant. But Augustine later described the church as a lecture room open
to both sexes and all ages (*ep.* 138.10), and that presented a far greater
challenge than he had faced in teaching literature and rhetoric, and discussing philosophy, with a self-selected educated group. Augustine was
an experienced teacher, with the teacher's characteristic belief that you
can always find a way to explain so that everyone can understand and
everything is as interesting to your students as it is to you. Even so, in
retrospect, he saw the early dialogues as still 'puffed up' by the habits of
secular literature (*Retr.* Prol. 1.3). The reference is to 1 Corinthians 8: 1,
'knowledge puffs up, love builds up.' The dialogues display learning and
ability to debate, and Augustine did not in fact bring everyone into the

40. See chapter 6 for other examples.

discussion. Lartidianus and Rusticus do no more than register agreement, and presumably were baffled when Augustine changed from discussion mode to lecture mode.

A philosophical dialogue should be a clear and helpful way to set out arguments and to make them memorable by association with different characters. But some people find argument and counterargument confusing, especially when it is not clear who is speaking. A century after Augustine, Theodoret, bishop of Cyrrhus in Syria, wrote a dialogue on the nature of Christ. To make it easy for his readers, he called one of his speakers Orthodoxus and the other Eranistes, 'the ragbag man' who collects his arguments from anywhere and everywhere. He explained in the prologue that, for clarity, their names were written in the margin each time they spoke. Apparently that was unusual: in dialogues, as in dramatic texts, there was only a dash (*paragraphos*) in the margin to mark a change of speaker, and readers had to work it out. In Augustine's time, Jerome made his position clear by calling one of his works *Dialogue against the Pelagians* and saying at the start which speaker was right. Augustine decided instead to change his mode of writing. After his baptism at Easter 387 CE, he wrote more treatises than dialogues, and after his ordination to the priesthood in 391 there are no dialogues.[41]

The first book in Augustine's list of his own works is *Against the Academics*. Here Monica makes a brief appearance. Augustine, his friend Alypius, and his student Licentius go out to the meadow on a beautiful day, help with some farm work, then turn back for lunch, discussing the Academics. Eventually they reach home and Monica intervenes (*c.Acad.* 2.4.10–5.13): 'Alypius was going to go on, but my mother (we were now at home) pushed us in to lunch so that there was no scope for discussion.' They eat enough to satisfy their hunger, then go back to the meadow and their debate. Monica's role is, apparently, to provide a break in the discussion by insisting on practicalities: even if nothing is certain, and the senses cannot be trusted, philosophers need lunch. In the next dialogue in the list, *The Happy Life*, Monica has a larger role and a different relationship both to food and to Academic philosophy. The discussants are also different. Alypius, Augustine's friend and intellectual equal, is absent, and Augustine is surrounded by people of lesser

41. See on this question Gillian Clark, 'Can We Talk? Augustine and the Possibility of Dialogue', in Goldhill, ed. (n. 17), pp. 117–34.

intellectual status. His son Adeodatus is very intelligent, but young; his students Licentius and Trygetius are still being educated; his mother and cousins are not educated beyond the basics; and his brother, who has been to a *grammaticus*, at first seems reluctant to debate.

The Happy Life takes its start from Augustine's birthday lunch. The participants agree, after some hesitation from Navigius, that human beings are composed of soul and body. The body needs food: what food does the soul need? Augustine asks 'do we think that knowledge is its food?' and Monica makes her first contribution: 'Clearly [*plane*], the soul is nourished, I believe, only on understanding and knowledge' (2.8). Trygetius looks doubtful, and Monica reminds him that part way through lunch, he said he had only just noticed which container (*vasculum*) they were using. (Was it something special for a birthday?) 'Where was your mind,' she asks, 'while it was not attending to what you were eating? Believe me, these are the meals on which the soul feeds, that is, its own reflections and thoughts, if it can get anything from them.' Everyone starts talking, and Augustine intervenes, but says nothing about difficulties in the statement that had seemed so clear to Monica. He develops the metaphor of food, and offers another kind of lunch, food for the mind, provided they want to eat.

Of course they do, and Augustine begins 'We want to be happy.' "Happy" translates as *beatus*, literally "blessed": this is happiness as a condition, not as a feeling. Everyone agrees that we want to be happy. 'Do you think someone is happy who does not have what he wants?' They all say no. 'So is everyone happy who does have what he wants?' Monica's answer is admirably clear and concise: 'If he wants good things and has them, he is happy. But if he wants bad things, he is wretched, although he has them.'[42] Now comes an important exchange between Augustine and Augustine's Monica:

> I smiled at her with delight, and said, 'Certainly [*prorsus*], Mother, you have laid hold on the citadel of philosophy. No doubt you lacked the words just now to spread yourself like Cicero: these are his words on this question. In the *Hortensius*, a book he wrote to praise and defend philosophy, he says "Look, not only philosophers, but everyone who is eager to debate, says that those who live as they want are happy.

42. *Si bona, inquit, velit et habeat, beatus est, si autem mala velit, quamvis habeat, miser est.*

But that is false, for wanting that which is not right is utter wretchedness. Nor is it as wretched not to get what you want as it is to want to get what you ought not. A corrupt will brings more evil than chance brings to any good person."'
She was exclaiming at these words in such a way that we, completely forgetting her sex, believed that some great man was sitting with us, while I understood, as far as I could, from what source, and from how divine a source, those words flowed. Then Licentius said 'But you need to say, for everyone to be happy, what they should want and for what things they ought to long.' (*b.vita* 2.10)[43]

Monica cannot be expected to have read Cicero, or to have heard of his dialogue *Hortensius*, and she has not been trained to speak in expansive Ciceronian style, but she has made the same point. The quotation from Cicero which follows does indeed take longer, but it is clearly expressed. Augustine's comment after the quotation is not entirely clear. Does Monica exclaim at the words of Cicero, or at the words of praise spoken by her son? The words of Cicero seem more likely, both because 'she was exclaiming at these words' picks up 'these are his words on this question', and because it is her immediate understanding which makes the men forget that she is a woman.[44] This is high praise, which Augustine repeats in *Confessions*: 'mother stayed close to us, in womanly clothing but with manly faith, with the serenity of an old woman, maternal love, and Christian devotion' (*Conf.* 9.11.8). To call a woman 'manly' meant that she had overcome female weakness of body and mind. But when Augustine understands, as best he can, 'from what source, and from how divine a source, those [words] flowed', does he mean Monica's words of exclamation, which he does not give, or Cicero's words, which he has just quoted? Possibly Cicero's words; Augustine wrote later, in

43. *Cui ego arridens atque gestiens: Ipsam, inquam, prorsus, mater, arcem philosophiae tenuisti. Nam tibi procul dubio verba defuerunt, ut non sicut Tullius te modo panderes, cuius de hac sententia verba ista sunt. Nam in Hortensio, quem de laude ac defensione philosophiae librum fecit: Ecce autem, ait, non philosophi quidem, sed prompti tamen ad disputandum, omnes aiunt esse beatos qui vivant ut ipsi velint. Falsum id quidem: Velle enim quod non deceat, id est ipsum miserrimum. Nec tam miserum est non adipisci quod velis, quam adipisci velle quod non oporteat. Plus enim mali pravitas voluntatis affert, quam fortuna cuiquam boni. In quibus verbis illa sic exclamabat, ut obliti penitus sexus eius, magnum aliquem virum considere nobiscum crederemus, me interim, quantum poteram, intellegente ex quo illa, et quam divino fonte manarent.*
44. I translate this passage differently from Conybeare (n. 1), p. 74, who thinks that it is Monica who protests that they have forgotten her sex.

Christian Teaching, that pagan works may offer sound teaching,[45] and in *The Happy Life*, Cicero, the mainstay of higher education, says at greater length what Monica already understands. But later in the dialogue (4.27, quoted below) Augustine contrasts 'many and various doctrines' with 'a soul most attentive to God', that is, Monica's soul, and asks 'Whence come those words we admire, if not from there?'

The student Licentius raises the next question: what are the good things that people should want? Everyone agrees that it is not possible to be happy in having temporal goods which may be lost. Monica's contribution, once again, is clear and concise, in a style less elaborate than Augustine's own, and once again she immediately sees the point of an argument:

> 'Even if someone is sure that he will not lose everything, he still cannot be satiated with such things. So he is wretched, because he is always needy.' I asked her 'Suppose he is lavishly supplied with all these things, but sets a limit to his desires, is satisfied with what he has, and enjoys them properly and pleasantly: don't you think he is happy?' 'Then he is happy not in those things,' she said, 'but in the moderation of his soul.' 'Excellent,' I said, 'that is the only reply which should be given to that question and by you.' (*b.vita* 2.11)[46]

Everyone then agrees that the happy man must have that which bad fortune cannot take away, and that is God. So Augustine asks who has God. The two students jump in with answers, and Adeodatus follows, but Augustine ensures that everyone is asked what they think:

> Licentius said 'He who lives well has God.' Trygetius said 'He who does what God wants to be done has God.' Lartidianus agreed with him. But that youngest boy of all said 'He who does not have an unclean spirit has God.' Mother approved everything, but especially this. Navigius was silent. I asked

---

45. *Doc. Chr.* 2.144–7 (2.11.60–61). Augustine uses the Bible story of the Israelites borrowing gold, silver, and precious fabrics from the Egyptians, and using them to worship the true God.

46. *Hoc loco autem mater: etiamsi securus sit, inquit, ea se omnia non esse amissurum, tamen talibus satiari non poterit. Ergo et eo miser, quo semper est indiguus. Cui ego: quid, si, inquam, his omnibus abundans rebus atque circumfluens cupiendi modum sibi statuat eisque contentus decenter iucundeque perfruatur, nonne tibi videtur beatus? Non ergo, inquit, illis rebus, sed animi sui moderatione beatus est.*

him what he thought, and he said he liked the last reply. It
seemed also that I should not neglect to ask Rusticus what his
opinion was on this great question, because he seemed to be
kept quiet by modesty rather than by deliberation. He agreed
with Trygetius. (*b.vita* 2.12)

Everyone had been involved in the discussion, if only to agree, until
Augustine mentioned the Academics. The three people who knew what
he was talking about (the two students and, presumably, Adeodatus)
sat up and looked keen (2.12–13). There follows a quick-fire debate, as
in *Against the Academics*, with reference to the absent Alypius. But
this time there are others present, and Augustine notices (2.16, quoted
at the start of this chapter) that they were left out. The men might be
embarrassed to say they had never heard of the Academics, but nobody
expected a woman to know. So Augustine smiled at Monica, who
responded at once, asked her question, and brought the discussion to a
close by calling the Academics *caducarii*, people who have the 'falling
sickness'.

This comment, unacceptable now, has been characterized as
"earthy", both because of the word used and because Monica brings
Academic philosophy down to earth, just as she did in the previous
dialogue by insisting on lunch.[47] But is it so earthy? The same comparison was used by Macarius Magnes, earlier in the fourth century,
in an elaborately written refutation of anti-Christian arguments. He
described his opponents as 'babbling *epilēpta*': presumably he meant
that they made unintelligible or incoherent sounds, as can happen in an
epileptic seizure when muscles contract and force air out of the lungs. It
is also possible that Augustine's Monica was not just name-calling. The
Academics argued that we cannot trust our sense perceptions, and she
could have meant the aura which may precede an epileptic seizure or
the confusion which may follow one, when (as Pliny put it, *NH* 11.146)
the eyes are open, but the mind is darkened.

In the next day's discussion Monica again requests an explanation
of a complicated argument. Augustine asks Adeodatus what he meant
by 'he who does not have an unclean spirit has God', and Adeodatus
decides that he did not mean someone who is not possessed by a demon,

47. Peter Brown's comment is often quoted: 'She can dismiss a whole philosophical school
in a single vulgar word', *Augustine of Hippo* (1967), p. 111. It is not always realized that "vulgar"
means "in common use", as in "vulgar [*vulgaris*] Latin".

and did mean someone whose spirit is pure and who holds only to God (3.18). Everyone agrees that such a person must necessarily live well, and that someone who lives well must necessarily be like that. They further agree that God wants people to seek him, that someone who seeks God does not live badly, and that an unclean spirit cannot seek God (Navigius, once again, hesitates before agreeing). Now Augustine poses a problem:

> 'So if someone who seeks God does what God wants, and lives well, and does not have an unclean spirit; but someone who seeks God does not yet have God; then it is not the case that whoever lives well or does what God wants or does not have an unclean spirit must necessarily [*continuo*] be said to have God?' The others laughed, tricked by their concessions. My mother was stunned [*stupida*] for some time, then she requested that I should explain to her and disentangle what, in the necessity of the conclusion, I had put in a complicated way. When that was done, she said 'But no one can come to God unless he has sought God.' 'Excellent', I said, 'but the one who is still seeking has not yet come to God, and is already living well. So it is not the case that whoever lives well has God.' 'It seems to me', she said 'that there is no one who does not have God, but he who lives well has God favourable, and he who lives badly has God hostile.' 'Then' I said 'we were wrong to concede yesterday that he who has God is happy, if everyone has God, yet not everyone is happy.' 'Then add "favourable"', she said. (3.19)

Now the usually silent Navigius has something to say, and shows that he too is aware of language and can construct an argument. 'Do we all agree,' Augustine asks, 'that he who has God favourable is happy?'

> 'I'd like to agree', Navigius said, 'but I fear the one who is now asking the question. I fear especially that you will conclude that the Academic is happy. In yesterday's conversation the Academic was called *caducarius*: the word is common speech and bad Latin, but seemed to me most appropriate. For I cannot say that God is against a man who seeks God; and if it is wrong for that to be said, God will be favourable, and he who has God favourable is happy. Then he who seeks

will be happy; but everyone who seeks does not yet have what he wants: so the man who does not have what he wants will be happy. Yesterday that seemed absurd to all of us, and we believed that Academic darkness had been dissipated. So Licentius will triumph over us, and will warn me, like a wise doctor, that the sweets I rashly accepted against the interests of my health are now inflicting this punishment on me.' (3.20) ['Sweets' refers to an exchange at 2.14, just before Monica asks about the Academics.]

Even mother smiled at this. 'I don't concede', said Trygetius, 'that if God is not favourable to someone, he is necessarily against him. I think there is something in between.' I replied 'This man in the middle, to whom God is neither favourable not hostile: do you concede that in some sense he has God?' He hesitated, and mother said 'It is one thing to have God and another not to be without God.' 'Which is better, then', I said 'to have God or not to be without God?' 'So far as I can understand', she said, 'this is my opinion: he who lives well has God, but has God favourable; he who lives badly has God, but against him; he who still seeks and has not yet found does not have God either favourable or hostile, but is not without God.' (3.21)

Augustine's Monica, who was temporarily stunned by a complicated argument with double negatives, here offers another clear, concise distinction. For the first time, she offers it tentatively, but that may be because she is talking about God, not about people. Everyone accepts her formulation, and they further concede that God is favourable to those who seek him. Now Augustine returns to the problem posed by Navigius: a seeker does not have what he wants, but God is favourable to him, so he is happy even though he does not have what he wants. For the first time, Monica apparently loses an argument:

'I really don't think someone is happy', said my mother, 'when he doesn't have what he wants.' 'Then', I said, 'not everyone who has God favourable is happy.' 'If that is what reason requires', she said, 'I can't deny it.' (3.22)

Augustine does not here develop an answer Monica could give: someone who seeks God, and has God favourable, is objectively happy. They are still needy, but they are not objectively wretched, because they know that they are needy and they are trying to find what they still lack. When they find God they will be truly happy.

The third day is beautiful, so instead of sheltering in the bathhouse, they sit in the nearby meadow. The argument starts from what Monica said the day before: 'it was said by my mother that wretchedness is nothing other than neediness, and it was agreed among us that all who are needy are wretched. But there is a question whether all who are wretched are needy, and yesterday we were not able to settle it' (4.23). Once again there is a quick-fire discussion, this time with Trygetius, and Augustine realizes that 'some of them are rather slow to understand', so he explains as best he can in words better suited to them. In practice, he goes into lecture mode, making a long speech in formal style, with two quotations from Terence (another classic author) and an example from Cicero. Eventually there is a brief discussion with Licentius, from which Augustine concludes that 'someone who was afraid [of loss] was wretched, although he was not needy; so it is not the case that everyone who is wretched is needy.' Now Augustine's Monica does something she has not done before: instead of answering a question, she asks one. She puts it tentatively and tactfully, not throwing down a challenge or raising an objection as the students do, but she does suggest that Augustine's conclusion is mistaken:

> She whose opinion I was defending approved with the rest,
> but said, with a little hesitation, 'I don't know, but I don't
> yet clearly [*plane*] understand, how wretchedness can be
> separated from neediness or neediness from wretchedness.
> For the one who was rich and wealthy and, as you say, longed
> for nothing more, was still in need of wisdom, because he
> was afraid of losing [his wealth]. Are we to call him needy
> if he lacks silver and money, but not if he lacks wisdom?'
> Everyone cried out in admiration, and I was delighted,
> because what I was preparing to put forward from the books
> of the philosophers as something great and the last word, had
> been said, and said by her. 'Do you see', I said, 'that many and
> various doctrines are one thing, and a soul most attentive to
> God is another? Whence come those words we admire, if not
> from there?' (*b.vita* 4.27)

Monica has apparently followed the lecture, or at least the discussion with Licentius which follows it. But though everyone praises her, and though Augustine refrains from saying 'I was just about to make that point', she remains silent while Augustine continues in lecture mode. He drops in references to Sallust and Cicero, and sometimes exchanges a few words with Licentius or Trygetius. The others only smile and agree. At last he concludes that 'the complete satisfaction of souls, that is, the happy life, is to recognize devoutly and completely by whom you are led into the truth, what truth you enjoy, and through what you are linked to the supreme definition [*summus modus*]. These three show one God, to those who understand God, and one substance, excluding the follies of different superstitions.' His language is complicated, but Monica (had she previously been stunned?) responds to words which are together in the Latin, 'three one God':

> Here my mother, recognizing the words so thoroughly fixed
> in her memory, and as if waking up to her own faith, joyously
> cited the line of our priest 'Nurture us praying, Trinity', and
> added 'This, no one doubts, is the happy life, which is the
> perfect life, and we must presume that we who hurry towards
> it can be brought there by secure faith, lively hope, and blazing
> love.' (4.36)

A line from one of Ambrose's hymns, quoted by Monica, says what needs to be said about the happy life, and the dialogue comes to an end.

The third dialogue in Augustine's list is *Order*. It is the most personal in what it says about his feelings and his state of health. He explains to his friend Zenobius (1.2.5) that he was at the villa of his kind friend Verecundus. There was discussion, recorded by 'the pen', with Alypius, Augustine's brother Navigius, Licentius, and Trygetius; no mention yet of Monica. The dialogue begins (1.3.6) with Augustine lying awake in the dark, taking some time for his own thoughts. He has encouraged the students to do the same, instead of giving all their attention to books. He hears the sound of water running behind the baths, sometimes more distinctly and sometimes faster. Why is that? Then it becomes clear that the students are awake too (there is no comment on the fact that Augustine does not have his own room), so the whole *schola* is there, since Alypius and Navigius have gone to the city (1.3.7). The discussion moves from the explanation of the irregular water flow (leaves blocking the drain) to the order of the universe, and in the course of discussion Licentius is converted from poetry to philosophy. Daylight (1.8.22) brings a wonderful scene, in which the spiritual exaltation of Licentius and the joy of Augustine are interwoven with the disconcerted reaction of Trygetius and with visits to the lavatory. The students get up; Augustine, left alone, prays fervently, then hears Licentius singing a psalm-verse under his breath. This prompts the first, reported, appearance of Monica in the dialogue:

> The day before, after dinner, when he had gone outside for the needs of nature, he sang it rather too loudly for my mother to bear the fact that such things should be sung, over and over, in that place. He sang nothing else, because he had recently learned the tune and, as happens, loved the unfamiliar melody. She is, as you know, very devout, and she scolded him, saying that place was unsuitable for chant. Then he said, in fun, 'So God would not hear my voice if an enemy shut me in there!' So in the morning he came back alone (for each of them had gone out for the same reason) and came up to my bed. (*Ord.* 1.8.22–23)

Licentius wanted to know what Augustine really thought of him. The three continue their discussion, in the bathhouse, then Augustine writes it up (1.8.26). They continue the next day, but the students get into an argument about the relationship of Christ to God, then into a further argument about whether a wrong statement should be recorded. Augustine is distressed by their competitive spirit and their concern for reputation. At this point (had she heard raised voices?):

> My mother came in and asked us what progress we had made, for she too knew about the enquiry. When I gave the order to write down her entry and question, as was our custom, she said 'What are you doing? Have I ever heard, in those books you read, that women too were brought in to this kind of debate?' (1.11.31)

Augustine begins a long answer. Some people judge books as they judge the people they visit, not by what they are but by the splendour of their clothes and surroundings. But some do reach the inner sanctum of philosophy through gilded and decorated doors. Amongst these are the older Latin authors [*maiores nostri*] Monica has heard read, and in his own time Theodorus:

> If my books [*libri*: divisions of Augustine's writing] come into the hands of one of these, and when they read my name they don't say 'who's he?' and throw the book [*codex*: a spine-hinged book] away, but from curiosity or zeal they disregard its modest entrance and go on inside, they will not be offended that I talk philosophy with you, nor, perhaps, will they despise any of those whose words are mixed with my writings. For they are not only free men [*liberi*], which is enough for any liberal discipline, let alone philosophy; they were born in the highest place among their own. But the writings of very learned men include shoemakers who do philosophy, and [people of] far lower levels of fortune, who nevertheless shone with such light of intellect and virtue that they would not want to exchange on any terms, even if they could, their goods for any high status in this world. And believe me, there will be people who will be more pleased by the fact that you are talking philosophy with me than with anything else amusing or serious that they find here. In the old authors [*apud veteres*] women did philosophy, and your philosophy pleases me greatly. Just so you know, mother, this Greek word "philosophy" means "love of wisdom" in Latin. Hence the divine scriptures which you fervently embrace teach that it is not philosophers in general, but the philosophers of this world who must be avoided and mocked. [. . .] So I would despise you in these writings of mine if you did not love wisdom; but I would not despise you if you loved it moderately; and far less if you loved wisdom as much as I do. As it is, you love wisdom much more than you love me, and I know how much you love me; and you have progressed so far in it that you are not frightened by the dread of any misfortune or even of death, which is very difficult for very learned men, and everyone acknowledges that this is the highest citadel of philosophy; shall I not gladly give myself to you as a student?

> She said, kindly and dutifully [*blande ac religiose*], that
> I had never uttered so great a falsehood [*numquam me tantum
> mentitum esse*]. (1.11.32–33)[48]

Augustine was quite right: there are, now, people who are more pleased by the fact of Monica's presence in his dialogue than by anything else they find there. Some of them are reading this book. But what could he have meant by the 'old authors' in whose works [*apud veteres*] women did philosophy? The most convincing answer is that the plural 'old authors' refers to a comment by a speaker in Cicero's dialogue *Hortensius*, now lost, which had inspired Augustine, aged 18, to study philosophy (*Conf.* 3.4.7): 'My grandmother used to say what the Stoics say, that everything happens by fate, but my mother, a wise woman, did not think so.'[49]

The second book of *Order* begins with another tribute to Monica:

> A few days later Alypius came, and the brilliant sunshine and
> mild weather (so far as was possible in that place in winter)
> invited us to go down to the meadow we often used. My
> mother too was with us. I had already seen, from a long time
> of living together and from loving attention, her intelligence
> and her soul on fire for the divine; and in a discussion on an
> important question, which I had on my birthday with the
> people I lived with and related in a short book [*de beata vita*],
> her mind had appeared to me as so great that nothing seemed
> better suited to philosophy. So I had adopted the practice that,
> since she had ample leisure [*otium*], she should not be absent
> from our conversation. You know this from the first book of
> this work. (*Ord.* 2.1.1)

Monica, in retirement from domestic duties, uses her *otium* to study philosophy. At this point, though she is not absent from the discussion, she does not contribute. It ends only when a slave runs down from the house to say that lunch is ready (2.6.18). Readers who are pleased by Monica's presence will note that she is now among those interrupted

---

48. Almost ten years later (395 CE) in his book on lying, *De mendacio*, Augustine insisted that a liar is someone who has one thing in his mind but says or conveys another. But the Latin verb *mentiri* can also mean "to give a false impression" or "to mislead", not always intentionally.

49. O'Donnell (n. 14), 3. 123, on *Conf.* 9.10.23. Conybeare (n. 1), pp. 105–6 offers some other suggestions.

by a call to lunch, whereas in *Against the Academics* she interrupted. Discussion resumes after lunch, back in the bathhouse. Monica arrives only after it has started (2.7.21), and makes her first contribution when discussion moves to the justice of God.

Augustine begins by reminding Licentius of what he said earlier. This passage is a smoother read in Latin. In English, "bad" or "the bad" can mean a bad thing or bad people, but can also be abstract, whereas Latin shows by the number and gender of the word which of these is meant:

> I remember you said that the justice of God is that by which he distinguishes between good and bad [people] and gives each their own. [. . .] Does it seem to you that God was ever not just? 'Never', he said. 'So if God was always just', I said, 'then good and bad [abstract] always existed.' 'Certainly [*prorsus*]', said my mother, 'I can't see anything else that follows. For there was no judgement of God when bad [abstract] did not exist, nor, if at some time he did not give the good and bad [people] their own, can he be seen to have been just.' Licentius said to her 'So you think we must say that bad [abstract] always existed?' 'I don't dare to say that', she said. 'So what shall we say?' I said. 'If God is just because he judges between good and bad [people], when there was not bad [abstract], he was not just.' They were silent, and I noticed that Trygetius wanted to answer, and allowed him. 'Certainly [*prorsus*]', he said, 'God was just. For he could have distinguished good from bad [abstract] if it had already come into existence [*si extitisset*], and from the fact that he could have done, he was just. [Trygetius uses a human analogy: Cicero had the virtues of wisdom, self-control, justice, and courage, even if Catiline had not conspired against the state and Cicero had not had to deploy those virtues in response.] When bad came into existence [*extitit*] and he separated it from good, he did not defer giving each his own; for he did not at that time have to learn justice, but to make use of justice which he had always had.' (2.7.22)

Augustine's Monica is in some difficulty. First she accepts that if God's justice has always existed, 'certainly' good and bad [abstract] must always have existed; but she does not venture to say that bad [abstract] has always existed. Augustine does not spell out why she does not venture to say it: the problem is that if bad [abstract] has always existed, it is not part of the order God created, but is a rival power, just as the Manichaeans argued. Trygetius offers a solution. Bad [abstract] has not always existed, but God's justice has always existed because God could always have exercised it. Licentius and Monica have to accept this argument, but then Augustine challenges Licentius: what becomes of his claim that nothing is outside order? 'For what was done so that bad was born was surely not done in God's order, but when it was born, it was included in God's order.' Licentius begins a response with *prorsus*: 'Certainly, I say that order began from the time when there began to be bad [abstract].' He is then caught in a dilemma: if order began when bad began, then either bad began outside order, or bad is part of God's order. He falls silent, and Monica says 'I don't think anything [nothing?] could have happened outside God's order, because bad itself [abstract], which was born, was in no way born in God's order, but justice did not allow it to be disordered, and compelled it back to the order it deserved' (2.7.23).[50]

This declaration is unusual for Augustine's Monica. It begins with an emphatic *ego non puto*, 'I don't think', and it apparently does not advance the discussion, if Monica has simply reaffirmed the contradiction that nothing happens outside God's order and that bad [abstract] was not born in God's order. But what Monica actually says is *ego non puto **nihil** potuisse praeter Dei ordinem fieri*, literally 'I don't think **nothing** could have happened outside God's order.' *Nihil* could be a negative reinforcing *non*, but it could have a deeper meaning. Augustine came to think that evil was not a separate force, as the Manichaeans argued, but a lack of good, *privatio boni*. If that is so, evil can only be a corruption of good, so where there is no good left to corrupt, there is nothing.[51] Evil, then, was not born outside God's order: it is a falling away from God's order. But instead of engaging with this, Augustine goes into lecture mode. For the rest of the dialogue, apart from two

50. *Ego, inquit, non puto nihil potuisse praeter Dei ordinem fieri, quia ipsum malum quod natum est nullo modo Dei ordine natum est, sed illa iustitia id inordinatum esse non sivit et in sibi meritum ordinem redegit et compulit.*

51. Rowan Williams, 'Insubstantial Evil', in Robert Dodaro and George Lawless, eds., *Augustine and his Critics* (2000), pp. 105–23.

brief exchanges with Alypius, he discourses on reason and the liberal arts. At one point he reassures Monica:

> But as for what we need from these [arts] for that which we seek, please do not, mother, let this huge forest of subjects deter you. Some things will be selected from them all, very few in number, very powerful in force; difficult to grasp for many, but for you, whose intelligence is new to me every day, and whose mind I know to have risen far up, distanced through age or through admirable self restraint from all trivialities, and emerging into itself from the great stain of the body: for you these things will be as easy as they are difficult for those who are sluggish and live wretchedly. If I say that you will easily attain the style which is free from faults of speech and expression, evidently I would lie. Even I, who had great need to learn all this, am still often harassed by the Italians about the sound of words, and I blame them in return so far as the sound is concerned. For it is one thing to be negligent on purpose, another to be negligent because of where you come from. An educated person, listening attentively, will perhaps find in my speeches what we call solecisms; for there was not lacking someone to persuade me that Cicero himself, with the greatest skill, made some such mistakes. As for barbarism, that is understood in our time in such a way that the very speech which saved Rome seems barbarous.[52] But you, disregarding these things which are childish or irrelevant to you, understand the near-divine force and nature of grammar in such a way that you seem to have grasped its soul and left its body to clever people. (2.17.45)

Then the lecture continues, except for a brief final exchange with Alypius.

Augustine believed, at the time of writing these dialogues, that the liberal arts are training for wisdom, because they teach students to free

---

52. A solecism is a grammatical mistake, "barbarism" is incorrect pronunciation. In *Christian Teaching* (2.44–45 = 2.13.19) Augustine gave examples: it is a solecism to say *inter hominibus* not *inter homines* (in grammatical terms, the preposition *inter*, "among", is followed by the accusative, not the ablative case) but this does not matter to a student of scripture who correctly understands "among people"; it is a barbarism to pronounce *ignoscere* ("to forgive") with the third syllable long, but this does not matter to someone who is asking God's forgiveness.

their minds from their immediate surroundings and experiences, and to move from the particular to the underlying principle. He planned to demonstrate this with treatises on all seven arts, but finished only the book on grammar; he subsequently lost both this and what he had written on dialectic, rhetoric, geometry, arithmetic, and philosophy, but he did complete, on his return to Africa, six books on rhythm as part of the theory of music (*Retr.* 1.6).[53] He did not think that Monica needed to work on the technicalities, for she did not need the skills of public life. He presents her as someone whose everyday domestic life provided the ethical training which was a necessary preparation for philosophy. In retirement from domestic duties, she has moved beyond the concerns of the world and the body. She has the intelligence to grasp philosophical principles, and she engages in discussion with God through scripture and prayer, just as Augustine did in *Confessions*.

Augustine wrote that Monica went faithfully to church, twice a day, 'so that she should hear you [God] in your discourses, and you should hear her in her prayers' (*Conf.* 5.9.17). This philosophical training makes it possible for her, shortly before her death, to share with her son a vision in which the mind ascends to God:

> As the day approached in which she was to leave this life
> (which you knew and we did not) it came about, I believe by
> your management in your hidden ways, that she and I were
> standing alone, leaning on a window from which could be
> seen the garden inside the house where we were, there at
> Ostia on the Tiber, where, removed from the crowds, after the
> effort of a long journey, we were restoring ourselves for the
> sea voyage. So we were talking together alone, very pleasantly,
> and, forgetting the past and intent on what lies before us (Phil.
> 3:13), we were jointly seeking in the presence of truth, which
> you are, what the future eternal life of the saints is like, the
> life which 'eye has not seen nor ear heard, nor has it ascended
> into the heart of man' (1 Cor. 2:9). We were thirsting with the
> mouth of the heart for the celestial streams of your fount,
> the fount of life which is in you, so that, sprinkled from it

---

53. See the papers collected in *Augustine and the Disciplines: From Cassiciacum to Confessions*, Karla Pollmann and Mark Vessey, eds. (2005); O'Donnell (n. 16), 2. pp. 269–78.

according to our capacity, we might somehow think about so great a question. (*Conf.* 9.10.23)

In their conversation, Augustine and Monica move beyond sensory delights and everything bodily, and beyond their own minds to God's eternal wisdom in which there is neither past not future. 'And while we speak and yearn after it, we touch it, just a little [*modice*], by a complete impact [*ictus*] of the heart' (9.10.24). They return to the 'noise of our speech' where words begin and end, and Augustine continues with what 'we were saying': suppose everything that God has made was silent, and we could hear God himself, without the mediation of any voice, as just now when we touch eternal wisdom, that is what eternal life will be like, when we rise again (9.10.25). Then he moves from 'we were saying' to:

> I was saying something like this, even if not in this way and
> with these words; but you know, Lord, that on that day when
> we were saying such things, and as we spoke this world and all
> its delights became insignificant to us, she said 'My son, so far
> as I am concerned, I no longer delight in anything in this life.
> What I am doing here now, and why I am here, I do not know,
> now that hope in this world is used up. There was one thing
> for which I wanted to remain a little in this life, to see you
> a catholic Christian before I died. God has given me this in
> heaping measure, so that I see you his slave, earthly happiness
> disregarded. What am I doing here?' (9.10.26)[54]

Many commentators have pointed to the differences between this shared experience and the ascent of the mind described by Augustine in *Conf.* 7.17.23.[55] In Book 7, Augustine has been reading Platonist philosophy, which tells him to enter into himself. He goes beyond bodily senses to the reason which assesses the reports of the senses: reason understands that immutability, changelessness, is better than its own mutability; so reason must somehow know immutability, and 'in the impact [*ictus*] of a trembling glance' it attains, for a moment, that which is.

---

54. See chapter 1 for some modern reactions to Monica's concern for her son.

55. O'Donnell (n. 16), 3. pp. 122–37; John Peter Kenney, *The Mysticism of Saint Augustine* (2005), especially pp. 73–86; and a brief but important note to the translation by Maria Boulding (1997), p. 228, on 9.10.25.

Porphyry, in his *Life* of the philosopher Plotinus, said that Plotinus had achieved such union with the divine four times in the years when Porphyry was with him, and Porphyry himself had achieved it once (*Life of Plotinus* 23). Both men had devoted their lives to philosophy in that they lived austerely, read and discussed philosophical works, lectured, and wrote. In Book 7 Augustine withdraws into himself and tries to see, but in Book 9 his account is full of phrases from scripture, and he and Monica, together, try to hear God's eternal wisdom. They respond differently to their moment of encounter. Both find that all earthly delights are now irrelevant, but Augustine reflects on the nature of eternal life and on themes he will pursue later in *Confessions*, whereas Monica expresses her own readiness to die. She has achieved what philosophers try to achieve: she has overcome the desires of the body and the concerns of this world, she is in contact with the divine, and she is not afraid of death.

5

Monica's Religion

Augustine's Monica is consistently Christian. She is a baptized member of
the Catholic Church,[1] and her prayers and tears connect Augustine with
the Church and with its bishops, even when he is intellectually and physically absent. In one of his last works, Augustine asked:

> Now which of my little works became more often or more
> delightfully known than the books of my *Confessions*? [. . .]
> And do you not remember that what I told in those same books
> about my conversion, when God converted me to the faith I was
> wrecking by wretched raving talk, I told in such a way as to show
> how I had been granted to the faithful and daily tears of my
> mother, so that I should not perish? There I proclaimed that God
> by his grace converts to it the wills of men which were not only
> turned away from right faith, but turned against it. (*persev.* 20.53)

In *Confessions*, Monica goes regularly to church to hear scripture read
and expounded; at home she prays and follows up the scripture readings. At Thagaste, she is a faithful worshipper who takes her young
son to church. Her household is Christian except for her husband, and
eventually her example makes her husband Christian too, but there is
no mention of household religious practice in addition to, or instead of,
churchgoing.[2] When Augustine grows up and joins the Manichaeans,

---

1. This means the universal (Greek *katholikos*) church. The division between (Roman)
Catholic and Protestant is a sixteenth-century development.
2. On the possibilities for household religion, see Kim Bowes, *Private Worship, Public Values*
(2008).

FIGURE 5.1. Mother Church: Mosaic from Tabarka.
© Bardo Museum.

who believed that their teaching was true Christianity, Monica considers refusing to share a house or to eat with him; she pleads for help from a bishop who had been Manichaean in his own youth, and for many centuries she was remembered chiefly for his reply: 'the son of those tears cannot be lost' (*Conf.* 3.12.21).[3] In the years when Augustine teaches rhetoric at Carthage, still a Manichaean, Monica continues to weep and pray for him. When he deceives her and slips away to Italy, he leaves her at the shrine of St Cyprian, the martyred bishop of Carthage; she prays there, and returns to her usual life.[4] At Milan, when she follows Augustine to Italy, she joins the congregation of Bishop Ambrose, who praises her commitment to churchgoing and good works. Augustine, no longer Manichaean, hears Ambrose preach, but struggles to understand the central Christian doctrine that Christ is God incarnate, 'the Word made flesh': he thinks of Christ as a man of unsurpassed wisdom (*Conf.* 7.9.25). Monica is undisturbed by debates about the divinity of Christ. She is concerned about different church traditions on fast days and on the right way to honor the dead, but she willingly follows the advice of Ambrose; and she bravely joins supporters of Ambrose in occupying a church that is wanted (see below) by an empress who has different theological views.

Augustine does not suggest any other possibilities for Monica, but they were always there. Thagaste was probably more pagan than

3. See chapter 6 for 'the son of those tears'.
4. On this episode, see chapter 1.

Christian. Monica may have grown up as a Donatist, a member of a rival church that claimed to be the true Catholic Church. The Manichaeans claimed that theirs was the true Christian teaching, and Augustine, who convinced some of his friends to join them, suggested to his mother that she might do so too (*Conf.* 3.11.20). Ambrose had rivals at Milan, where the boy-emperor's mother and the Gothic imperial bodyguard supported the Arian interpretation of Christianity (see below). Pagans, Donatists, Manichaeans, Arians, are all names imposed by opponents on people who in their own view worshipped the divine in accordance with truth. The opponents won and the names have stuck, but it was not so obvious in Monica's lifetime which way was right. Recent scholarship has made great efforts to understand how it seemed to the other side.

Monica was born (331 CE) late in the reign of Constantine, the first Roman emperor to give open support to Christianity. At the end of his life (337) Constantine was baptized. For almost all of Monica's lifetime, Constantine's successors followed his example of support for Christianity (the exception is Julian, discussed below), but they did so with greater or lesser commitment and with different interpretations of Christian doctrine. They made donations to churches, and they intervened in Church concerns by summoning councils of bishops, exiling bishops of whom they disapproved, and denouncing people who in their view were heretics. In Greek philosophical and medical tradition, a *hairesis* (literally "choice") was a school of thought, and adherents of one school did no more than argue against the others. But in Christian tradition *hairesis* became heresy, false belief which endangered the soul, and heresy was blamed on intellectual arrogance and demonic activity. Disputes about heresies sometimes led to violence, which meant that Roman officials had to intervene to maintain public order. Christian emperors recognized a duty to ensure that the true God was rightly worshipped. But how could they ensure that people held the right beliefs, especially when one emperor regarded as heresy beliefs which his successor, or even his colleague, regarded as orthodox? Constantine ruled as sole emperor, but for much of Monica's lifetime there was one emperor in the Latin-speaking west and another in the Greek-speaking east, and sometimes there were three emperors at once.

An example from 380 CE, when Monica was almost 50 and Augustine was teaching at Carthage, shows the general problem of ensuring that people held the right beliefs. It also helps to explain the difficult situation Augustine, and therefore Monica, encountered a few years later at

Milan. In 380 CE Theodosius I had recently achieved power in the eastern Roman Empire, at the invitation of Gratian, who was emperor in the west together with his young brother Valentinian II. In the names of all three, Theodosius issued an edict to the people of Constantinople, capital of the Eastern Empire, saying that the emperors wished all their subjects to accept the teaching that Father, Son, and Spirit are one god. This doctrine of the Trinity (Latin *trinitas*, "threeness") is affirmed in what is now called the Nicene Creed.[5] "Creed" comes from Latin *credo*, "I believe", and "Nicene" from Nicaea, the town to which, in 325 CE, Constantine summoned a council of bishops to produce an agreed statement of Christian belief. Nicaea was conveniently near his new capital Constantinople, and he attended the council, where the bishops affirmed that God the Father and Christ the Son are "of the same substance" (Greek *homoousios*). This technical term of Greek philosophy was intended to convey that the divinity of Christ does not differ from the divinity of God, for if it differed, God and humanity were not fully reconciled in Christ. But some theologians, who were known as "Arians" because they (supposedly) agreed with Arius, a priest of Alexandria, held that this is not what scripture says. They argued that Christ as son of God, 'begotten not made', is superior to all created beings, but derives his being from his father.

Constantius II (ruled 337–61), son of Constantine, was pro-Arian. So was Valens (ruled 364–78), predecessor of Theodosius I in the eastern empire, and so was Justina, mother of the young emperor Valentinian II. Gratian, like Theodosius, was pro-Nicene, but by the time Augustine was appointed professor of rhetoric at Milan, in 384 CE, Gratian had been killed in a rebellion. Meanwhile, at the Council of Constantinople in 381 CE, the assembled bishops had reaffirmed the teaching of Nicaea and clarified that the divinity of the Holy Spirit does not differ from the divinity of God the Father and God the Son. What was to become of those who held different views? In the edict of 380 CE Theodosius had declared:

We order them to follow this law and embrace the name of Catholic Christians, and the rest, judging them to be crazy,

5. Strictly speaking, the "Niceno-Constantinopolitan" creed, as explained below, because it was the council of Constantinople which affirmed the equal divinity of the Holy Spirit. On the debate about the relationship of Christ the Son to God the Father, see Lewis Ayres, *Nicaea and its Legacy* (2004).

we order to bear the *infamia* [loss of some legal rights] of heretical teaching; their gatherings are not to have the name of churches; and they are to be brought low first by divine punishment, then by the vengeance of our strong feeling [*motus*], which we have taken from the heavenly will. (*C.Th.* 16.1.2.1)

What exactly was the 'vengeance of our strong feeling'? The edict of Theodosius I survives, in part, in a compilation of legal material made on the orders of his grandson Theodosius II. This compilation, known as the Theodosian Code (from Latin *codex*, a spine-hinged book), was designed to be a clear, authoritative, and accessible statement of the law. The legal commission was told to start from the time of Constantine, to distinguish authentic laws from forged or corrupt documents, to remove inconsistencies, and to extract material that was relevant to the empire as a whole and arrange it under headings. This was necessary and useful work, but it is often difficult to reconstruct the content and purpose of the laws which were excerpted. In this instance, Theodosius I may not have specified what the imperial vengeance would be. Law in this period was often a warning, or a statement of imperial views, rather than a precise set of rules and penalties.[6] Moreover, an edict issued by one emperor in Constantinople, in the names of all current emperors, had not always been agreed, or even discussed, by them all, and did not necessarily reach other parts of the empire. It could happen that officials at Carthage, or even at Rome or Milan, did not know what an emperor had said at Constantinople.

Christians differed both about the interpretation of Christianity and about the right way to deal with traditional Graeco-Roman religion. In retrospect, the fourth century from Constantine on shows a sequence of Christian emperors, with the one brief exception of Julian, who reigned for eighteen months (361–3) when Monica was in her early thirties and Augustine (born 354 CE) was a child. But when Julian came to power, many people must have seen a return to normality. Julian was brought up as a Christian, but as soon as he achieved power, he declared his support for the traditional religion. He recalled bishops

6. On the Theodosian Code, see Jill Harries, *Law and Empire in Late Antiquity* (1999), especially pp. 59–64. Neil McLynn discusses the edict of 380 in '*Genere Hispanus*: Theodosius, Spain, and Nicene Orthodoxy', in Kim Bowes and Michael Kulikowski, eds., *Hispania in Late Antiquity* (2005), pp. 77–120.

who had been exiled, and left Christians to settle their own disputes. He saw no reason to give Christian clergy exemption from civic duties. When he was asked whether he wished to appoint the holders of publicly funded teaching posts, he declined, but said that the names of those chosen by the cities should be sent to him for formal approval, so that he could show how important he thought teachers were. In a follow-up letter he wrote that teachers must have high moral standards, and Christians could not with integrity teach classical literature when they condemned its religious and ethical teaching. He was interpreted as forbidding Christians to teach literature or rhetoric (*Conf.* 8.5.10), and even his supporters objected to that. But Julian spent his short reign in Constantinople and Antioch, in the Greek-speaking Eastern Empire, before dying on campaign in Persia. He did not have time to explain to his Latin-speaking subjects in the western empire what he meant by saying that 'Hellenism' was the true religion, expressed in divinely inspired Greek literature and philosophy. In Africa, he was remembered chiefly for his effect on the Donatist dispute, because he refused to intervene in support of either side, and because he required property that had been confiscated in earlier stages of the dispute to be returned to its previous owners. He did not reign for long enough to disrupt Monica's hopes for her clever son.[7]

Most emperors were Christian, but it does not follow that Roman Africa in Monica's lifetime was a Christian country. There were some legal constraints on the public practice of traditional religion, especially on blood sacrifice. Constantius II said that he was following the precedent of his father Constantine in banning sacrifice (*C.Th.* 16.10.2, dated 341 CE), and some years later he ordered the closing of temples to ensure that sacrifice should not happen (*C.Th.* 16.10.4). Julian reversed these policies. After Julian, emperors varied in their willingness to intervene or to tolerate, and practice could be very different in different parts of the empire.[8] Thus Valentinian I (reigned 364–75) was tolerant, but in the eastern empire his brother Valens, an Arian Christian, sometimes took action against Nicene Christians. In the city of Rome traditional cult was maintained, but in the early 380s CE Gratian withdrew financial support, renounced the title of *pontifex maximus* (chief priest),[9] and

7. On Julian, see further Shaun Tougher, *Julian the Apostate* (2007).

8. On changes over time, and local variation, see Garth Fowden, 'Polytheist Religion and Philosophy', in Averil Cameron and Peter Garnsey, eds. *The Cambridge Ancient History XIII: The Late Empire AD 337–425* (1997), pp. 538–60.

9. Roman priesthood was not a vocation. Priests were members of the governing elite,

ordered the altar of Victory to be removed from the Senate House. The altar and statue of Victory had been set up by Augustus, who became the first emperor of Rome. According to tradition, this was where senators took oaths of loyalty, and also burned incense and offered libations before meetings. Symmachus, prefect of the city, led the protests of pagan senators; Damasus, bishop of Rome, led the counter-protest of Christian senators, with the help of Ambrose, bishop of Milan. These religious differences led to lobbying rather than violence, but in the Eastern Empire the prefect Cynegius (in office 384–8) made violent attacks on traditional cult and on temples.

It was not until 391/2 CE, four years after Monica's death, that Theodosius I, now sole emperor, banned public and private worship of the traditional gods. He told the prefect of Rome, and the count in charge of Egypt, that no one was to sacrifice, go to shrines or temples, or revere manmade images (*C.Th.* 16.10.10, 16.10.11). Nor was anyone to venerate, with incense and wine and lights, the gods of a household (*lares* and *penates*) or the guardian spirit (*genius*) of its head (16.10.12) This legislation is sometimes presented as the decisive outlawing of paganism, but even when local officials were aware of the latest legislation, law enforcement depended on their willingness to take action themselves or to respond to complaints.[10] Christian emperors did not insist on appointing Christian officials, and whatever their own religious beliefs, people might be reluctant to cause trouble either in towns or among workers on the land. So pagans were not persecuted as Christians had been: they did not risk death, or even loss of property and status, for their religious beliefs and practices.

But who counted as pagan? The word is a Christian label for people who worshipped the traditional gods of Rome, and it is still in use, often in scare quotes, because nobody has found a satisfactory alternative. One of Augustine's philosophical friends called himself "pagan" (*ep.* 234), but his style is so elaborately deferential that it sounds like irony:

> Blessed am I, and bathed in the pure light of your radiant
> virtue, because you thought me worthy to be crowned with

and were responsible for maintaining specific temples and rituals. Until the time of Augustus, Rome's first emperor, the *pontifex maximus* was a senior priest among others. Augustus took the title, which was inherited by his successors, and made the *pontifex maximus* head of all the colleges of priests.

10. Harries (n. 6), pp. 77–98.

the honour of your divine utterance. But, reverend lord, you have laid upon me a heavy burden, and a most difficult task of replying, especially to your questions, and in explaining such matters at this time in accordance with my own view: that is, of a pagan man.

Most people did not call themselves pagan, but said 'I have always worshipped the gods.' Some recent scholarship uses "polytheist", but that name accepts the Christian charge that pagans worshipped many gods, whereas it was common for pagans to insist that they did not. Maximus, a teacher of literature at Madauros where Augustine was sent to school, wrote to him that the forum was full of visible gods, but everyone knew that these gods were manifestations or aspects of the one divine power.[11] To judge from the commentary of Servius, which dates from the late fourth century, that is what teachers usually said as they took their classes through the poems of Virgil; so that was what Augustine heard when he was away at school. There was no alternative to classical education, and it is understandable that Monica helped to fund Augustine's.[12] If she knew enough to warn him against its content, or to ensure that he lived in a Christian household at Madauros and attended church there, he did not say so; but if all her household was Christian, presumably he had a Christian slave as his *paedagogus*.

Monica grew up at a time when blood sacrifice was forbidden by law, but pagans could still make a public commitment to traditional religion by holding the priesthood of a local deity, subsidizing the annual festival, leading the procession, and sitting in the theatre in the seats reserved for priests. Patricius, as a member of the *curia*, was expected to take part in traditional ceremonies and civic banquets; Monica, a baptized Christian, is less likely to have attended shows and festivals (see below). Augustine remembered watching at Carthage the procession in honour of its patron goddess Caelestis (*civ.* 2.4), which included musicians and singers; this was in the 370s or the early 380s CE when he lived in Carthage as a student and later as a teacher.[13] Even

11. The letter survived in Augustine's correspondence as *ep.* 16.
12. See chapter 2.
13. On the persistence of Romano-African paganism, see David Riggs, 'The Continuity of Paganism between the Cities and Countryside of Late Roman Africa', in T. Burns and J. Eadie, eds., *Urban Centers and Rural Contexts in Late Antiquity* (2001), pp. 285–300; 'Christianizing the Rural Communities of Late Roman Africa', in H. A. Drake, ed., *Violence in Late Antiquity: Perceptions and Practices* (2006), pp. 297–308.

when stronger legislation was in place, pagans could still show commitment to the heritage of their town by restoring a temple or a statue and by maintaining a traditional popular festival, for they could claim that this was civic tradition, not cult. In 399 CE the sons of Theodosius sent an instruction to the governor of Africa:

> Just as we have already removed profane rites by a salutary law, so we do not permit the festive gatherings of citizens and the general happiness of all to be removed. So we decree that without any sacrifice or any damnable superstition, pleasures shall be provided for the people in accordance with ancient custom, and if public wishes require it, festival banquets too shall take place. (*C.Th.* 16.10.17)

They had already said that although they wanted sacrifice to stop, they also wanted the ornaments of cities to be preserved (*C.Th.* 16.10.15, also dated 399 CE). These "ornaments" were temples that were also public buildings, and cult images that were also works of art; for example, the statue of Victory in the Senate House at Rome, which was not removed, because without its altar it posed no threat. We do not know what happened out of view in pagan households, but there too, if someone tried to cause trouble, a statue or a shrine could be described as a work of art passed down in the family.

At the start of the fifth century, replying to a letter from the town council of Madauros, Augustine said that pagans were no longer allowed to worship their gods in public, but they had not destroyed the idols in their hearts (*ep.* 232.1). Like other preachers, he frequently complained that even people who called themselves Christian were not distinctively Christian. Some (like Augustine himself) were only a generation away from paganism: he commented in a sermon that when Christ said 'I have come not to bring peace, but a sword', the sword 'separated every one of the faithful from his father who did not believe in Christ, or from a mother who was likewise an unbeliever; or if he was born of Christian parents, then at least from earlier generations of the family; for there is not one of us who did not have a grandfather or a great-grandfather or an earlier ancestor among the Gentiles' (*En.Ps.* 96. 7). Scripture told Christians that 'the gods of the nations are demons' (Psalm 96: 5), but they were far too ready to expose themselves to these demonic presences, who could not openly say 'come to the idol, come to my altars' (*ser.* 62.10.15), but used more devious means. In a sermon preached at Carthage, probably in 399 CE, Augustine said that Christians were seen 'reclining [i.e., dining] in the place of idols' (1 Cor. 8:10). The context shows that this was a civic banquet, and the Christians said they were afraid of offending some powerful person if they refused the invitation (*ser.* 62. 4.7–5.8). Anyway 'it's not a god, they say, because it's the Genius of Carthage' (ibid. 6.10). If it is not a god, Augustine demanded, why is there an altar? Christians knew it was not a god, but pagans thought it was, so there was a danger both that Christians would be exposed to pagan arguments and that pagans would think 'why should we leave the gods whom Christians worship with us?' (ibid. 6.9).

Christians watched immoral shows at the theatre, even though these shows were instituted to please the false gods, who wanted to corrupt their worshippers; Christians sought advice from soothsayers who relied on the powers of demons, and Christians wore amulets that invoked the powers of demons.[14] In a small town such as Thagaste, it was obvious who did and who did not go to church, but without that evidence of commitment it was not obvious who thought of himself or herself as Christian. There were no external markers in clothing or speech; and even churchgoers went to shows at the theatre, and compromised in dealing with problems of everyday life: 'Don't tell me "Yes, I go to idols, I get advice from visionaries and soothsayers, but I don't leave the church of God: I am a catholic"' (*En.Ps.* 88.2.14):

> There are people who say 'God is good, great, supreme,
> invisible, eternal, incorruptible; he will give us eternal life, and
> the incorruption he promised in the resurrection; but these
> worldly and temporal matters are the province of demons and
> the powers of this darkness.' In saying this, when they are
> entangled in the love of these things, they dismiss God, as
> if these things were not his province; and they seek by
> unspeakable sacrifices, and by some sort of remedies, or by
> some sort of unlawful persuasion of people, to provide for
> themselves temporal things, such as money, a wife, children,
> and anything else that is either a comfort in this transitory
> life, or an impediment to those going through it. (*En.Ps.* 34.1:7)

14. Examples in F. Van der Meer, *Augustine the Bishop* (1961), pp. 56–67; see also chapter 1 on the martyr who refuses amulets.

There were also people who said they were Christian, took an intelligent interest, perhaps were catechumens who came to church, but who were still not prepared to come forward for baptism and to live by Christian moral teaching.[15]

Monica was born into a Christian household (*Conf.* 9.8.17), but her name is sometimes taken to indicate that there was in her family an older religious devotion. Monnica, or Nonnica, is a name found in her part of Africa; it is a diminutive of Monna, a local deity who is mentioned in an inscription from Thignica (now in Tunisia). Nonnica, wife of Nubel prince of Mauretania, was a contemporary of Augustine's mother, whose name is often spelled Monnica in modern scholarship. Scholars in postcolonial times have been eager to find traces of pre-Roman and non-Roman cultures in the Roman Empire, and to move on from any assumption that Romanization was always a process of civilizing the uncivilized. This eagerness has been especially strong in relation to Roman Africa, where some earlier work by French and Italian scholars was seen as too closely connected with foreign military occupation.[16] Archaeologists and historians have argued for continuities from the local Libyan culture to the Berbers of their own time. Thus William Frend, in his much challenged study of the Donatist church (see below) asked 'Is Donatism part of a continuous native religious tradition, as fundamentally unchanging as the Berbers themselves in the routine of their daily life?'[17] So it is sometimes affirmed that Monnica (with this spelling) was Berber, in the sense that she belonged to the local Numidian peoples who predated not only the Roman conquest of Africa (from the second century BCE) but the arrival of settlers from Phoenicia in the seventh century BCE.

But what does it mean to say that "Monnica was Berber"? Who, in this context, were the Berbers? Ethnic descent and cultural identity were complicated, long before the Roman conquest, by the varying

15. For example, Firmus, who was eager to have the latest books of *City of God: ep.* 2*.
16. Elizabeth Fentress, 'Romanizing the Berbers', *Past & Present* 190 (2006), 3–33, is a concise and helpful survey of the debates. See also David Mattingly and Bruce Hitchner, 'Roman Africa: An Archaeological Review', *Journal of Roman Studies* 85 (1995), 165–213, at pp. 169–70, on reaction against the work of French and Italian officials.
17. W.H.C. Frend, *The Donatist Church* (1952), xvi; for a recent assessment, see Eric Rebillard, 'William Hugh Clifford Frend (1916–2005): The Legacy of *The Donatist Church*', in Markus Vinzent, ed., *Studia Patristica LIII* (2013), pp. 55–71. On the distinctive religious tradition of Africa, see Brent Shaw, 'Cult and Belief in Punic and Roman Africa', in Michele Salzman, ed., *The Cambridge History of Religions in the Ancient World* 2 (2013), pp. 235–63.

relationships of Numidians, Libyans, Mauri, and Punic-speaking settlers. Many people spoke more than one language and adopted elements of more than one culture, depending on their circumstances.[18] The evidence for Libyan comes from inscriptions; some, from the first and second centuries CE, were found at Thagaste. But there are no inscriptions to show the continued use of Libyan in Monica's lifetime, and it is difficult to demonstrate a connection between ancient Libyan and modern Berber. The evidence for Punic, a Semitic language brought by pre-Roman settlers from Phoenicia, comes from references in literature. It was still spoken in country districts in Augustine's time, but he had difficulty finding Punic-speaking bishops for these areas in his diocese, and himself had only a limited and passive knowledge of Punic.[19] 'Let the people of Mappalia hear us both', he wrote to a rival bishop: 'let what we say be written down, and let what I write be translated into Punic' (*ep.* 66.2). Evidently the nurses who helped him to learn language (*Conf.* 1.8.13) did not speak Punic. Monica was *Afra*, African in that she came from Africa, just as Augustine was *Afer*, and since Augustine after all his training had an identifiable regional accent (*ord.* 2.17.45), no doubt Monica did too. But she and her household spoke Latin, and their culture was Roman.

The name Monnica does not in itself show that a family had recently worshipped Monna rather than Christ. Most people in late antiquity had names which were traditional in the family, and Christian families did not feel the need to give children Christian names. Basil of Caesarea, for example, was named for his father, and his sister Macrina, the eldest daughter, was named for their father's mother. Gorgonia, sister of Gregory of Nazianzus, was named for their mother's mother, and had a daughter named Alypiana after her husband Alypius, and another named Nonna after her own mother.[20] Monnica too was probably named for a grandmother. Her sons Navigius and Augustinus did not have explicitly Christian names, and the son of Navigius was

18. See C.R. Whittaker, 'Berber', in Glen Bowersock, Peter Brown, Oleg Grabar, eds., *Late Antiquity: A Guide to the Postclassical World* (1999), pp. 340–1.

19. Eric Rebillard, 'Punic', ibid. pp. 656–7. The epigraphic evidence for Libyan and the literary evidence for Punic are discussed by Fergus Millar, 'Local Cultures in the Roman Empire: Libyan, Punic and Latin in Roman Africa', *Journal of Roman Studies* 58 (1968), 126–34. See further J.N. Adams, *Bilingualism and the Latin Language* (2003), pp. 200–45 on Punic, especially pp. 237–40 on Augustine's knowledge of Punic, and pp. 245–7 on Libyan and Berber; Brent Shaw, *Sacred Violence* (2011), pp. 427–33 on Punic speakers and interpreters.

20. Raymond Van Dam, *Families and Friends in Late Roman Cappadocia* (2003), pp. 122–3.

called Patricius after his grandfather. Some people in Roman Africa did have religious names. Augustine called his son Adeodatus, 'given by God', and corresponded with a deacon called Quodvultdeus, 'what God wills'. But these names are ambiguous: which god? 'Adeodatus' was the equivalent of Punic 'Iatanbaal' and of Greek 'Diodoros'.[21] Augustine did not urge his congregation, as John Chrysostom once did (in Gen. 21.3), to name their children after saints.

Monica's dreams are another possible connection with local religion.[22] The evidence is slight, and is scattered across many centuries; this may be one more example of efforts to find survivals of pre-Roman culture. But there is some evidence for a tradition of divination by dreams, associated with cult for the dead, and practised especially by women. Monica followed African custom by bringing food and wine to share at the tombs of the dead. Some Christian leaders interpreted this as cult of the dead, rather than commemoration of the dead, and Monica gave up the practice in Milan when she was told that Ambrose had forbidden it; Augustine thought that she would not have done so as willingly for anyone else (Conf. 6.2.2).[23] But Augustine does not associate Monica's dreams with visits to the dead, and Augustine's Monica thinks of her dreams as sent by the Christian God in answer to prayer. The first dream he reports in Confessions is a reassurance when Augustine was Manichaean:

> Whence came that dream [somnium] by which you consoled
> her, so that she agreed to live with me and to have the
> same table with me in the house? She had begun to refuse
> this, turning away from the blasphemies of my error and
> denouncing them. She saw herself standing on a wooden
> rule, and a radiant young man coming towards her, cheerful
> and smiling at her, when she was grieving and worn out
> with grief. He asked her the reasons for her sadness and her
> daily weeping (to teach her, as is usual, not to learn), and she
> replied that she was lamenting my perdition. He told her to

21. Iatanbaal: see Adams (n. 19), p. 238. On the absence of specifically Christian names, see Eric Rebillard, 'Religious Sociology: Being Christian', in Mark Vessey, ed., A Companion to Augustine (2012), pp. 40–53, at p. 45.

22. William Klingshirn, 'Comer y beber con los muertos', Augustinus 2007: 127–31. I am most grateful to Professor Klingshirn for a copy of this paper.

23. See also chapter 1 for Monica's practice. On "cult of the dead" see Eric Rebillard, The Care of the Dead in Late Antiquity (English translation, 2009), pp. 144–53.

be free from care, and advised her to look, and she would see that where she was, I was also. And when she looked, she saw me standing beside her on the same rule. Whence did this come, unless because your ears heard her heart, O good and almighty one? (*Conf.* 3.11.19)

Monica told Augustine about her vision [*visum*] (3.11.20). He tried to interpret it as meaning that she should not lose hope of being what he was, that is, Manichaean, but she replied with characteristic clarity 'No. I was not told "where he is, you will be", but "where you are, he will be"' (not *ubi ille, ibi et tu, sed ubi tu, ibi et ille*). At the time, he was more impressed (*commotus*) by 'your *responsum* through my mother when awake' than he was by the dream (*somnium*) which consoled her. *Responsum* is often used of an oracle given to an enquirer, and Augustine remembered another *responsum*, given through a bishop who had been brought up as a Manichaean (3.12.21): 'it cannot be that the son of these tears shall perish.'[24] Monica used to tell Augustine that she had received this as if it had sounded from heaven.

There were other reassurances, all in the context of Monica's faithful Christian practice:

> Would you, merciful Lord, reject the contrite and humble
> heart of a chaste and sober widow, generous in almsgiving,
> respectful and helpful to your saints, letting no day pass
> without an offering at your altar, twice a day coming to your
> church, morning and evening, without a break, not to engage
> in idle stories and old ladies' chatter, but so that she could hear
> you in your discourses and you could hear her in her prayers?
> Would you reject and exclude from your help those tears with
> which she sought not gold and silver, no unstable and mutable
> good, but salvation for the soul of her son: you, by whose
> gift she was like that? No, Lord. No, you were there, hearing
> her and acting in the order in which you had predestined
> what was to be done. Heaven forbid that you were deceiving
> her in those visions and responses of yours [*visionibus et
> responsis tuis*], those I have already mentioned and those
> I have not mentioned, which she kept in her faithful heart

24. See further chapter 6.

and, constantly praying, presented to you like a bond you had signed. (*Conf.* 5.9.17)

On the sea crossing from Africa to Italy, Monica was able to reassure the sailors:

My mother had already come to me, strong in her devotion, following me on land and sea and confident in you in all dangers. Even at critical moments on the sea she was reassuring the sailors, by whom travellers inexperienced in the deep are usually reassured when they are anxious, promising them a safe arrival because you had promised it to her in a vision [*per visum*]. (*Conf.* 6.1.1)

But it was different when Augustine asked Monica to pray for a vision about his marriage:

Both at my request, and by her longing, every day there were prayers to you, with a loud cry of the heart, that you would show her in a vision [*per visum*] something about my future marriage; but you were never willing. She saw some empty phantasms [*videbat quaedam vana et phantastica*], to which she was driven by the force of the human spirit that was active on this matter, and she told them to me not with the confidence she used to have when you showed her something, but with contempt. She said that she could tell by a kind of flavour [*sapore*], which she could not explain in words, the difference between your revelation and her soul dreaming. (*Conf.* 6.13.23)

Phantastica are the product of *phantasia*, the capacity of the human mind for forming images, which may or may not be images of real things. In the mid-sixth century CE, Gregory the Great generalized Monica's experience: 'holy men [*sic*] distinguish illusion from revelation, through the very words and images of the visions, by an inward flavour, so that they know what they receive from the good spirit and what they experience from illusion' (*Dial.* 4.48).[25] Augustine's marriage

25. *Sancti autem viri inter illusiones atque revelationes ipsas visionum voces ut imagines quodam intimo sapore discernunt, ut sciant vel quid a bono spiritu percipiant vel quid ab illusione patiantur.*

was not going to happen, and perhaps Monica had moved on from the local tradition of dreaming, just as she had moved on from the local cult of the dead.[26]

It was not unquestionable that Monica, born into a Christian household, would remain untouched by local religious tradition or by acceptance of the gods of Rome. But according to Augustine, this was a Christian household in the strong sense. He wrote that Monica was born *in domo fideli*: he used *fidelis*, "faithful", to mean a baptized Christian.[27] He did not say at what age Monica herself was baptized, but one observation suggests that it was not an infant baptism, but a commitment made when she was older: 'I do not venture to say that, from the time when you gave her new birth in baptism, no word escaped her lips which was contrary to your teaching' (*Conf.* 9.13.34). In later debates with followers of the theologian Pelagius, Augustine used infant baptism as a demonstration that salvation depends on the grace of God, not on human merit; but infant baptism was not then standard practice, though it was possible when the child was dangerously ill.[28]

Monica showed her Christian commitment by taking Augustine (and presumably his brother and sister) to church from the start of his life. But he was not baptized in infancy or as a child:

> When I was still a child [*puer*, older than *infans*] I had heard
> about the eternal life promised to us through the humility
> of our Lord God descending to our arrogance, and I was
> already being signed with the sign of his cross and seasoned
> with his salt from the time I left my mother's womb, for she
> had great hope in you. You saw, my Lord, when I was still a
> child and one day had a sudden fever, with stomach cramps,
> which brought me close to death; you saw, my God, for you
> were already my guardian, with what intensity of soul and
> with what faith I begged the baptism of your Christ, my lord
> and God, from the piety of my mother and of your church,
> the mother of us all. The mother of my flesh was distraught,
> because she was yet more lovingly in labour for my everlasting
> salvation, with a pure heart and with faith in you. She would

26. Klingshirn (n. 22).

27. Examples in J. O'Donnell, *Augustine: Confessions*, 2. 121–3, on *Conf.* 2.3.6.

28. William Harmless, 'Baptism', in Allan Fitzgerald, ed., *Augustine Through the Ages* (1999), pp. 84–91, at pp. 89–90.

have hurried off to see that I was initiated into your saving sacraments and washed clean, confessing you, Lord Jesus, for the remission of sins, if I had not immediately recovered. So my cleansing was deferred, as if it was necessary for me to stay dirty if I lived, because after that washing my guilt would be greater and more dangerous in the squalor of wrongdoing. [. . .] Even now, on all sides, we hear people say 'let him be, let him do it: he's not baptized yet'. (*Conf.* 1.11.17–18)

The child Augustine was a catechumen, 'under instruction'. The two verbs 'signed' and 'seasoned' are imperfect tenses, indicating repeated actions each time he was taken to church. Catechumens were not yet baptized, so they left the service before the distribution of bread and wine at the Eucharist. They were given the sign of the cross on the forehead, laying-on of hands with prayer, bread that had been blessed, and salt, a token of purification, which perhaps was placed on the tongue.[29] It was expected that they would eventually become *competentes*, asking for baptism, but this could take many years, because of the fear that post-baptismal sin was worse, and because baptized Christians were expected to live by a higher moral standard. Augustine often urged the catechumens in his audience to make the commitment to baptism. Preaching in Bulla Regia, a town too small to use the argument that it was only the non-Christians who filled the theatre, he said:

And this is done by Christians. I don't want to say 'and by the faithful [i.e. baptized]'. Perhaps a catechumen thinks poorly of himself. 'I'm [only] a catechumen', he says. 'You're a catechumen?' 'Yes, a catechumen.' Do you have one forehead which receives the sign of Christ, and another you take to the theatre? (*ser.* 301A.8)

For boys and men 'let him be, let him do it, he's not baptized yet' has a particular reference to sowing wild oats (an image Augustine would have liked) in adolescence and to having a sexual partner other than a wife.[30] Baptism, in Augustine's interpretation, carried a commitment

29. Van der Meer (n. 14), pp. 353–7.
30. For "wild oats", compare the metaphor of a vine running to seed, *Conf.* 2.1.1.

FIGURE 5.2. Theatre at Bulla Regia.
Wikimedia Commons.

to marital fidelity, such as his father made when he was at last baptized (*Conf.* 9.9.22). When Augustine was in his early thirties, Monica hoped that he would be baptized when he married (*Conf.* 6.13.23). But girls and women were expected to remain virgins until marriage and faithful within marriage, so for them there was no such reason to defer baptism. Some rigorist Christians held that postbaptismal sin cannot be forgiven, but there is nothing to suggest that Monica thought this, and Augustine certainly did not. But the complaints of Monica's neighbours, and her own anxieties as Augustine reached puberty (*Conf.* 2.3.7), show that many men in Thagaste were unconcerned for premarital chastity or marital fidelity. Monica may have accepted, for her sons, the conventional wisdom that baptism could wait until people were better able to follow the rules. She warned Augustine to avoid fornication and especially adultery, but she did not try to arrange an early marriage, which would have been an obstacle to his further studies. As Augustine put it, she had fled from the midst of Babylon, the great sprawling city which symbolizes earthly concerns in contrast to the heavenly Jerusalem; but she was still on the outskirts of Babylon and was moving more slowly (*ib.* 2.3.8).[31] When she arrived at Milan, she was confident that before she died she would see Augustine a baptized member of the Catholic Church (*Conf.* 6.1.1), and hoped that baptism would follow his marriage. Augustine expressed this in an oddly constructed sentence:

> There was unrelenting pressure for me to marry. I was already seeking a wife, and one was already promised, my mother especially applying herself so that salvific baptism would wash me, once married; she rejoiced that day by day I was more fitted to this, and was aware that her prayers and your promises were being fulfilled in my faith.[32] (*Conf.* 6.13.23)

Many commentators assume that the unrelenting pressure to marry came from Monica, but why would Augustine not say so? This passage is preceded by his report of his own thoughts about a marriage which both would help his career (6.11.19) and meet his sexual needs (6.12.22). These too were unrelenting pressures.

There is also a question whether Monica's effort went into negotiating the marriage, rather than into associating marriage with baptism. The sentence could be read either way, depending on the punctuation, and early texts of *Confessions* were not punctuated.[33] Commentators who think that Monica negotiated the marriage wonder how this woman from a small town in Africa was able to do that. Perhaps she used her contacts in Ambrose's congregation, or followed up a suggestion from one of Augustine's contacts? Augustine does not say. He goes on to report that he asked Monica to pray for a dream about his marriage, but no dream came. 'Nevertheless the pressure continued, and a girl was sought whose age was almost two years less than the age of marriage, and because she was pleasing, she was waited for.' Again, Augustine used passives: who sought the girl, and to whom was she pleasing?[34] Not long after he abandoned his marriage plans, Augustine

31. On Babylon as a symbol, see Frederick van Fleteren, 'Babylon', in Fitzgerald (n. 28), pp. 83–4. See chapter 6 for different interpretations of Monica's warnings.

32. *et instabatur impigre ut ducerem uxorem. Iam petebam, iam promittebatur, maxime matre dante operam quo me iam coniugatum baptismus salutaris ablueret, quo me in dies gaudebat aptari et vota sua ac promissa tua in mea fide compleri animadvertebat.* James O'Donnell punctuates *iam promittebatur maxime matre dante operam, quo me iam coniugatum . . .* This strengthens the interpretation that it was Monica who negotiated the marriage.

33. On early texts without punctuation, or even word-division, see M. B. Parkes, *Pause and Effect* (1992), pp. 276–7.

34. Maria Boulding translates 'I liked her, though, so we decided to wait', Philip Burton 'as she was pronounced satisfactory, a period of waiting ensued.'

represented Reason asking him whether he still likes the idea of a wife: pretty, modest, obliging, educated (*litterata*), or someone he could easily teach himself? Especially if, through her family connections, he could achieve a post which enabled him also to achieve posts for his friends, and if she had enough money that they could all live in cultivated leisure and study philosophy? (*Sol.* 1.10.17–11.18). He replies that he had never wanted more than a wife who would give him pleasure combined with a good reputation; but in *Confessions* (6.11.19) he represented himself thinking that he had influential friends, but would also need a wife with money.

The most notorious passive comes near the end of Book 6: 'the one with whom I was accustomed to sleep was torn from my side as an obstacle to marriage, and my heart, to which she clung, was cut and wounded, trailing blood' (6.15.25). Readers, understandably moved, tend to blame Monica. But despite his deep attachment, Augustine had not married his partner, because she was not suitable as a wife for a man with ambitions.[35] He had lived decently, faithful to one woman, but he knew that it was not acceptable to continue such a relationship now that his marriage was arranged.[36] Perhaps this passive, like the others, indicates that he did not want to take responsibility for the marriage and its consequences, or that he was too uncertain to feel that he was making a decision: it was just the expected thing if he continued his career.

Augustine, in Milan at the age of 30, was presented with an example of a celibate life committed to religion. He thought that Ambrose was fortunate in being honoured by powerful people: 'only his celibacy seemed to me effortful' (6.3.3). Monica, in Thagaste in her teens, had no such example. It was taken for granted that she would marry, and her Christian parents did not insist on a Christian husband. A church wedding was not in question, for Christian marriage rituals are a later development, but perhaps the local bishop was among those invited to witness the marriage contract.[37] Perhaps there were few, if any, suitable Christians, and Monica's parents hoped that Patricius would follow his wife's example, as he eventually did. The choice of a husband may

---

35. There have been many attempts to tell the story of Augustine's partner. For an assessment of Augustine's language and of the social and legal position, see Danuta Shanzer, 'Avulsa a latere meo', *Journal of Roman Studies* 92 (2002), 157–76.

36. See chapter 3 on wives and concubines.

37. David Hunter, 'Augustine and the Making of Marriage in Roman North Africa', *Journal of Early Christian Studies* 11 (2003), 63–85; see chapter 3.

also have been limited by divisions among Christians. Two churches in Africa claimed to be the catholic, that is the universal, church.[38] The division began in the time of the "Great Persecution" in the early fourth century (303–5), when the emperor Diocletian targeted Christian clergy and property. Christians in Africa suffered less than those in some parts of the Eastern Empire, but they differed about what to do in time of persecution. Some absolutely refused to hand over copies of the scriptures or church possessions. Others were prepared to avoid the problem, perhaps in collusion with officials who did not want to persecute, by handing over other impressive-looking texts, or by claiming not to have any information. The hardliners called this second group "handers-over," *traditores*, a word which also means "traitors"; and they argued that a *traditor*, having betrayed the faith, could not validly baptize or ordain to the priesthood. In particular, they said, Caecilianus was a *traditor* and should not have become bishop of Carthage in 306 CE. Anyone he had ordained, or anyone ordained by someone he had ordained (and so on), was not validly a priest, could not give absolution for sins, and could not consecrate the bread and wine used in the Eucharist; anyone they had baptized needed rebaptism. They were not Catholics, but Caecilianists.

When the emperor Constantine restored church property, and sent donations to the Catholic (i.e., universal) Church, he found that in Africa there were rival claimants. Every detail of every episode, especially the occasional outbreaks of violence, was bitterly remembered and contested, and each group accused the other of invoking the government to deal with the concerns of the church. Constantine and his sons tried, unsuccessfully, to resolve the dispute by legislation and official missions. In Monica's lifetime, many towns and even villages had two church buildings and two bishops, each claiming to be Catholic. The biographer of the Roman heiress Melania, writing in the early fifth century CE, said that the estate she owned outside Thagaste had two churches, one for the Catholics and one for the heretics. The "heretics" were the hardliners, labelled by their opponents "the party of Donatus", who was one of their leaders.

Augustine became involved in this controversy as a priest, and then a bishop, at Hippo, where his church was in the minority. There is

38. Shaw (n. 19) offers an authoritative study of the verbal and physical violence of this dispute.

no explicit mention of Donatism in *Confessions*, but his account of his own life, and of Monica's, is implicitly anti-Donatist. Two memorable images used in other writings show how he thought of Donatists and of the Catholic Church. The Donatists wanted the church to be like Noah's Ark, sealed inside and outside against the sea of the world; they forgot that the Ark contained all kinds of creatures (*cath.* 5.9; Genesis chs 6–8).[39] Augustine saw the church as a net floating in the sea, containing good and bad fish, which swim together; they will be separated only when the net is drawn in at the end of time (*civ. Dei* 18.49; Mt 13:47–50). Nobody, he argued, is free from sin, before or after baptism, and only God knows the human heart, so we cannot say for certain who truly loves God rather than themselves. Monica lived as a baptized Christian, but Augustine could not claim that she never said anything that was not in accordance with Christian teaching. He prayed for her sins, which he believed God had forgiven (*Conf.* 9.13.34–5).[40] In Augustine's view, it is simply not possible to have a church of the pure: we do not know.

Augustine thought at first that Donatists must be persuaded by argument, but, he said, he was convinced by examples of people who were frightened into conversion, then found that horror stories about the rival church were simply untrue. One such example was 'my town', *civitas mea*, that is, Thagaste. He wrote to a Donatist 'My town belonged entirely to the party of Donatus, but was converted to catholic unity by fear of the imperial laws. Now we see that it abhors the menace of your animosity to the point that one would think it had never belonged' (*ep.* 93.5.17). He did not specify the imperial laws which frightened Thagaste into conversion, but a likely context is the "Macarian times" of 347 CE, when Monica was sixteen.[41] The emperor Constans, son of Constantine, sent two envoys, Paul and Macarius, who used a combination of threats and promises to achieve reunion of the churches. The Donatists remembered this as a time of persecution.

Augustine himself was kin to a Donatist, Severinus (*ep.* 52.1, 52.4), and this made him regret even more that they were divided. In a letter to the Donatist bishop of Hippo, he wrote of households where husband and wife, parents and children, were divided (*ep.* 33.5); and in a sermon he said 'in one house are found daughter-in-law and mother-in-law,

---

39. It is not certain that Augustine wrote this 'letter to Catholic brothers', but the image of the Church as a sealed Ark expresses his view of Donatism.

40. See chapter 6.

41. Shaw (n. 19), pp. 162–94.

heretic and catholic' (*ser.* 44.11). If that was a factor in the hostile gossip of the slave women who tried to turn Monica's mother-in-law against her (*Conf.* 9.9.20), it is very unlikely that Augustine would say so. But it is possible that Monica grew up and was baptized as a Donatist, and that the conversion of Thagaste happened when she was of an age to be aware of it. The conversion might not in practice have made much difference. One of the saddest aspects of the conflict was that the rival churches were so similar:

> We are brothers, we call upon one God, we believe in one
> Christ, we hear one gospel, we sing one psalm, we reply
> with one Amen, we sound one Alleluia, we celebrate one
> Easter: why are you outside and I am inside? (*En.Ps.* 54.16)

How exactly did Thagaste "convert", and how many of the churchgoers in Thagaste could have explained what was at issue? At the conference of 411 CE which was supposed to end the Donatist problem, Augustine's friend Alypius, who by then was bishop of Thagaste, was able to say 'we have Catholic unity': that is, he had no Donatist rival. Perhaps a Donatist bishop withdrew, or was exiled, in 347 CE, and did not come back in 362 CE when Julian recalled the exiles and required the return of any property transferred in 347 CE. Julian's actions prompted further disputes, some of them violent.[42] But perhaps only a few people cared very much, and most people chose to be at peace with their neighbours, forgetting past disputes about who was the rightful bishop or who had started a fight. Religious differences are most dangerous when they become the markers of ethnic or economic social conflict, and it has been argued that Donatism was linked with the African culture of the countryside, and the self-styled Catholic Church with the colonial Roman culture of the towns. But, as always, these divisions between African and Roman, town and country, are too simple.[43]

---

42. Augustine wrote to a Donatist opponent that Julian gave back 'the basilicas of the unity', but this has no specific reference to Thagaste. *C.litt. Pet.* 2.83.184.

43. The argument was advanced by William Frend in *The Donatist Church* (1952). It has been repeatedly challenged, notably by Peter Brown in papers reprinted in *Religion and Society in the Age of St Augustine* (1972). Brown points to the dangers of looking for 'permanent Africans', and emphasizes that Africa was part of the Roman Empire, Donatist leaders (for example Optatus of Timgad) came from Roman towns, and Latin was the language of culture. See now Rebillard (n. 17 above).

Monica, then, was a baptized Christian. She was not a follower of the traditional gods, and it cannot be shown that she was a bearer of local African religious tradition. If she grew up Donatist, she changed when Thagaste changed, and she did not share the beliefs Augustine ascribed to Donatists. Was it unquestionable that she would marry at the appropriate age? Almost certainly there was no other way of life on offer. From the earliest Christian times, some Christians had argued that it is better for men and for women not to marry, but to be concerned only to please God.[44] At the provincial capital, Carthage, there were consecrated virgins at the time of Tertullian, in the early third century, but according to Augustine religious communities came later: he said that he wrote *On the work of monks* (*de opere monachorum*, c. 400 CE) at the time when there began to be monasteries at Carthage (*retr.* 2.21). There is no evidence for Christian ascetic communities in or near Thagaste until Augustine returned from Italy and lived with his friends in the family house, engaged in prayer and study.[45] Monica, had she lived, would have been part of this group, following the same pattern as some other, grander widows who had waited to see their children established in life before changing their own lifestyle; but there is no evidence that she had even heard (for example) of the Roman aristocrat Paula.[46] Some years after Monica's death, her widowed daughter was the leader of a community of women at Hippo (*ep.* 211.4). It was probably the first in the region.

Augustine himself, as a young man, offered Monica another possibility. He became a Manichaean, believing that this was the true, profound understanding of Christianity. Why was Augustine's Monica so distressed? Augustine wanted, of course, to show the constant presence in his life of a mother who rejected Manichaeism as strongly as he came to do, but without need for the long process of philosophical argument which eventually convinced him. But it is still worth asking why, until she was reassured by a dream that he would rejoin her, Monica thought of refusing to share a house with him or to eat with him (*Conf.* 3.11.19).

---

44. On changing forms of asceticism, see Peter Brown, *The Body and Society* (1988, rev. ed. 2008).

45. Richard Finn, *Asceticism in the Graeco-Roman World* (2009), pp. 143–9, sets Augustine's monastic communities in the North African context. He suggests that such communities were a late development in Roman Africa, perhaps because Donatists preferred to think of holy Christians grouped around their bishop.

46. See chapter 6.

Was it dangerous to be a Manichaean? Augustine was only a "Hearer", the usual word for someone who attends the teaching of a philosopher but does not make a commitment to the philosopher's way of life. Manichaean leaders, the "Elect", were celibate, and had their food prepared by others so that they would not themselves take any life, not even vegetable life. Augustine later wrote that when he was a Hearer in Carthage, people did not challenge the scandalous behaviour of some Elect because of fear 'that at a time when their gatherings were forbidden by law, they would betray something if provoked' (*mor.* 2.19.69). In 381 CE, shortly before Augustine's move to Italy, an imperial law banned Manichaeans from accepting or bequeathing property by will (*C.Th.* 16.5.7), and this was reaffirmed, in more dramatic language, in 383 CE (16.5.9). A Donatist opponent claimed that Augustine left Carthage for Italy because the governor had exiled him (*c.litt.Pet.* 3.25.30). Augustine replied that the dates were wrong, but perhaps he was indeed safer among influential Manichaeans at Rome. He stayed in the house of a Manichaean, and Manichaean contacts helped him to be appointed by Symmachus, prefect of Rome, as professor of rhetoric at Milan.

Augustine may not have tried to explain to Monica the complex mythologies which expressed Manichaean understanding of the universe (*Conf.* 3.6.11). Even so, there was much to shock her in Manichaean teachings. Jesus promised to send his followers an Advocate (the Paraclete, from Greek *paraklētos*) to lead them into all truth, and mainstream Christians believed that the promise was fulfilled when the Holy Spirit came to the apostles at Pentecost (Acts 2:4). Manichaeans held that it was fulfilled in Mani, apostle of Jesus Christ, in the third century in Mesopotamia (*Conf.* 5.5.8–9), and that his teachings were true Christianity, whereas much of the Bible had been contaminated by false teaching. Mani taught that there is a rival power of evil which resists the providential order of God; the world is not God's good creation, but a battleground of good and evil; we should avoid entrapping souls in it by procreation, and some foods should not be eaten; and Christ did not die on the cross, for he was a purely spiritual being.[47] So Augustine the Manichaean wanted Monica to condemn her own motherhood and the food she had provided for her family, the scriptures she studied, and

47. For a helpful survey, see Johannes van Oort, 'Augustine and the Books of the Manichaeans', in M. Vessey (n. 21), pp. 188–99. See further Jason BeDuhn, *Augustine's Manichaean Dilemma: Conversion and Apostasy 373–388 CE* (2010); and Nicholas Baker-Brian, *Manichaeism: An Ancient Faith Rediscovered* (2011).

the teaching of the church she attended twice daily that God created all there is and that Christ reconciled human and divine.

Finally, was it obvious that Monica, on reaching Milan, would be a devoted follower of Ambrose? Augustine had good reason to present her in this way, because Monica connected him with Ambrose, who baptized him but, apparently, took no further notice of him. Augustine wrote the *Confessions* in the year of Ambrose's death (397 CE). By that time Theodosius I had shown his support for pro-Nicene theology and his respect for the spiritual authority of Ambrose. But when Augustine came to Milan in 384 CE, the position of Ambrose was much less secure. He had rivals who were supported by the imperial court, and he had also recently opposed an official request from his relative Symmachus, the prefect of Rome who had appointed Augustine professor of rhetoric. Augustine was in a difficult position. His duties included speeches in praise of important people, one of whom was the boy emperor Valentinian II (*Conf.* 6.6.9). Valentinian's mother Justina was Arian, and so were the Gothic troops who formed the imperial bodyguard. Augustine hoped for a post in the imperial service: it was probably an advantage that he did not arrive with a commitment either to Arian or to pro-Nicene theology, and if Symmachus knew that Manichaean friends had used their influence (*Conf.* 5.13.23), Augustine's Manichaean sympathies may have been a factor in the appointment.

In the summer of 384 CE, before Augustine arrived in Milan, Symmachus reopened the question of the altar of Victory, in the hope that the situation had changed with the death of Gratian. He submitted to the court at Milan an official paper (a *relatio*), which included an impressive plea for religious toleration:

> It is just that whatever all people worship should be thought of as one. We look at the same stars, the sky is common, the same world enfolds us: what difference does it make by what wisdom each one seeks the truth? So great a mystery cannot be reached by one road. (*Rel.* 3.10)[48]

Ambrose wrote a response, and succeeded in having the *relatio* rejected.[49] But it does not follow from this dispute that Ambrose and

48. *Aequum est, quidquid omnes colunt, unum putari. Eadem spectamus astra, commune caelum est, idm nos mundus involvit: quid interest, qua quisque prudentia verum requirit? Uno itinere non potest perveniri ad tam grande secretum.*
49. The complete *relatio* of Symmachus, and the relevant letters of Ambrose, are translated

Symmachus were personally on bad terms. Augustine wrote that when he came to Milan, 'that man of God [Ambrose] took me up in a fatherly way, and showed, as befitted a bishop, affection for one who was away from home' (*Conf.* 5.13.23).[50] Welcoming visitors and incomers was one of the duties of a bishop, as Augustine recognized when he became one (*ser.* 355.1.2). Monica may simply have taken the view that Ambrose was the bishop of the Catholic Church in Milan, which, of course, she attended. She may not previously have encountered the Arian interpretation of Christianity: when Augustine returned to Africa, he did not find it necessary to preach against Arianism until the arrival of refugees from Italy in 411, and Arian interpretation is not a theme of his preaching until nearer 418.[51] But Ambrose in 384 did find it necessary. Perhaps Monica could also have learned from the discussions of Augustine and Alypius about the nature of Christ, although according to Augustine the question which most concerned them at that time was the human soul or mind of Christ (*Conf.* 7.19.25). Augustine made only a rapid allusion to the Arian dispute:

> It was not long since the Milanese church had begun to practise this kind of consolation and exhortation, the brothers singing together with hearts and voices, with great zeal. It was a year, or not much more, since Justina, mother of Valentinian the boy king, was persecuting your servant Ambrose for the sake of the heresy into which she had been led by the Arians. The faithful people slept in the church, ready to die with their bishop, your slave. There my mother, your slave, took the lead in anxiety and keeping watch, and lived by prayer. I was still cold, not warmed by your spirit, but was nevertheless stirred by the tension and disturbance of the city. At that time the practice began of singing hymns and psalms according to the custom of the eastern regions, so that the people should not be worn down by the exhaustion of grief. It has been retained to this day, and many if not all of your flocks have imitated it in other parts of the world. (*Conf.* 9.7.15)

with notes in Wolf Liebeschuetz, *Ambrose of Milan: Political Letters and Speeches* (2005), pp. 61–94. See further Neil McLynn, *Ambrose of Milan* (1994), pp. 166–7.

50. *Suscepit me paterne ille homo Dei et peregrinationem meam satis episcopaliter dilexit.*
51. Suzanne Poque, *Le langage symbolique dans la prédication de Saint Augustin* (1984), 1. p. 357.

Augustine mentioned this episode out of sequence, in connection with the effect of hymn singing at the time of his baptism, and did not explain further why the faithful people slept in the church. Historians continue to debate Ambrose's version of the complicated events of 385/6 CE. Justina wanted a church for public worship in accordance with Arian theology. At one point imperial curtains (*vela*) were put in place, to show that the church belonged to the court, and it was surrounded by troops from the Gothic bodyguard; most Goths were Arian.[52] Even if Ambrose, an experienced politician, expected a stand-off, there was a risk of immediate violence, and it took courage for his followers to occupy the church.

Monica strengthened Augustine's connection with Ambrose, who recognized her piety and often congratulated Augustine on having such a mother (*Conf.* 6.2.2). In *Confessions* Augustine wrote that he found it difficult to consult Ambrose about the interpretation of scripture (6.3.3), but two letters show that he did manage to seek advice on behalf of Monica, who was concerned about the difference between fast days in Africa and fast days in Milan. But why did not Monica ask her bishop herself? Did she want Augustine to visit him?

I shall tell you what the venerable Ambrose, bishop of Milan, by whom I was baptized, replied when I asked him about this. My mother was with me in that city; I was still a catechumen and not much concerned about these matters, but she was anxious about whether she should fast on the sabbath in accordance with the custom of our city, or eat in accordance with the custom of the church of Milan. To free her from this hesitation, I asked this man of God. But he said 'What better advice can I give than what I do myself?' I had thought he meant by this reply only to tell us that we should eat on the sabbath, since I knew he did so, but he added 'When I am here, I do not fast on the sabbath; when I am at Rome, I do fast on the sabbath. Observe the custom of whatever church you come to', he said, 'if you want not to experience or to cause difficulty.' I took this reply back to my mother, and she was satisfied and had no doubt in obeying, and I followed the

52. The relevant letters of Ambrose are translated, with commentary, in Liebeschuetz (n. 49), pp. 124–73; see further McLynn (n. 49), pp. 170–208.

same practice. But since it happens, especially in Africa, that in one church, or in the churches of one district, some people eat on the sabbath and some people fast, I think we should follow the custom of those to whom rule over the assembly of these peoples has been entrusted [that is, follow their bishop]. (ep. 36.32; the same story in ep. 54.3)

Was Monica also influenced by Ambrose's strong support for celibacy?[53] He had established a monastic community outside the walls of Milan (*Conf.* 8.6.15), and it was in Milan that Augustine heard for the first time about the ascetic life of Antony of Egypt (8.6.14). According to Augustine, Monica rejoiced when he told her of his decision to abandon marriage and career (8.12.30), which meant the end of her worldly ambition for him. At Cassiciacum, he described her as having risen above the great stain of the body.[54] She was already devoting much of her life to prayer and the study of scripture, and if she had lived to return to Thagaste, she would have been part of a celibate (though not single-sex) religious community.

In Monica's lifetime there were women who renounced great wealth and status, acquired great learning in the study of scripture and philosophy, and adopted lifestyles of great austerity which sometimes entailed rejection of marriage or separation in widowhood from their children. Augustine's Monica was charitable, but did not give up the family property. She made progress in wisdom by faithful attendance at church, prayer, and Bible study, but she did not withdraw from her everyday domestic life. She was a devoted wife and mother, and there is no suggestion that she was reluctant to marry or that she hoped her husband would agree to postmarital celibacy when their family was complete; she did not remarry in widowhood, but neither did she leave her family. How, then, did this ordinary woman become Saint Monica?

53. Peter Brown, *The Body and Society*, pp. 341–65; David Hunter, *Marriage, Celibacy and Heresy in Ancient Christianity* (2007), pp. 219–30.
54. See chapter 4.

6

Saint Monica

Monica began to be commemorated as a saint almost eight centuries after her death in 387 CE. In the intervening years, some people may have responded to Augustine's prayer in the passage with which this book began:

> Inspire, my Lord, my God, inspire your slaves, my brothers,
> your sons, my masters, whom I serve with heart and voice and
> writings, that all who read this may remember at your altar
> Monica, your slave, with Patricius, once her spouse, through
> whose flesh you brought me into this life, how I do not know.
> May they remember with pious feeling [*affectus*] my parents in
> this transitory light; my brother and sister in our mother the
> Catholic Church under you, our father; my fellow citizens in
> the eternal Jerusalem,[1] for which your people sighs in absence
> from the time of leaving to the time of return; so that what
> she asked of me at the last should be granted to her more fully
> through my confessions, in the prayers of many, than through
> my prayers. (*Conf.* 9.13.37)

The words quoted here conclude Augustine's own memories of Monica and of his reaction to her death. They are also the conclusion to Book 9 of his *Confessions* and to his narrative of God's action in his life; writing in

---

1. Augustine thought that the name Jerusalem means "city of peace". The heavenly Jerusalem is the city of God (Revelation 21:2), and its citizens are all the angels and humans who love God. See further Frederick Van Fleteren, 'Jerusalem', in Allan Fitzgerald, ed., *Augustine Through the Ages* (1999), pp. 462–3.

397 CE, Augustine did not take the narrative part of *Confessions* further than Monica's death ten years earlier. All of *Confessions* is addressed to God, and this passage is a prayer to inspire prayers. It is not a prayer to "remember Monica" in the sense "remember who she was, how she lived, and what she was like". It is a response to what she told her sons in her final illness:

> In her illness, one day she had a loss of consciousness, and
> for a little while she was withdrawn from those present. We
> rushed to her, but she soon returned to her senses and saw me
> and my brother standing there, and said to us, like someone
> asking for information, 'Where was I?' Then, looking at us
> who were struck with grief, she said 'You put your mother
> here.' I was silent, holding back tears. My brother said
> something to show his hope that she would die not abroad but
> in her homeland, as if that were better. When she heard this,
> her face was troubled; she fixed her gaze on him with reproach
> for thinking like that, then looked at me and said 'See what he
> says!' Soon after she said to us both 'Put this body anywhere.
> Don't worry about it. All I ask is, wherever you are, remember
> me at the altar of the Lord.' (*Conf.* 9.11.27)[2]

"Remember me at the altar" means "remember me when you share in the Eucharist".[3] Then as now, there were prayers for the faithful departed, in which some might be individually named.[4] Many churches now use the general prayer, name the recently departed and those whose anniversary of death falls at that time, then leave time for people to think about those who are important to them.

Prayers for the dead, and offerings in their memory, were ancient traditions of the Church. In the *Handbook* he wrote more than twenty years later than *Confessions*, Augustine explained why these prayers and offerings do not conflict with the saying of St. Paul that 'we must all

---

2. See also chapter 1 on Augustine's presentation of Navigius.
3. The Eucharist (from the Greek for "thanksgiving") is also known as Holy Communion, and as Mass (from Latin *missa*, "sending", because the closing words send the people out into the world). It is the sharing of bread and wine in accordance with Christ's instruction 'do this in memory of me'. Different churches have different ways of doing this, and interpret it differently. Monica and her sons expected that people who were not yet baptized would leave the church before the bread and wine were consecrated at the altar and shared by the baptized.
4. Eric Rebillard, *The Care of the Dead in Late Antiquity* (English translation, 2009), p. 160.

appear before the tribunal of Christ, so that each may receive according to what they did in the body, whether good or bad' (2 Cor. 5:10). He argued that some people live in such a way that they can benefit from prayers and offerings after their death, and others do not:

> We must not deny that the souls of the dead are given relief by the piety of their living family, when the sacrifice of the Mediator is offered for them, or there is almsgiving in the church.[5] But these actions benefit those who, in their lifetime, lived so that such actions could benefit them afterwards. There is a way of life which is neither so good that it does not need these things, nor so bad that they are of no benefit after death [. . .] So when sacrifices are offered for all the baptized dead, whether at the altar or in almsgiving, they are thanksgiving for the very good, propitiation for those who were not very good, and for those who were very bad, even if they are no help to the dead, they are some consolation to the living. For those whom they benefit, they benefit toward full remission, or at least toward more bearable condemnation.[6] (*Ench.* 29.110)

Augustine thought that Monica was right not to mind where her body was buried, because in his view the only way to help the dead is by prayer, or by sacrifice in the sense that the Eucharist or alms are offered for their sake. He made this clear when Paulinus of Nola consulted him about Flora, who (it seems) lived in Africa and was known to Augustine. Her son died near Nola, in southern Italy, and she asked to have him buried near the tomb of St. Felix, who was a confessor: that is, he was ready to die rather than deny his faith, but he was not in fact martyred.

Flora wanted this burial because of the widely held belief that, even if other souls were asleep until the resurrection of the body, martyrs after the death of the body were immediately alive with God.[7] So martyred saints could intercede for the living and for the dead; their

---

5. The Mediator is Christ, who brings together God and humanity, and the sacrifice is the Eucharist, which commemorates or reenacts Christ's offering of himself.

6. Augustine appears to mean that there may be different degrees of suffering among the damned, though all will suffer eternally; see also *en.Ps.* 105.2.

7. "Resurrection" (from Latin *resurgere*) literally means "getting up again" after sleep. Hence Christian burial places were called "cemeteries" (Greek *koimētēria*), literally "sleeping places". For debates about the sleep of the soul after the death of the body, see Matthew Dal Santo, *Debating the Saints' Cult in the Age of Gregory the Great* (2012); for a brief account of relics, see Gillian Clark, *Christianity and Roman Society* (2004), pp. 54–9.

spiritual power could be manifested, especially in healing; and their relics, that is their bodily remains and former possessions and even the dust from their tombs, were also charged with the spiritual power which had overcome their human fear of pain and death and united them body and soul to God. Augustine was more cautious about the powers of martyrs. When he preached at celebrations of martyrs, he said that their prayers can help us to follow their example. He thought at first that the age of miracles was over (*vera rel.* 46), but later found that in his own part of Africa there were healing miracles, associated especially with the relics of St. Stephen.[8] But he insisted that Christian veneration of martyrs was different from pagan cults of dead heroes who were believed to have special powers. Christians, he said, do not sacrifice to martyrs, because saints do not want worship for themselves, but for God alone. The prayers of saints may help, but it is always God who acts, though God may choose to act through a saint or an angel or a living human being.[9] People are not always as clear as Augustine was about the difference between "praying to" a saint and asking for the saint's prayers. Flora hoped that burial near the holy body of a saint would somehow protect or benefit her son, and Paulinus was not sure what to say to her. Augustine's response was that burial is a consolation for the living, not for the dead, who are souls not bodies. So the only benefit to the dead person, if they had lived so as to benefit from prayer, is that the tomb of the martyr prompts the living to pray.[10]

Augustine prayed for forgiveness of Monica's sins, because he could not know for certain that she did not need forgiveness (*Conf.* 9.13.35). He believed that God had already done what he asked (9.13.36), but he still asked God to inspire prayers for her at the Eucharist (9.13.37). He could be confident that she had lived so as to benefit from prayers and offerings after her death. Remembering how, when she died, he and his friends had restrained the weeping of his son Adeodatus, he wrote that it was not fitting to mourn her as people mourn 'the misery of the dying, or death as complete extinction. She did not die in misery, nor

---

8. *Civ. Dei* 22.8 collects reports of miraculous healings. Relics believed to be those of St. Stephen, the first martyr (Acts 6-7), were found at Jerusalem in 415 CE, and soon after were distributed in Africa.

9. No sacrifice to martyrs: *Civ. Dei* 8.27. It is always God who acts, ibid. 22.9. See further Paul Schrodt, 'Saints', in Fitzgerald (n. 1), pp. 747-9. On the development of cult see Peter Brown, *The Cult of the Saints in Late Antiquity* (1981) and James Howard-Johnston and Paul Hayward, eds., *The Cult of Saints in Late Antiquity and the Middle Ages* (1999).

10. On Augustine *De cura* see Dennis Trout, *Paulinus of Nola* (1999), pp. 244-7.

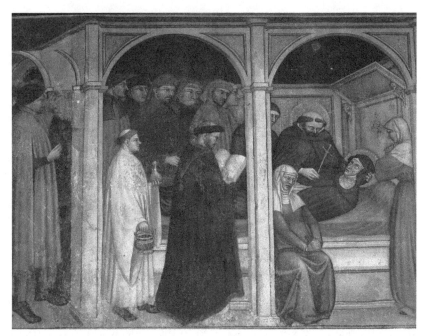

FIGURE 6.1. Augustine at Monica's deathbed. Ottaviano Nelli, c. 1420s.

Gianni Dagli Orti / The Art Archive at Art Resource, NY

did she die entirely. We held this with good reason from the evidence of her conduct and her sincere faith' (*Conf.* 9.12.29). By 'misery' he did not mean pain or distress: he meant the pitiable state of those who are alienated from God, just as by 'happiness' he meant the blessed state of those who love God. What then did Augustine think was the situation of Monica's soul, and of all souls of the dead, as they waited 'patiently and with longing' (*civ. Dei* 13.20) for the resurrection of the body?[11] He was cautious in interpreting the passages of scripture that bear on this question.[12] A little earlier in Book 9 of *Confessions,* reporting the death of his dear friend Nebridius, he wrote:

> Not long after my conversion and regeneration through your
> baptism, you released him from the flesh, a baptized Catholic,
> serving you in perfect chastity and continence at his home
> in Africa, having made his whole household Christian. And
> now he lives [*vivit*, 'he is alive'] in the bosom of Abraham.

11. Discussed in Serge Lancel, *St. Augustine* (English translation, 2002), pp. 443–56.
12. *Ep.* 164, written 414/5 CE to Evodius, is a good introduction to the difficulties of exegesis.

Whatever it is that is signified by that bosom, there my
Nebridius lives, my dear friend, and your adoptive son, Lord,
formerly a freed slave: there he lives. What other place is
there for such a soul? There he lives in the place about which
he used to ask me many questions, poor ignorant man that
I am. He no longer puts his ear to my mouth, but his spiritual
ear to your fountain, and drinks all the wisdom he can in his
eagerness, happy without end. (9.3.6)

The 'bosom of Abraham' comes from Jesus' story of Dives, 'the Rich
Man', and Lazarus, the beggar who sat at his door (Luke 16:22). The beggar died and was carried by angels to the bosom of Abraham. The rich
man died, and from his place of torment in the underworld he could
see Abraham and Lazarus far off. He begged Abraham to send Lazarus
with a drop of water to cool his thirst, but Abraham replied that there
was a 'great gulf fixed' between him and them. Nebridius was not alone
in finding this story problematic: other passages of scripture were interpreted to mean that Christ descended to the underworld to free those
who were to be released (*Gn.Litt.* 12.34.66), but Abraham and Lazarus
were not in the underworld.

There was also debate on whether the souls of all the dead, or at
least the souls of all the dead who were not saints, were asleep until the
general resurrection of bodies. Without bodily sensation, what awareness could they have? In *Care for the Dead*, writing in response to a
plea from a mother, Augustine used Monica as proof that the souls of
the dead do not know about the living: if they did know, and could
appear in dreams, she would never miss a night.[13] But this need not
mean that souls after death are wholly unaware. In the passage quoted
above, Augustine envisaged the soul of Nebridius as alive and recep-
tive of wisdom, and in a letter to his friend Evodius (*ep.* 159, written
414/5 CE) he told a story to counter doubts. Gennadius, a doctor well
known in Rome, now lived at Carthage. He was a good man, religious
and charitable, but in youth he doubted that there was life after death.
So God sent him a dream, in which a young man took him to a city
where he heard wonderfully beautiful melodies: he was told they were
the hymns of the blessed. The next night the young man reappeared,
and in answer to his questions, Gennadius said that he recognized

13. See chapter 1 on this passage as evidence of Monica's devotion to her son.

him and remembered all that had happened in the dream. The young man asked:

> 'Where is your body now?' He replied 'In my bedroom.' 'Do you know', the young man said, 'that your eyes are now held fast in that same body, closed and not in use, and that you are not seeing anything with those eyes?' He replied 'I know.' Then the young man said 'What then are the eyes with which you see me?' He could not think what to say, and was silent. As he hesitated, the young man revealed what he sought to teach by these questions, and immediately said 'Just as those eyes of your flesh are now at leisure and do no work, while you sleep and lie in your bed, and yet there are those eyes with which you see me, and you make use of that vision; so, when you are dead, and the eyes of your flesh are inactive, there will be in you life by which you live, and senses by which you sense. So in future do not doubt that life remains after death.' (*ep.* 159.4)

When he wrote Book 21 of *City of God*, probably in 426/7, Augustine thought it possible that some souls experienced purgation before they were reunited with their bodies and faced the Last Judgement. 'Some suffer temporal [as opposed to eternal] penalties only in this life, others after death, others both now and then, but before that most severe and final judgement. But those who endure temporal penalties after death do not all go to everlasting punishment' (*civ. Dei* 21.13). He did not reject the suggestion that:

> After the death of this body, until that final day is reached which, after the resurrection of the body, will be the day of condemnation and reward: if in this interval of time the spirits of the dead are said to experience a kind of fire which is not felt by those who did not in the life of this body behave and love so that their 'wood and hay and straw' is [to be] burned up, but others do feel it, because they have carried with them that kind of building . . . (*civ. Dei* 21.26; see also *Ench.* 69)

The 'wood and hay and straw' which will be burned by the fire of judgement (1 Cor. 3:13–14) signifies attachment to transitory things; and

Monica had in the course of her life been attached to worldly success for her son (*Conf.* 2.3.8) and to having him physically with her (5.8.15). Augustine did not suggest that Monica was one of the 'very good' who, according to the *Handbook*, do not need prayers and offerings; or that she was a martyr who bore witness to her faith whatever the cost, and who should be asked for her prayers.[14] Augustine's writings provided all the material there is for Saint Monica, but Augustine's Monica is not a saint, and this is the great contrast with the other lives of holy women that were produced during and soon after Monica's lifetime.

What makes a saint? In the early centuries of Christianity, "saint" (Latin *sanctus/a*) meant "Christian". The Latin word, like its Greek equivalent *hagios/a*, means "holy" in the sense "belonging to God". The letters of Paul of Tarsus are among the earliest surviving Christian documents, and the "saints" he greets in them are not saintly: he frequently rebukes them for immoral behaviour and partisan quarrels. Saint Paul himself did not claim to be saintly, but he and the people to whom he wrote had made a commitment to God, and Augustine's Monica is certainly a saint in this sense. In late antiquity, a saint was someone who had given up his or her life for God, by martyrdom or by the "long martyrdom" of the ascetic life. In the present day, there are still people who die for their faith, and there are still people who live in a way that most people do not find possible: they are focussed on God, not on self, so they are able to hear God, and to allow God's love to shine through, without all the usual noise and distractions that beset human life.[15] Andrew Louth asks some key questions in his introduction to a collection of papers on *Saints and Sanctity*:

> Is a saint a role model? Someone with special powers?
> A patron and intercessor? Is sanctity something that is
> perceived in contemporary human beings? Or are saints the
> noble dead? Who decides? Throughout Christian history we
> can detect an ambiguity between sanctity as the goal, perhaps
> rarely achieved, of the Christian life, that is, something to do

14. On Augustine's distinction between prayers for the dead and asking for the prayers of martyrs, see Rebillard (n. 4), pp. 157–61.

15. On this second kind of sainthood, see Rowan Williams' chapter on 'Saints', in Rowan Williams and Joan Chittister OSB, *For All That Has Been, Thanks* (Canterbury Press, 2010), pp. 65–77. He emphasizes that saints are not free from faults, and that in most cases they are known only to a few people.

with the inner life of the Christian, something hardly claimed by anyone for themselves (though there are exceptions to this), and sanctity as an aura of power, claimed for individuals by their friends, or more often by those who want to make use of the power this acknowledged.[16]

Augustine's Monica does not have an aura of power, and Augustine did not make claims about her inner life as a Christian, because he was so sharply aware of the complexity of the human heart, which is known only to God. But he said of Monica 'Whoever of your servants knew her praised her greatly, and honoured and loved you, because he was aware of your presence in her heart, attested by the fruits of her holy way of life.'[17] If he had chosen to present her as a saint, the material was there.

Monica was a confessor, ready to die in Milan for her faith if the troops sent by the empress Justina were ordered to use force to take over a basilica for Arian worship.[18] Monica was also a martyr in the sense Augustine urged on his congregation, in that she resisted temptation and showed that she lived by Christian principle.[19] The "long martyrdom" or "white martyrdom" of the ascetic life was another way of bearing witness to faith, and Augustine could have made a case that Monica was in later life an ascetic.[20] Ascetics "died to the world" by giving up worldly wealth and ambitions for themselves and their families; living in celibacy, and often in extreme austerity, they gave up their lives to the service of God. Monica did not retreat from the world or from her family, and at Milan she continued to mother her son's friends as well as the family members in the group (*Conf.* 9.9.22). But she was a devout and celibate widow.[21] At Cassiciacum she had leisure [*otium*] to devote to the love of wisdom, and Augustine praised the moral qualities of her

16. Andrew Louth, in Peter Clarke and Tony Claydon, eds., *Saints and Sanctity* (2011), xx; see also his paper 'Holiness and Sanctity in the Early Church', ibid., pp. 1–18.

17. *quisquis eorum [servorum tuorum] noverat eam, multum in ea laudabat, et honorabat et diligebat te, quia sentiebat praesentiam tuam in corde eius sanctae conversationis fructibus testibus, Conf.* 9.9.22. *sancta conversatio* comes from 2 Peter 3:11; *conversatio* is an exact translation of Greek *anastrophē*, and covers both "way of life" and "association with others".

18. See chapter 5. Brent Shaw, *Sacred Violence* (2011), pp. 731–2, which shows how easily this event could be presented as martyrdom.

19. See chapter 1.

20. 'White martyrdom': Jerome, *Epitaphium Sanctae Paulae* 22.

21. Widows could take vows of celibacy; see Kevin Wilkinson, 'Dedicated Widows in *Codex Theodosianus* 9.25?', *Journal of Early Christian Studies* 20 (2012), 141–66, for a careful assessment. Augustine does not suggest that Monica did so.

soul and its escape from what he then regarded as the 'great stain of the body'.[22] If she had lived to return to Africa, she would have been one of the group who led a celibate life of prayer and study in her family house. Instead, she achieved with her son a spiritual ascent beyond all earthly things and a moment of contact with the eternal wisdom of God, and she died without fear and without concern for the burial of her body.[23]

In late antiquity, the "aura of power" of martyrs and ascetics was manifested in many ways: discernment, healing, foretelling and preventing disasters, speaking a few words which transformed a life. But someone had to write a saint's life to make these manifestations more widely known, especially when an ascetic withdrew from the demands of human contact, or practised austerities in secret to avoid the danger of pride in reputation, or led the home-based life of a modest woman who was known only to her family and friends.[24] When martyrs were commemorated on the anniversary of their death, by celebrations at their shrines and by naming in prayers, people wanted to hear what the martyr had done and suffered; so when relics of saints were distributed, texts came too. Writing the life of a saint acquired a special name, hagiography (Greek *hagios/a* is the equivalent of Latin *sanctus/a*), and a special reputation for excessive and unqualified praise.[25]

Some of Augustine's contemporaries, who like him were trained in rhetoric, wrote hagiographies of women. Around 380 Gregory of Nyssa wrote a life of his elder sister Macrina, who lived as a virgin ascetic in their mother's house and took the lead in a community of women which was paired with a community of celibate men. Like Augustine, Gregory does not name his mother; her name, Emmelia, is mentioned by his friend Gregory of Nazianzus. Ten years earlier, Gregory of Nazianzus delivered a funeral speech for his married sister Gorgonia, which Virginia Burrus sees as the first hagiography of a woman.[26] He also praised his mother Nonna, not in a separate speech but in funeral speeches for his father and his brother, and in his autobiographical

22. See chapter 4.
23. On the shared experience of Monica and Augustine, see chapter 4.
24. On the importance of saints' lives, see James Howard-Johnston, 'Introduction', in Howard-Johnston and Hayward (n. 9 above), pp. 1–24, at pp. 5–7.
25. Thomas Head, *Medieval Hagiography* (2001) is an anthology of translated texts, starting from late antiquity, with a helpful introduction.
26. Virginia Burrus, 'Life after Death: the Martyrdom of Gorgonia and the Birth of Female Hagiography', in Jostein Børtnes and Tomas Hägg, eds. (2006), *Gregory of Nazianzus: Images and Reflections*, pp. 153–70.

poems. These works are in Greek, and nothing suggests that Augustine read them, but there is also hagiography in Latin. In 404 CE, a few years after Augustine wrote *Confessions*, Jerome wrote a *Funeral Speech for Saint Paula* (*epitaphium sanctae Paulae*) to commemorate his friend, the Roman lady who left her home and family to finance his monastic community in Bethlehem and to live next door, with her daughter Eustochium, in a community of women. In what looks like an attempt to have her remembered as a saint, he added a note on the date of her death and the location of her tomb, and by the end of the fifth century CE, if not earlier, her feast day was included in a liturgical calendar.[27] Jerome also wrote shorter tributes to the Roman aristocrats Asella, a dedicated virgin (*ep.* 24) and to Marcella, an ascetic widow (*ep.* 127). These various writings about women show the distinctive quality of Augustine's Monica.

Just as Augustine is known as Augustine of Hippo, so three of his contemporaries are known by the names of the towns where they became bishops: Basil of Caesarea, his brother Gregory of Nyssa, and his friend Gregory of Nazianzus. (Together, they are called the Cappadocian Fathers, because these towns were in Cappadocia, now part of Turkey.) Basil and Gregory of Nyssa came from a much grander family than Augustine did. The marriage of their parents, Basil and Emmelia, brought together families from two adjoining eastern provinces, Pontus and Cappadocia. The elder Basil was a well-connected teacher of rhetoric, and the couple produced nine (or perhaps ten) children. Their eldest child, Macrina, was a few years older than Monica: she was born around 327 CE and died in 379. Emmelia was widowed soon after her youngest son was born, and outlived her husband by perhaps thirty years.[28] Like Monica, she managed the family property, but this property included landholdings in three provinces. She funded the studies at Athens of her son Basil, helped others of her children to careers or marriages, and had a choice of country estates to be used as retreats by those who experimented with the ascetic life. Gregory observed that his paternal and maternal grandfathers had both been deprived of their property, but through God's goodness the family prospered to the extent that when the inheritance was divided among the nine children of Basil and

27. Andrew Cain, *Jerome's Epitaph on Paula* (2013); see also his 'Rethinking Jerome's Portraits of Holy Women', in Andrew Cain and Josef Lössl, eds., *Jerome of Stridon* (2009), pp. 47–57, on Jerome's tributes to Asella and Marcella.
28. Raymond Van Dam, *Families and Friends in Late Roman Cappadocia* (2003), p. 99.

Emmelia, even a ninth share surpassed what their parents had (*Life of Macrina* 20). It is all very different from the family house at Thagaste, the 'little fields' of a modest inheritance shared among three children, and the struggle to fund Augustine's education while also meeting the obligations of a city councillor.[29]

It is also different in that Emmelia and her husband came from a long tradition of committed Christianity. Augustine's father Patricius was not Christian until late in his life; Monica's parents were Christian, but Augustine said nothing about earlier generations. The paternal grandparents of Basil and Gregory acknowledged their faith in time of persecution in the early fourth century; in the 340s CE their parents maintained a Christian household; in widowhood Emmelia withdrew from the city to a country estate, and around the age of 50 she made further progress in the ascetic life:

> So, when concern for child-rearing was over for her mother,
> together with worries about educating the children and
> establishing them in life, and most of the resources for
> material life had been divided among the children, then,
> as was said earlier, the life of the virgin [Macrina] became
> her mother's adviser in moving toward a philosophical
> and non-material way of life. Having given up all the usual
> [amenities], she brought her mother to her own level of
> humility, preparing her to be equal in status to the assembly of
> virgins, so as to share equally with them in food and sleeping
> place and all necessities of life, all difference of rank being
> removed from among them. (*Life of Macrina* 11)

The 'assembly of virgins' included their women slaves. Emmelia, according to Gregory, had wanted to lead a pure life, but married because her parents were dead and her beauty put her at risk of abduction (*Life of Macrina* 2). Macrina too was very beautiful in her twelfth year, when her father chose an excellent young man to be her husband when she reached the appropriate age. (This age is not specified, any more than Augustine specified it for Monica.) She was also very skilled at wool-work.[30] But when her fiancé died, she argued against both her parents that betrothal was equivalent to marriage, and she expected to

29. See chapter 2.
30. See chapter 2 on wool-working.

rejoin him in the resurrection (*Life* 5). Macrina decided never to leave her mother; she set her an example of the philosophic life, and when Emmelia was widowed she helped with all the tasks of managing the property and bringing up the other children (*Life* 6). With the help of Peter, the youngest child, the community came to include celibate men, to care for children, and to welcome visitors.[31]

Gregory's *Life of Saint Macrina* shows how Augustine's commemoration of Monica differs from a saint's life. Augustine always refers to 'mother'; Gregory refers, not to 'my sister', but to 'the great Macrina', 'the virgin', or 'the teacher'. Augustine's Monica is not faultless; Gregory's Macrina is always exemplary as she progresses, through philosophy, to the height of human virtue (*Life* 1).[32] Monica is able to move on from worldly concerns for her son and from too much maternal love. Macrina is already free from worldly concerns; she loves her family, but she bravely withstands the shock of her brother's death and strengthens her mother to endure it (*Life* 10). Kim Bowes comments on the privacy of Macrina, who lived in retirement on a country estate;[33] Monica was a well-known member of a town congregation, in Thagaste and Milan, and perhaps also in Carthage when visiting her son. Augustine does not suggest any unusual austerity in Monica's life, either as wife or as widow; she advises wives to think of themselves as the slaves of their husbands, but she does not live or work as her slaves do. Macrina takes on the servile task of making her mother's bread (*Life* 5), urges her mother to live in the same way as their slaves, and increases her own austerity after her mother's death. Even in her final illness she lies on a plank covered with sacking, her head supported on another piece of wood (*Life* 16). She has only one set of clothes: a dark cloak, a head covering, and a pair of worn-down shoes (*Life* 29).

Augustine's Monica takes some part in the discussions at Cassiciacum, sometimes with confident assertion, sometimes tentatively; she flatly rejects her son's suggestion that he could be her student (*ord.* 1.11.33). Gregory's Macrina is teacher and adviser to her mother, her brothers, and her fellow nuns, and in the dialogue *On the Soul and*

31. On the development of Macrina's asceticism, see Susanna Elm, *Virgins of God* (1994), pp. 78–105; on home-based asceticism in her family, Anna Silvas, *The Asketikon of St Basil the Great* (2005), pp. 51–83.

32. On this aspect of the lives of philosophers, see Patricia Cox, *Biography in Late Antiquity* (1983), pp. 17–44; and see chapter 4.

33. Kim Bowes, *Private Worship, Public Values* (2008), pp. 208–12.

Resurrection she, 'the teacher', confidently deploys philosophical debate and exposition.[34] Monica, dying of fever, manages to say a few words to her sons, then 'when she had made her view clear in such words as she could, she fell silent and was put to the test [*exercebatur*] as the illness worsened.' Macrina, dying of fever, has a long conversation with the brother she has not seen for eight years, and even on her deathbed discourses on the soul and resurrection (*Life* 17).[35] Gregory, on his way to see Macrina, dreams that he is carrying relics of martyrs (*Life* 15). He relates an eyewitness account of Macrina refusing medical help and healing an abscess in her breast by prayer (ibid. 31), and another of Macrina healing the eye disease of a little girl (ibid. 37–8); and he says that he will not mention other miracles which might not be believed. Augustine makes no such claims about Monica, and centuries passed before healing miracles were associated with her relics.

Gregory of Nazianzus also came from a landowning family. His parents, Gregory and Nonna, sent him and his brother Caesarius to study at Athens, where he met Basil. He later became assistant bishop to his father. Susanna Elm sums up his use of funeral orations: 'He epitomized his brother as the model public official, his sister as the perfect wife and mother, and his parents as the exemplary married couple, blessed with exceptional children and grandchildren.'[36] Gorgonia, the 'perfect wife and mother', has some characteristics in common with Augustine's Monica, but like Macrina she is exemplary.[37] Gregory of Nazianzus adapted the conventions of a funeral oration to praise the committed Christian life of Gorgonia, just as Gregory of Nyssa adapted the conventions of a philosophical biography to praise the life of Macrina. Gregory's Gorgonia brought together all that is best in marriage and celibacy, living in the world but concerned for the kingdom of God. She regarded her husband as her head and called him "lord", but she knew that Christ is the head of all, and she brought her husband to Christ. She was a good wife and manager of her household, like the good wife in the Book of Proverbs.[38] She was self-controlled and gentle.

34. See chapter 4.
35. See chapter 4.
36. Susanna Elm, 'Family Men: Masculinity and Philosophy in Late Antiquity', in Philip Rousseau and Manolis Papoutsakis, eds., *Transformations of Late Antiquity* (2009), pp. 279–301, at p. 294.
37. Gregory's Oration 8, for Gorgonia, is translated with commentary by Brian Daley, *Gregory of Nazianzus* (2006), pp. 63–75.
38. On the "good wife", see chapter 3.

She rarely appeared in public and did not care for adornment. She was generous in charity, and practised great personal austerity. Gregory told how, after an accident when her mules ran away with her carriage, she healed by prayer injuries which she was too modest to show to (male) doctors, and how she cured by prayer an illness which baffled them. As she died, she spoke the words of a psalm verse, which the priest was just able to hear. Virginia Burrus observes that these are the only words Gorgonia speaks.[39]

Gregory of Nazianzus did not give a separate funeral oration for his mother Nonna, but both parents (then still living) are praised in the oration for Gorgonia, and Nonna is an important presence in the oration for his father, whom she brought to Christ.[40] Gregory also wrote far more epitaphs for his mother than he did for other family members: thirty-five for his mother, sixteen for his brother, eleven for his father, three for his sister. Nonna, like Monica, had two sons and a daughter, but only Gregory outlived her. He said in a poem (*epitaph.* 71 = *Anth.Gr.* 8.30) that she preferred him to his brother. Nonna prayed for her sons to return together from study overseas, and they did (*or.* 7.8). She wanted Gregory to be a priest; she had a vision of him bringing bread (*or.* 18.41), and he had a vision of her rescuing his ship from a storm (ib. 31). She died while praying in church.[41]

At Rome there were examples of women who did their duty as wives and mothers, then led the ascetic life in widowhood. Melania the elder, widowed at 22, spent some years ensuring the place of her surviving son in the world of senatorial Rome, then set off to visit the monks of Egypt and to settle in the Holy Land.[42] Marcella, widowed after seven months, did not have children, but refused to remarry, and according to Jerome (*ep.* 127) made her family house into an ascetic community of widows and virgins engaged in Bible study.[43] Paula, born in 347 CE, was married in the early 360s, bore four daughters and a son, and was

39. Burrus (n. 26), p. 166.
40. The elder Gregory had been a Hypsistarian, a worshipper of the 'Highest God': on the debates about this cult, see Stephen Mitchell, 'Further Thoughts on the Cult of Theos Hypsistos', in Stephen Mitchell and Peter Van Nuffelen, eds., *One God* (2010), pp. 167–208.
41. On the funeral orations of Gregory of Nazianzus, see also Susanna Elm, 'Gregory's Women: Creating a Philosopher's Family', in Børtnes and Hägg (n. 7), pp. 171–91, and Tomas Hägg, 'Playing with Expectations: Gregory's Funeral Orations on His Brother, Sister and Father', ibid. pp. 133–51. His autobiographical poems are translated by Carolinne White (2005).
42. Kevin Wilkinson, 'The Elder Melania's Missing Decade', *Journal of Late Antiquity* 5.1 (2012), 166–84.
43. Cain 2009 (n. 27), pp. 52–6.

widowed around 381.[44] In the next year she met Jerome, and when he left Rome in 385 CE, she and her daughter Eustochium, a consecrated virgin who (like Macrina) never left her mother's side, joined him in the Holy Land. Paula died there in 404, and Jerome, in his 'Funeral Oration for Saint Paula', emphasized her rejection of status, her use of wealth in charity and in building projects (so that Eustochium inherited only debts), her extreme austerity, her exceptional piety, and her remarkable knowledge of scripture, which included Hebrew. He also described in detail her travels in the Holy Land and her visit to the monks of Egypt. He told Eustochium that Paula had been 'crowned by a long martyrdom' (*epit.* 22); he asked for Paula's prayers (ibid. 33); and by adding the date of her death and the place of her burial, he helped to establish her as a saint.

All these women came from a much higher social level from Monica, and made much more dramatic commitments to the ascetic life. The men who wrote about them presented them as faultless.[45] Augustine, also a trained rhetorician, knew how to give a funeral oration, but he did not follow the conventions in his memories of Monica and of his own response to her death. He was also distinctive in his handling of the convention "ah, such a mother!" He reported Ambrose's praise of Monica in the course of explaining how, in Milan, she willingly gave up her African custom of taking offerings of food and drink to memorial shrines, when she was told that the bishop had forbidden it:

> But it seems to me, Lord my God (and on this matter my heart
> is in your sight) that perhaps my mother would not easily have
> yielded to this abolition of custom if it had been forbidden
> by another whom she did not love as she did Ambrose. She
> loved him greatly for the sake of my salvation, and he loved
> her for the sake of the deeply religious way of life and spiritual
> fervour with which she undertook good works and was
> constantly in church; so that when he saw me he would often
> burst out in praise of her, congratulating me on having such
> a mother, but not knowing that she had such a son, who was

---

44. On the *epitaphium sanctae Paulae* (Jer. *Ep.* 108), see Cain 2013 (n. 27).
45. Elizabeth Clark, 'Holy Women, Holy Words', *Journal of Early Christian Studies* 6.3 (1998), 413–30, at p. 416, makes the point that saints' lives were written about women of wealth and status.

in doubt about all these things and did not think it possible to find the way of life. (*Conf.* 6.2.2)

Public praise of someone else's mother was evidently acceptable, even though it was not polite to name her. John Chrysostom's mother Anthousa, widowed at 20 and struggling with tax demands, greedy relatives, and reluctant slaves, refused to remarry because of the risk to her children's inheritance (*On the Priesthood* 5). John, writing to a young widow (*ad viduam iuniorem* 2), said that even pagans respected widowhood. His own teacher, hearing that he was the son of a widow, asked how old she was and for how long she had been widowed. The answer was that she was 40 and had been a widow for 20 years. The teacher exclaimed 'What women there are among the Christians!' Probably the teacher was Libanius, who in his *Autobiography* praised his own widowed mother. She too was left with children to raise; her father died; she did not trust guardians, and she chose to be everything to her children. She paid for their education, but could not bring herself to be severe against idleness: 'she thought that a loving mother should never distress her own in any way' (*Autob.* 4). She wept at the thought of Libanius going to Athens for his studies (13). He was distressed at not being with her in her old age (58–9), and when he reported her death he said that she was everything to him (117). All this leaves very little impression of what she was like. Another teacher of rhetoric, Ausonius of Bordeaux, similarly leaves little impression of his admirable mother Aemilia Aeonia in his collection of poems on family members:

> Next are you, Aeonia who gave me birth, of mixed descent,
> your mother from Tarbellae, your father of the Aedui. Every
> virtue of the compliant wife was yours: a reputation for
> chastity, hands that worked wool, loyalty to your husband,
> concern for bringing up your children; dignified but friendly,
> serious but cheerful. Now for ever, embracing the peaceful
> shade of your husband, as you once cherished his bed in life,
> cherish in death his tomb. (*Parentalia* 2)

Monica too was a compliant wife and devoted mother, who had wished to be buried with her husband. But Augustine did not present "such a mother!" as an unqualified good. In a letter to Laetus, who asked for advice on leading the religious life (*ep.* 243.3–10), Augustine cited the words of Jesus in Luke 14:26: 'If anyone comes to me and does not hate his father, and mother, and wife, and children, and brothers, and sisters, and even his own life, he cannot be my disciple.' He drew a contrast:

> ... in that a woman is now your mother, by that very fact she
> is not mine. So this is temporal and transitory: you see how it
> has already passed that she conceived you, carried you in her
> womb, gave birth to you, fed you with milk. But in that she
> is a sister in Christ, she is yours and mine, and is promised
> in the same association of love to all who have one heavenly
> inheritance, whose father is God and whose brother is Christ.
> (Aug. *ep.* 243.3)

She holds Laetus back in that she is his own mother; she should not plead 'the ten months for which you burdened her entrails, and the pains of childbirth, and the effort of rearing.' The church is the mother of both mother and son. Augustine does not offer the example of his own mother, but, as the quotation at the start of this chapter shows, after his baptism he was her brother in the church as well as her son.

Even Mary mother of Jesus might seek to distract her son from the work he had to do. The theme "such a mother!" makes a remarkable appearance in one of Augustine's sermons (*ser.* 72A.3):

> As he [Jesus] said this to the crowds (I am following the
> Gospel) his mother and brothers were standing outside,
> wanting to speak to him. Someone told him, saying 'Look,
> your mother and your brothers are outside, they want to
> speak to you.' And he said 'Who is my mother? Or who are
> my brothers?' And stretching out his hand over his disciples
> he said, 'These are my mother and my brothers. And whoever
> does the will of my Father who is in heaven, he is my brother,
> my sister and my mother.' (Mt. 12: 46–50) I would have liked
> to talk only about this, but, because I did not want to pass over
> the earlier part, I have used, I think, much time. This passage
> which I have just set before you has many complexities and
> difficulties to investigate: how the Lord Christ could with
> piety disregard his mother, not just any mother, but in so
> much as she was a virgin mother, so much more a mother
> to whom he had brought fertility in such a way that she did
> not lose [bodily] integrity; a mother who conceived as a
> virgin, gave birth as a virgin, remained for always a virgin.

He disregarded such a mother, lest maternal feeling should enter into the work he was doing and impede him. What was he doing? He was speaking to groups of people, destroying the old human beings and building up the new, freeing souls, releasing those who were bound, enlightening blind minds; he was doing good work, eager with act and speech in good work. In the midst of this, the affection of the flesh is announced to him. You heard what he replied: why should I repeat it? Let mothers hear, so that they do not hamper with fleshly affection the good works of their children. For if they do choose to hamper them, and break in upon them as they take action, so as to interrupt work which should not be delayed, they are disregarded by their children; I venture to say, they are disregarded; out of piety they are disregarded. And when will a woman be angry with her son, who is concentrating on his good work and for that reason disregards his mother's arrival: when will she be angry, whether wife or widow, when the virgin Mary was disregarded? But you will say to me 'So you compare my son to Christ?' I don't compare him to Christ or you to Mary. The Lord Christ did not condemn maternal affection: he gave in himself a great example of disregarding a mother for the sake of God's work. He was a teacher in speaking and a teacher in disregarding; he deigned to disregard his mother to teach disregard of you, and of a father, for the sake of God's work.

Augustine preached Christmas sermons in celebration of Mary, focussing on her faith and on her virginity, which meant that Christ's humanity was conceived without the transmission of sin.[46] He developed the paradox of the virgin mother whose son was her creator. He did not write a treatise on Mary or advocate a cult of Mary, and he did not ask for her prayers.[47]

For Augustine, then, mothers may be admirable in their devotion to their children. They may resemble Mother Church in their constant concern for children who stray; they may even have qualities shared with Mary the mother of the Lord.[48] But the physical bond of mother and child should not be overvalued. God brought Augustine into this life through the flesh of his parents (*Conf.* 9.13.37), just as God created Monica, whose parents did not know what kind of person would come from them (9.8.18); God filled with milk the breasts of Augustine's mother and nurses (1.6.7). There is always a risk that a mother will love her son too much, and will hold him back because she wants him with her. Monica was able to let go at the end of her life, when she knew that Augustine was safe as a committed and baptized Christian, but letting go took time and the unseen workings of the grace of God. Monica was not always a saint.

When and how did Monica become a saint? In late antiquity, saints were made by local recognition, and were more widely acknowledged as their story was transmitted and (if possible) their relics were distributed. Soon after Augustine's death in 430 CE, Possidius wrote a *Life*; by the end of the fifth century, at Carthage, Augustine's name was on the list of those read out for special veneration, and according to tradition his body had been moved from Hippo to a place of safety. The earliest evidence for recognition of Monica, still as Augustine's mother not as herself a saint, has been dated to the late sixth or early seventh century CE. It is part of a text, engraved on a broken marble slab which was found at Ostia in 1945. The full text appears in various manuscripts, the earliest dating from the ninth century, which include a collection of seven verse epitaphs. Monica's epitaph reads:

> *Hic posuit cineres genetrix castissima prolis,*
> *Augustine, tuis altera lux meritis,*
> *Qui servans pacis caelestia iura sacerdos*
> *Commissos populos moribus instituis.*
> *Gloria vos maior gestorum laude coronat*
> *Virtutum mater felicior subole.*

Here the most chaste mother of her offspring placed her ashes, a second light, Augustine, for your merits. You, as a priest keeping the heavenly laws of peace, teach with your conduct the peoples entrusted to you. The glory of your virtues, greater than praise of your deeds, crowns you both, mother more fortunate in your offspring.[49]

---

48. Mother Church: Joanne McWilliam, 'The Cassiciacum Autobiography', *Studia Patristica* 18.4 (1990), 14–43. Qualities shared with Mary, Kim Power, *Veiled Desire* (1995), p. 91.

49. Dating and text from Douglas Boin, 'Late Antique Ostia and a Campaign for Pious

One of the manuscripts adds a note that a former consul, Bassus, wrote these verses on Monica of sainted memory, mother of Saint Augustine. There were three consuls called Bassus in the late fourth and early fifth century CE, but even if the note is reliable, it would be remarkable if this tribute to Monica was offered so soon after her death. Douglas Boin suggests instead that the inscription was part of an effort, perhaps two centuries later, to reaffirm the Christian history of Ostia.

It took several more centuries for Monica to be celebrated as a saint. The material is collected in the *Acta Sanctorum*, the impressive project, begun in the seventeenth century, for a critical edition of the lives of the saints.[50] The sequence of lives follows the feast days of the saints in the church year, so the entry for 'Saint Monica, widow, mother of Saint Augustine' is in the volume that includes May 4th. This date was chosen, according to the editors, because Augustine did not mention his mother's birthday; so when her cult (which, as the editors observed, was unknown to the more ancient martyrologies) began to be celebrated at Arrouaise in Artois (northwestern France), the day before the feast of Augustine's conversion seemed appropriate.[51] (In later church calendars, Monica is celebrated on August 27th, the day before Augustine's feast day.) The community of Arrouaise took Augustine's rule for monastic life as the basis for their austere practice. They elected their first abbot in 1121, and the rule of Arrouaise spread to other monastic houses. Gauthier of Arrouaise told how in 1162, on a visit to Italy, he was guided to bring back from Ostia the relics of Monica, and how at the request of his brothers he wrote an account of this event and compiled a life of Monica, mostly taken from the *Confessions*, to accompany the relics.[52] His preface to the Life reminds readers that not all saints are associated with miracles, and some are shown by the quality of their lives: in this instance, 'how chaste, how pious, how sober, how gentle, how kind, how modest, how patient she was, and how assiduous

Tourism', *Journal of Roman Studies* 100 (2010), 195–209, at p. 200. My translation differs from his, especially in the last two lines, but this affects only one aspect of his interpretation.

50. The project is led by the Bollandists, a group of Jesuit scholars named for the first editor, John van Bolland.

51. The entry is in *Acta Sanctorum* Maii i.473–92; cult unknown before Gauthier of Arrouaise, p. 480.

52. Clarissa Atkinson, 'Your Servant, My Mother,' in Clarissa Atkinson, Constance Buchanan, and Margaret Miles, eds., *Immaculate and Powerful* (1987), pp. 139–72, at pp. 144–5. Gauthier's compilation of excerpts from *Confessions*, and his account of the transfer of relics, are in *Acta Sanctorum* l.c. (n. 51).

and devout in prayers, vigils, fasts, and almsgiving, so that she lacked nothing for perfection, is plainly read in the *Confessions*.' The story of Monica and her 'son of tears' was made more generally known by the life of Augustine in the *Golden Legend* of Jacobus de Voragine, written around 1260 and very widely distributed in manuscript and later in print. Another source was a pseudo-Augustinian letter, addressed to Augustine's sister, describing Monica's religious life and holy death; the editors of the *Acta Sanctorum* remark that 'nobody would say [the letter] was Saint Augustine's unless they had never read Augustine's writings.'[53]

Saint Monica now became part of a complicated story involving the Augustinian Canons and the Augustinian Hermits, who had different views of Augustine's theology and of his teaching on the monastic life.[54] In 1327 the Hermits were allowed to share with the Canons guardianship of the tomb of Augustine in the church of San Pietro al Ciel d'Oro in Pavia. Why Pavia? Augustine had no connection with the town, but Bede, writing early in the eighth century, gave the answer at the end of the world chronicle he included in his work *The Reckoning of Time*:

> Hearing that the Saracens had depopulated Sardinia and
> had dug up the place where the bones of the holy Bishop
> Augustine had once been moved on account of the barbarian
> raids and honorably buried, Liutprand sent and paid a great
> price [for them], received [them] and transported them to
> Pavia, and reburied them there with the honour due to so
> great a Father.[55]

The first move was made to escape the 'barbarian raids' of the Vandals, who were besieging Hippo when Augustine died in 430 CE, and soon took control of Africa. They were Arian Christians who expelled many Catholic bishops; some of these (notably Fulgentius, bishop of Ruspe at the start of the sixth century) were thought to have taken Augustine's

---

53. *Acta Sanctorum* l.c. p. 473; on Jacobus and on Jordan of Quedlinburg, who also wrote about Monica, see Diana Webb, 'Eloquence and Education: A Humanist Approach to Hagiography', *Journal of Ecclesiastical History* 31.1 (1980), 19–39, at p. 31.

54. Eric Saak, 'Augustine in the Western Middle Ages to the Reformation', in Mark Vessey, ed., *A Companion to Augustine* (2012), pp. 465–77, at pp. 467–74; see further Eric Saak, *Creating Augustine* (2012a).

55. *Bede: The Reckoning of Time*, translated by Faith Wallis (2004), p. 237.

FIGURE 6.2. Augustinian Hermits carry the body of Monica. Arca di Sant'Agostino, Pavia.

Scala / Art Resource, NY

remains with them when they were exiled to nearby Sardinia. The second move happened around 720 CE, when Liutprand was king of the Lombards, who had established a kingdom in north Italy. His uncle Peter was bishop of Pavia.[56]

At Pavia in the fourteenth century, the Hermits built a new tomb, the Arca, decorated with sculpture and relief panels showing scenes from Augustine's life. Monica is present at the scene of Augustine's baptism, and in another panel her body is carried towards a church by men and women members of the Order of Hermits.[57] She also appears

56. On the bones of Augustine, see Konrad Vössing and Harold Stone, 'Cult of Augustine', in Karla Pollmann and Willemien Otten, eds. (2013), 2: 846–9. On Vandal Christianity, see Robin Jensen, 'Christianity in Roman Africa', in Michele Salzman, Marvin Sweeney, and William Adler, eds., *The Cambridge History of Religions in the Ancient World*, Vol. 2 (2013), pp. 264–91, at pp. 277–81.

57. On the *arca* and its decoration, see Meredith Gill, *Augustine in the Italian Renaissance* (2005), pp. 4–48 and plates 2–4; see also http://www.cassiciaco.it/navigazione/iconografia/cicli/trecento/pavia/pavia.html, accessed 24 June 2013.

in an early fifteenth-century sequence of frescoes, painted by Ottaviano Nelli, on the walls and vault of the church of the Hermits at Gubbio in Umbria. Monica, marked as a saint by her halo, sends Augustine off to school, dreams of his salvation while he reads, and consults a bishop. With Augustine and Alypius, she listens to Ambrose preaching; Augustine tells her of his conversion; she is present at his baptism; and Augustine brings a crucifix to her deathbed.[58] Similarly, in the frescoes painted by Benozzo Gozzoli, in the 1460s, in the Hermits' church of Sant'Agostino in San Gimignano, Monica sends Augustine to school, is present at his baptism, and is shown on her deathbed.[59] She is much more prominent in these frescoes than in earlier cycles, but in all the sequences of Augustine's life, the focus is of course on Augustine, and Monica appears in episodes which show his and her sanctity. She is not shown as a child raiding the wine barrel or as a mother with worldly ambitions.

By the time Gozzoli painted his sequence of frescoes, there had been a further discovery of relics at Ostia. The editors of the *Acta Sanctorum*, clearly unconvinced, remark that religious people at Ostia had no doubt kept quiet about the activities of Gauthier three centuries earlier. The Hermits were given permission to move these bones to San Trionfe, their church in Rome. The "translation" (literally "carrying across', a technical term for moving the body of a saint) took place on Palm Sunday in 1430, and was reported by Andrea Biglia, an Augustinian friar. Monica was not a new saint, so there was no need for formal "canonization", that is, a declaration by the Pope that, having entered into glory, she was enrolled on the list (canon) of those who deserve veneration. But Biglia ascribed to Pope Martin V a sermon, preached to the Hermits, in which it was said that people had not known the

58. Gill ibid. pp. 60–8, with plates 8–29, especially 12, 13, 17, 19, 20, 21; compare the earlier stained-glass cycle in the Church of St Augustine at Erfurt: http://www.cassiciaco.it/navigazione/iconografia/cicli/trecento/erfurt/erfurt.html, accessed 13 May 2013. See further Saak 2012a (n. 54), pp. 154–5, and Diane Cole Ahl, 'The Life of Saint Augustine in San Gimignano', in Joseph C. Schnaubelt and Frederick Van Fleteren, eds., *Augustine in Iconography: History And Legend* (1999), pp. 359–82, at pp. 362–3.

59. Gill ibid. pp. 76–93, with plates 30–40, especially 32 and 33; see also http://www.cassiciaco.it/navigazione/iconografia/cicli/quattrocento/gimignano/gimignano.html, accessed 24 June 2013. The sequence includes the scene of Augustine reading before his conversion (Gill plate 39), a strong contender for the title of "most-used cover image in books about Augustine". Other contenders include Ary Scheffer, *Saints Augustine and Monica*, painted in 1854 and now in the National Gallery, London, but not currently on display: http://www.nationalgallery.org.uk/paintings/ary-scheffer-saints-augustine-and-monica, accessed 11 June 2013.

name of Monica, but when they realized who she was they rushed to be near her, and healing miracles accompanied the translation.[60] The most fervent admirer of Monica was the humanist Maffeo Vegio, who prepared the order for this translation. He organized a chapel of St. Monica, with a marble sarcophagus, in the church of Sant' Agostino, and a second translation to this chapel took place on Monica's feast day in 1455. Vegio described his own increasing devotion to Monica, whom he used as an example of the ideal mother and teacher, prepared for sanctity by her own rigorous moral education; his material came mostly from *Confessions*, but he also used *de beata vita*.[61] In 1440 the Pope approved the Confraternity of St. Monica (still in existence), a voluntary association for prayer and charity; and late in the fifteenth century the nuns of the convent of St. Monica, in Florence, commissioned for their chapel in Santo Spirito an altarpiece showing Monica seated among women.[62]

Tracing the reception history of Monica would, to borrow a favourite phrase of Augustine, require lengthy investigation and a long argument (e.g., *en. Ps.* 4.1). It would also require expertise in many languages and cultural contexts.[63] As Clarissa Atkinson points out, depictions of Monica depend on ideals of motherhood, a subject on which almost everyone has views, and these ideals have often been those of celibate men committed to the religious life. It is understandable that the relationship of mother and son was very important to them, especially if they were sheltered from the practicalities of raising children. When anxious mothers sought advice, they could be offered the example of Monica's constant prayers and tears. Pierre Courcelle undertook the immense task of tracing the literary reception of *Confessions*, primarily in French tradition, and found that from the twelfth century on, the theme most strongly associated with Monica is 'the son of those tears cannot perish'.[64] In nineteenth-century writing especially, Monica became the patron of mothers who hoped to save their children, or who needed reassurance that devoted motherhood is important work and

60. Webb (n. 53), pp. 21–22.
61. Webb (n. 53), pp. 28–32; Atkinson (n. 52), pp. 148–50. See also Meredith Gill, 'Remember Me at the Altar of the Lord: Saint Monica's Gift to Rome', in Schnaubelt and Van Fleteren (n. 58), pp. 550–76; Figure 3 shows Monica's tomb.
62. Gill (n. 57), p. 160.
63. My thanks to Karla Pollmann for advance information that the *Oxford Guide to the Historical Reception of Augustine* (2013) does not include an entry on Monica.
64. Pierre Courcelle, *Les Confessions de Saint Augustin dans la tradition littéraire* (1963).

that they had not really lost touch with sons who were physically or emotionally absent.[65]

But 'the son of those tears cannot perish' is usually separated from the preceding phrase in *Confessions*: 'go away' (3.12.21). That phrase is important, not only because it shows that the devotion of Augustine's Monica was not always well received, but also because it makes, once again, Augustine's point that God acts through people who do not know or intend the effect of what they say:

> You gave her another response that I remember [. . .] through
> your priest, a bishop nurtured in the church and trained by
> your books. She asked him to deign to talk to me, refute my
> errors, unteach me what was bad and teach me what was good
> (for he used to do that when he happened to find suitable
> people). He refused, very wisely, as I realized afterwards. He
> said that I was still unteachable, because I was still puffed
> up with the newness of that heresy and, as she had told him,
> had already harassed many inexpert people with quibbles.
> 'But', he said, 'leave him be there. Just pray the Lord for him.
> He will discover by reading what an error that is and how
> great an impiety.' He told how he too as a boy was given to
> the Manichaeans by his mother, who had been led astray, and
> had not only read but copied out almost all their books, and it
> had become clear to him, with no one arguing against it and
> convincing him, how much that sect was to be avoided: so
> he did. When he had said this and she would not accept it,
> but pressed him yet more, begging and weeping copiously, to
> see me and discuss it with me, he became somewhat irritable
> and tired of this, and said 'Depart from me: as you live, it
> cannot be that the son of those tears should perish.' She often
> remembered, in her conversations with me, that she heard this
> as if it had sounded from heaven. (*Conf.* 3.12.21)

Through the centuries, many other people heard this as if it had sounded from heaven. But in the early twentieth century, Freudian and post-Freudian psychology offered a different interpretation of the tears

---

65. Atkinson (n. 53), p. 159 notes especially Emile Bougaud, *Vie de Sainte Monique* (1865), with two English translations and many reprints.

of the devoted mother. Peter Walcot takes an epigraph from Freud's lecture on femininity:

> A mother is only brought unlimited satisfaction by her relation to a son; this is altogether the most perfect, the most free from ambivalence of all human relationships. A mother can transfer to her son the ambition which she has been obliged to suppress in herself and she can expect from him the satisfaction of all that has been left over in her of her masculinity complex. (Walcot 1996: 114)[66]

Present-day readers may want to locate Freud's observations in a particular context of time and place which was very different from the social and family patterns of fourth-century Africa; but in classical antiquity too, mothers were accused of trying to dominate and manipulate their sons. In this interpretation, 'the son of those tears' was controlled and constrained by Monica's devotion.

We have only Augustine's Monica, and cannot say what Monica herself intended, but it is Augustine's Monica who shows what Augustine felt, or wanted his readers to think he felt. His envisaged readers approved of devoted mothers who wept when their sons left home, and of devoted sons who, though they left home, were bereft by their mother's death. Augustine wrote that he was comforted by remembering how in her last illness Monica would call him a good son (*pium*) and say that she had never heard him fling a harsh or disrespectful word at her (*Conf.* 9.12.30). He did not envisage readers who would see danger signals in his account of the intense relationship between mother and son 'whom she loved uniquely'[67] and of his extreme grief when she died.

Garry Wills points out that Augustine was not in practice dominated by his mother: he was away from home for most of his adolescence, and she is absent from almost all his writings.[68] Augustine himself reports that he disregarded Monica's strong views on sex and

---

66. Peter Walcot, 'Plato's Mother and Other Terrible Women'. in Ian McAuslan and Peter Walcot, eds., *Women in Antiquity* (1996), pp. 114–33. See also Paul Rigby, 'Paul Ricoeur, Freudianism, and Augustine's *Confessions*', *Journal of the American Academy of Religion* 53.1 (1985), 93–114, with the comment by Donald Capps, 'Augustine as Narcissist', ibid. 115–28. Kim Power (n. 4), suggests some Kleinian approaches in her chapter on 'Augustine the Son' (pp. 71–93), but offers a balanced account.

67. On the interpretation of *unice*, "uniquely", see chapter 1.

68. Garry Wills, *Augustine's Confessions* (2011) p. 86, pp. 142–4.

on religion, dismissing as 'women's advice' her warnings against fornication and especially against adultery (*Conf.* 2.3.7), and remaining a Manichaean despite her shock and her continuing distress (3.11.19). She was distraught when he left for Italy, and did her best to stop him, but he went (5.8.15). But Monica followed, and it is possible that Augustine could not see, or did not acknowledge, psychological processes which are now more recognizable. He is exceptional among classical authors in discussing his infancy, childhood, and puberty, and he provides the material for deductions about these experiences and for arguments that Monica won: she succeeded in displacing her son's robust father (1.11.17), whose death Augustine notes out of context in a parenthesis (3.4.7), in dismissing his much-loved partner, and, eventually, in overcoming his sexuality.[69] According to Augustine, she hoped he would be a baptized Christian and a faithful husband and father, but she rejoiced much more in his decision to be celibate:

> We [Augustine and Alypius] went in to my mother, and
> told her: she rejoiced. We told her how it had happened: she
> exulted and triumphed and kept blessing you, who have the
> power to do more than we ask and understand, because she
> saw how much more you had granted her about me than
> she used to ask with wretched and tearful groans. For you
> converted me to you, so that I should not seek a wife or any
> hope in this world, standing on that rule of faith on which
> so many years before you had revealed me to her, and you
> converted her grief into joy far more abundantly than she had
> wished, and with much more love and greater chastity than
> she had sought in grandchildren of my flesh. (8.12.30)

Augustine's words link his mother's rejoicing in his celibacy with his father's rejoicing in his ability to beget children. When Augustine was fifteen, recently returned from school at Madauros, Patricius came back from the baths and 'as if he was already eager for grandchildren, told my mother, rejoicing', that their son had reached sexual maturity (2.3.6).[70] Augustine, in retrospect, blamed Monica for being less concerned to arrange an early marriage than she was to give him moral

---

69. Rebecca West, *St. Augustine* (1933) is a particularly forceful example of this approach. On blaming Monica for dismissing Augustine's concubine, see chapter 5.

70. *Gaudens matri indicavit*, 2.3.6; *ad matrem ingredimur, indicamus: gaudet*, 8.12.30.

warnings. 'There was fear' that marriage would impede his further education and his career; both parents were concerned for worldly success, but Monica, he thought, expected his studies to bring him closer to God (2.3.8). Present-day readers are more likely to blame Monica for her reaction to the news Patricius brought: 'she started up with pious fear and trembling' and with 'immense anxiety' (*cum sollicitudine ingenti*, 2.3.7) warned her son against fornication and especially against adultery with someone else's wife. Anxiety is a characteristic of Augustine's Monica. In Milan, she was anxious (*sollicitudinem gerebat, ep.* 36.32) about fasting rules, and she led the congregation in anxiety (*sollicitudinis . . . primas tenens, Conf.* 9.7.15) for the basilica which was threatened by the empress; Augustine knew how she had always been in a fever of concern (*quanta cura semper aestuasset*, 9.11.28) about burial beside her husband. Present-day readers are likely to think that Monica was made anxious by her son's sexuality, rather than by what she saw as moral and spiritual danger which also endangered a promising career and all that meant for the family.

Augustine expected a different response to 'she started up with pious fear and trembling'. 'Fear and trembling' is a phrase from scripture (2 Cor. 7:15): it refers to the fear of the Lord, which is the beginning of wisdom. Augustine was not yet baptized, so people said 'let him be, let him do it' (1.11.18), but Monica reminded him of Christian teaching. She was also alert to the social dangers of sexual activity, and she had good reason for warning especially against adultery. It was a serious crime, because, in the absence of effective contraception, an adulterous wife might conceive another man's child who would claim a share in her husband's property; worse still, her adultery raised doubts about the legitimacy of all her children. Such doubts would also wreck the chances of a marriageable woman who had a sexual relationship, so if Augustine had a relationship with a freeborn woman, he might be forced into marriage and thereby into taking his share of social duties in Thagaste. Augustine dismissed Monica's advice because he was more concerned to behave like his peer group, or at least to sound as if he was behaving like them (2.3.7). He did not say what exactly they claimed to be doing: trying to seduce married or marriageable women, having sex with slaves or low-class women, going to the local brothel? A younger contemporary, Paulinus of Pella, described his own decisions in his late teens: to avoid adding *crimina*, legal charges, to *culpa*, moral fault, 'I would never pursue an unwilling woman, or one who belonged to another [*iuris alieni*] ... and I would beware of yielding to freeborn who offered of their own choice, satisfied with the attractions of the house which were at my service [*domus inlecebris famulantibus*]' (*Euch.* 161–8). In other words, keep to the household slaves. Patricius might have offered his son the same advice.[71]

Psychological readings of Augustine offer an alarming collection of adjectives for Monica: manipulative, possessive, domineering, rigid, constrictive, controlling, devouring.[72] This is very different from what Augustine wrote about her, but those who offer the psychological readings argue that it is what he unwittingly revealed, or how she unwittingly behaved. Readers of *Confessions* should be wary of asking, in effect, "what would a psychiatrist conclude today if Augustine came for help?" but many readers think Augustine goes too far in expressing sexual guilt. He was in agreement with most philosophers of his time, both Christian and non-Christian, in holding that the proper use of sexual desire is for the procreation of children within marriage, so any other use is a victory for desire over reason;[73] but he behaved decently, by the standards of his time, in living before his marriage with one woman to whom he was faithful (4.2.2). But perhaps Augustine's own sexual anxieties, imposed or reinforced by Monica, contributed to his distinctive belief in "original sin"— that is, sin which derives from Adam, who as the first human being is the origin of the human race.[74]

Original sin is, in modern terms, a genetic tendency to go wrong. Augustine came to think that there is both a biological and a psychological transmission of sin at conception: the child's life begins with the father's semen, inherited from Adam who sinned and fell away from God, and semen is emitted when the father is overcome with desire and has lost all awareness of self.[75] In late antique medical theory, the

71. See chapter 3. Danuta Shanzer, 'Avulsa a latere meo', *Journal of Roman Studies* 92 (2002), 157–76, at pp. 166–9, offers an illuminating discussion of the risks at Thagaste.

72. Judith B. Miller, 'To Remember Self, to Remember God', in Judith Chelius Stark, ed., *Feminist Approaches to Augustine* (2007), pp. 243–79, at p. 263. All these adjectives come from papers in Donald Capps and James E. Dittes, eds., *The Hunger of the Heart* (1990).

73. See further Gillian Clark, 'Do Try This At Home: The Domestic Philosopher in Late Antiquity', in Amirav and ter Haar Romeny (n. 47), pp. 153–72.

74. Augustine emphasizes (*civ. Dei* 12.22) that according to Genesis 2, Eve, the first woman, was created *from* Adam: this is to show that all humanity is united in descent from Adam. Present-day feminist theologians point out that in Genesis 1: 26, "the adâm" is not the male human being, but humanity.

75. Miller (n. 72) discusses 'loss of self' and Augustine's relationships with other people and with God.

dominant view was that the mother's contribution to the embryo is the blood that would otherwise be shed in menstruation. Augustine may have shared (but did not discuss) the view of some doctors that conception does not happen unless the mother too experiences desire.[76] He thought that marriage, though less good than celibacy, is still good: God invented it, and Christ endorsed it.[77] But he also thought that human sexual response demonstrates the effects of "the Fall" of the first humans into sin and away from obedience to God. The body no longer obeys reason, which should guide it. Sexual response occurs when it is not wanted and does not occur when it is wanted (*civ. Dei* 14.16). People cannot decide to conceive a child. For women, intercourse is invasive, and childbirth is painful and dangerous (*civ. Dei* 14.26).

Do we now know better than Augustine, or than Monica, what was really at work in their efforts to live rightly and to think about human life? Peter Brown has the last word on psychological interpretations: 'the unexpected combinations, ramifications and resolutions that a properly sophisticated knowledge of modern psychology would lead us to expect, escape the historian.' A footnote gently adds 'The studies known to me [. . .] show that it is as difficult as it is desirable to combine competence as an historian with sensitivity as a psychologist.'[78] 'Competence as an historian' must include awareness of the social and intellectual context, and of the scriptures which Augustine quoted and evoked throughout the *Confessions*. For example, about Monica's displacement of his father, he wrote:

> So I and she and all the household were believers, except
> only my father; but he did not conquer in me the right of my
> mother's devotion, so that I should not believe in Christ in the
> same way that he did not yet believe. For she strove to ensure
> that you should be my father, my God, rather than he, and in
> this you helped her to overcome her husband, whom she, the

76. For relevant medical theory, see Gillian Clark, *Women in Late Antiquity* (1993), pp. 63–89. In *civ. Dei* 1.16–19 and 1.28, discussing women who committed suicide to avoid rape or the shame of rape, Augustine avoids explicit mention of pregnancy that results from rape, but insists that a raped woman does not lose her chastity unless her mind consented.

77. On Augustine's view of marriage, see Carol Harrison, *Augustine: Christian Truth and Fractured Humanity* (2000), pp. 158–93; on fourth-century debates, see David Hunter, *Marriage, Celibacy and Heresy in Ancient Christianity* (2007).

78. Peter Brown, *Augustine of Hippo* (1967) (rev. ed. 2000), p. 19 and n. 5. See also James O'Donnell, *Augustine: Confessions 2* (1992), 70–1 on mothers and fathers in *Confessions*.

better, served, because in this too she was serving you who gave the order. (*Conf.* 1.11.17)

Readers need to hear Psalm 26:10, 'my father and my mother have abandoned me, but the Lord has taken me up', and to be aware that Augustine emphasizes 'in this you helped her to overcome her husband', that is, in this all-important matter of his Christian faith. He was careful not to suggest that Monica overcame her husband in other ways.[79] These cautions do not mean that present-day readers must accept Augustine's interpretation of his experience and his representation of Monica, or that his personal experience is not relevant to his theological arguments and to the images he uses to express them. They do mean that Augustine and his envisaged readers had different expectations about mothers.

For Augustine, Monica's tears show her commitment to God and to her son. She is still a source of comfort for women anxious about their children, but Augustine's Monica took action as well as weeping and praying, and Augustine's own account shows a life that was not entirely focussed on her son. These are the aspects of Monica most likely to appeal in a time when many women have a far greater range of opportunities: thus Kate Cooper calls Monica's story 'the exploits of an unstoppable provincial heroine [. . .] who, despite an unpromising beginning, was able, by dint of vivid imagination and personal warmth, to make her way from a remote and minor town to the empire's capital.'[80] Monica took the opportunities she had. In the late fourth century she would not have made her way to Milan, or even to Carthage, without her clever son, and without Augustine we would not have heard of her unless by the chance survival of an epitaph commemorating the faithful and compliant wife of Patricius. We do not know what Monica thought and felt about her life, or about the lives of women. Did she bring up her own daughter as strictly as she had been brought up; what part did she play in arranging her daughter's marriage; and what advice did she give her on being a wife and mother? But Augustine's Monica shows what could be achieved by an ordinary woman progressing in faith, making the best of domestic life, and doing what she could for her family and friends. It is worth remembering Monica.

79. See further chapter 3.
80. Kate Cooper, 'Love and Belonging, Loss and Betrayal in the *Confessions*', in M. Vessey (n. 54), pp. 69–86, at p. 81.

Works of Augustine

References and Resources

Translations are my own unless it is otherwise stated.

References to the writings of Augustine follow the conventions set out in *Augustine Through the Ages: An Encyclopedia*, Allan D. Fitzgerald, ed. (1999), xxxv–xlii. These pages also give English titles, Latin editions, and English translations. More translations have since been published, especially in the series *Complete Works of Saint Augustine: A Translation for the 21st Century* [website], (http://www.newcitypress.com/Complete_works_Saint_Augustine_english.html), with introductions and notes.

Editions and translations up to 2011 are included in the tables in *A Companion to Augustine*, Mark Vessey, ed. (Wiley-Blackwell 2012), xxiv–xxxv.

Updated lists of editions and translations, with a wide range of further information, are available at www.augustinus.de, the website of the Zentrum für Augustinus-Forschung (Centre for Research on Augustine) at Wurzburg. This is a German-language website, but some pages offer English translations: for example, http://www.augustinus.de/bwo/dcms/sites/bistum/extern/zfa/lexikon/contents.html on the form and content of the *Augustinus-Lexikon* (in progress).

The *Augustinus-Lexikon* entry on Monica, by Larissa Seelbach, is in 4 fasc. 1/2 pp. 68–74.

The *Oxford Guide to the Historical Reception of Augustine*, Karla Pollmann and Willemien Otten, eds. (Oxford University Press 2013), offers valuable discussion of the transmission and reception of Augustine's writings, but does not include an entry on Monica.

Latin texts are freely available on line at www.augustinus.it (note that these are not the latest critical editions). A subscription is required for access to the online searchable texts and bibliography of the *Corpus Augustinianum Gissense*: see the English-language information at http://www.augustinus.de/bwo/dcms/sites/bistum/extern/zfa/cags/cag-online_en.html.

http://www9.georgetown.edu/faculty/jod/augustine/, James J.O'Donnell's pioneering site, includes his invaluable commentary on *Confessions* (Oxford University Press 1992). The commentary assumes knowledge of Latin, but readers without Latin can still benefit from it.

www.findingaugustine.org offers a bibliography. This is a project in progress at the Katholieke Universiteit Leuven and Villanova University.

www.cassiciaco.it is especially helpful on iconography (images of Augustine) in its historical context, in particular the medieval and early modern period.

Modern authors use varying forms of reference to the works of Augustine, but it is usually possible to understand what is meant. Three examples

De civitate Dei is here translated as *City of God* and abbreviated as *civ. Dei.* Some authors abbreviate as *civ.*, or as *DCD*, and some give a fuller version of the translated title, *The City of God Against the Pagans.*

De doctrina Christiana is here translated as *Christian Teaching* and abbreviated as *doc.Chr.* Some authors abbreviate as *doctr. Chr.* or *DDC*, and some translate the title as *Christian Doctrine*: this is less helpful than 'teaching', which covers both what should be taught and the way to teach it.

De Genesi ad litteram, here abbreviated as *Gn.Litt.*, is particularly difficult to translate. Augustine wrote eleven books of commentary on the opening chapters of Genesis up to the point where Adam and Eve were sent away from Paradise, then added a twelfth book on Paradise. *Ad litteram* contrasts with "allegorical", but Augustine thought that events themselves often had a hidden significance. *Literal Interpretation of Genesis* is the usual translation; sometimes *Genesis According to the Letter.*

Below, for convenience, are the abbreviations that occur in this book, with a brief explanation of each title. First, some general observations

Augustine's biographer Possidius listed over a thousand books, letters, and sermons.

Augustine provided an annotated list of his *books*, in chronological order, in his *Retractationes* ('re-readings'). 'Book' may mean a section of a text, or a complete text: for example, there are twenty-two books in *City of God*, but *Care for the Dead* is a single short book. Augustine had a sense of how long a single book should be, but did not further divide his text. Chapters (*capitula*, 'headings') and paragraphs are later subdivisions of texts, made to help medieval readers.

Letters were not private correspondence. Many were intended for public reading, some are short treatises, and it was expected that all letters would be shared with others. Letter-carriers might be entrusted with messages which really were private. Augustine kept copies of his letters, but did not have time to read through them, so there is no complete chronological list, and sometimes there are new discoveries. In 1969, for example, Johannes Divjak found a small group of letters, which are numbered 1*–29* to avoid confusion with the main collection. Augustine's *sermons* vary in formality. Sometimes he had time to dictate a sermon in advance of preaching, or to revise the transcript of the shorthand record taken by his *notarii*. Transcripts sometimes show how the audience reacted. As with letters, Augustine did not have time to read through all his sermons, and sometimes there are new discoveries.

Abbreviations Used in this Book

b.vita De beata vita (386 CE), usually translated 'On the Happy Life', sometimes (more accurately) 'On the Blessed Life'. Philosophical dialogue, one of Augustine's earliest writings and a major source for Monica.

C.Acad. Contra Academicos (386 CE). Usually translated 'Against the Academics', or sometimes 'Against the (Academic) Sceptics'. Philosophical dialogue on whether it is possible to achieve knowledge and truth. Monica briefly intervenes.

Cath. Ad catholicos fratres (?401 CE). A letter 'to Catholic brothers', also called *De unitate ecclesiae,* 'On the Unity of the Church'. Letter in answer to a pamphlet from the rival Donatist church; there is debate on whether Augustine wrote it.

civ. Dei De civitate Dei (c. 413–26). *City of God.* The city of God, the heavenly city, is the community of angels and humans, in all times and places, who love God and want to do God's will; the earthly city is the community of angels and humans, in all times and places, who want their own way. In Books 1–10 Augustine defends the city of God against those who prefer their own gods: he attacks traditional Roman religion (1–7) and Platonist philosophy (8–10), which is the greatest achievement of philosophy but still allows the worship of many gods. Books 11–22 set out the origins (11–14), progress (15–18), and destined ends (19–22) of the two cities.

c.Iul.imp. Contra Iulianum opus imperfectum (428–30). 'Unfinished Work against Julian'. This Julian (not the emperor), bishop of Aeclanum in Italy, challenged Augustine's view of sexual desire and its association with sin. The 'unfinished work' followed six books 'Against Julian' (c. 421 CE).

c.litt.Pet. Contra litteras Petiliani (c. 400 CE). 'Against the Writings of Petilian'. Petilianus, bishop of Cirta, wrote to his clergy a letter setting out the Donatist position on the purity of the church. Augustine wrote a response, followed by further discussion.

Conf. Confessiones (397 CE). *Confessions,* the major source for Monica. Augustine confesses (acknowledges) the glory of God as well as his own sins and errors. Books 1–9 trace God's presence in Augustine's life from infancy to baptism (aged 31); Book 10 reflects on his spiritual condition at the time of writing, Book 11 continues the discussion of memory and time, and Books 12–13 explore the narrative of creation in the book of Genesis.

Cresc. Contra Cresconium (405 CE). 'Against Cresconius', a Donatist teacher of literature who had challenged *c.litt.Pet.*

de cura De cura pro mortuis gerenda (c.421 CE). 'On Care [To Be Taken] for the Dead', a short response to questions from Paulinus bishop of Nola.

doc.Chr. De doctrina Christiana (books 1 to 3.25.35 c.395 CE, the rest of Book 3 and Book 4 completed late 420s), *Christian Teaching.* Book 1 is concerned with the content of Christian teaching, Books 2–3 with biblical interpretation, Book 4 with preaching technique.

ench. Enchiridion (c. 422 CE). 'Handbook'; also known as *Liber de fide, spe et caritate,* 'Book on Faith, Hope and Love'. Response to a request from a layman for a handbook on the basics of Christian faith.

en.Ps. Enarrationes in Psalmos (392–c.418 CE). 'Expositions of the Psalms', a collection of commentaries on all 150 psalms, ranging from sermons to notes.

ep. Epistulae (earliest 386 CE). 'Letters' (see general comment above). About 300 survive; some can be dated.

Gn.Litt. De Genesi ad Litteram (c. 400–15 CE). *Literal Interpretation of Genesis:* see previous comment.

Jo.Ev.Tr. In Johannis evangelium tractatus (between 408 and 420 CE). 'Tractates on the Gospel of John'. There are 124 tractates: some are sermons, some are dictated notes.

mor. De moribus ecclesiae catholicae et de moribus Manichaeorum (387–9 CE). 'On the Catholic and the Manichaean Ways of Life', two books contrasting the two traditions of asceticism and their basis in scripture.

nupt. et conc. De nuptiis et concupiscentia (c.420 CE). 'On Marriage and Concupiscence', arguing that marriage is good, but because humans have fallen away from God, the conception of children is affected by sin.

ord. De ordine (386 CE). 'Order', one of the early philosophical dialogues, on the order of the universe and the place of evil; a major source for Monica.

persev. De dono perseverantiae (428/9 CE), 'The Gift of Perseverance', arguing that we need God's grace to remain faithful.

qu.Gen. Quaestiones in Genesim (419 CE), 'Questions on Genesis', part of *Quaestiones in Heptateuchum,* 'Questions on the Heptateuch', that is, on the first seven books of scripture. Notes, often brief, on exegesis.

reg. Regula (397? CE). 'Rule': a rule of life for monks and nuns. It is not mentioned in the *Retractationes* (perhaps because it is a letter) or in the list of works compiled by Possidius, but many scholars accept that Augustine wrote it.

retr. Retractationes (426/7 CE). 'Reconsiderations' or 'Re-readings', a chronological list of all Augustine's books, with some comments on the context, and with corrections of errors or of words which might mislead.

ser. Sermones (from 393 CE). 'Sermons'. About four hundred survive; some can be dated.

sol. Soliloquia (386/7 CE). 'Soliloquies' (a word Augustine seems to have invented): a dialogue between Augustine and personified Reason on his spiritual state and progress towards wisdom.

vera rel. De vera religione (c. 390 CE). 'On True Religion', written before Augustine was ordained priest. He says that Platonism is very close to Christianity, discusses the origin of evil, and argues against Manichaeism.

v. Aug. Vita Augustini (?early 430s CE). Life of Augustine by his friend and fellow bishop Possidius, taking the story of his life on from the narrative of *Confessions*, and adding a catalogue of books, letters, and sermons.

Bibliography

Ahl, Diane Cole (1999) 'The Life of Saint Augustine in San Gimignano', in J. Schnaubelt and F. Van Fleteren, eds, *Augustine in Iconography: History and Legend*, 359–82. New York: Peter Lang.

Allen, Pauline (2007) 'Augustine's Commentaries on the Old Testament: A Mariological Perspective', in H. Amirav and B. H. Romeny, eds, *From Rome to Constantinople: Studies in Honour of Averil Cameron*, 137–51. Leuven, Belgium: Peeters.

Ameling, Walter (2012) '*Femina liberaliter instituta*: Some Thoughts on a Martyr's Liberal Education', in J. Bremmer and M. Formisano, eds, *Perpetua's Passions: Multidisciplinary Approaches to the* Passio Perpetuae et Felicitatis, 78–102. Oxford: Oxford University Press.

Amirav, Hagit, and Romeny, Bas ter Haar, eds (2007) *From Rome to Constantinople: Studies in Honour of Averil Cameron*. Leuven, Belgium: Peeters.

Arjava, Antti (1996) *Women and Law in Late Antiquity*. Oxford: Oxford University Press.

Atkins, E. Margaret, and Osborne, Robin, eds (2006) *Poverty in the Roman World*. Cambridge: Cambridge University Press.

Atkinson, Clarissa (1987) '"Your Servant, My Mother": The Figure of Saint Monica in the Ideology of Christian Motherhood', in C. Atkinson, C. Buchanan, and M. Miles, eds, *Immaculate and Powerful: The Female in Sacred Image and Reality*, 139–72. Wellingborough, UK: Crucible.

Atkinson, Clarissa, Buchanan, Constance, and Miles, Margaret, eds (1987) *Immaculate and Powerful: The Female in Sacred Image and Reality*. Wellingborough, UK: Crucible.

Ayres, Lewis (2004) *Nicaea and Its Legacy: An Approach to Fourth Century Trinitarian Theology*. Oxford: Oxford University Press.

Baker-Brian, Nicholas (2011) *Manichaeism: An Ancient Faith Rediscovered*. Edinburgh: T&T Clark.

Beaucamp, Joelle (1990) *Le statu de la femme à Byzance, 4e-7e siècles.* 2 vols. Paris: De Boccard.

BeDuhn, Jason (2010) *Augustine's Manichaean Dilemma: Conversion and Apostasy 373–388 CE.* Philadelphia, PA: University of Pennsylvania Press.

Birk, Stine and Poulsen, Birte, eds (2012) *Patrons and Viewers in Late Antiquity.* Aarhus, Denmark: Aarhus University Press.

Boin, Douglas (2010) 'Late Antique Ostia and a Campaign For Pious Tourism: Epitaphs for Bishop Cyriacus and Monica, Mother of Augustine', *Journal of Roman Studies* 100:195–209.

Børtnes, Jostein and Hägg, Thomas, eds (2006) *Gregory of Nazianzus: Images and Reflections.* Copenhagen, Denmark: Museum Tusculanum Press.

Boulding, Maria (1997) *The Confessions: Introduction, Translation and Notes.* Vol. 1.1, *The Works of Saint Augustine: A Translation for the 21st Century.* New York: New City Press.

Bowersock, Glen, Brown, Peter, and Grabar, Oleg, eds (1999) *Late Antiquity: A Guide to the Postclassical World.* Cambridge, MA: Harvard University Press.

Bowery, Anne-Marie (2007) 'Monica: The Feminine Face of Christ', in J. C. Stark, ed., *Feminist Interpretations of Augustine,* 69–95. University Park, PA: Penn State University Press.

Bowes, Kim (2008) *Private Worship, Public Values and Religious Change in Late Antiquity.* Cambridge, UK: Cambridge University Press.

Bowes, Kim (2010) *Houses and Society in the Later Roman Empire.* London: Duckworth.

Bowes, Kim, and Kulikowski, Michael, eds (2005) *Hispania in Late Antiquity: Current Perspectives.* Leiden, The Netherlands: Brill.

Bradley, Keith (1991) *Discovering the Roman Family.* New York: Oxford University Press.

Brakke, David, Deliyannis, Deborah, and Watts, Edward, eds (2012) *Shifting Cultural Frontiers in Late Antiquity.* Farnham, UK: Ashgate.

Bremmer, Jan, and Formisano, Marco, eds (2012) *Perpetua's Passions: Multidisciplinary Approaches to the Passio Perpetuae et Felicitatis.* Oxford: Oxford University Press.

Brown, Peter (1967, rev.ed. 2000) *Augustine of Hippo: A Biography.* London: Faber and Faber.

Brown, Peter (1972) *Religion and Society in the Age of St Augustine.* London: Faber and Faber.

Brown, Peter (1981) *The Cult of the Saints in Late Antiquity: Its Rise and Function in Latin Christianity.* Chicago: University of Chicago Press.

Brown, Peter (1988, rev. ed. 2008) *The Body and Society: Men, Women and Sexual Renunciation in Early Christianity.* New York: Columbia University Press.

Brown, Peter (1992) *Power and Persuasion in Late Antiquity.* Madison: University of Wisconsin Press.

Burns, Tom and Eadie, John, eds (2001) *Urban Centers and Rural Contexts in Late Antiquity.* East Lansing: Michigan State University Press.

Burrus, Virginia (2004) *The Sex Lives of Saints: An Erotics of Ancient Hagiography*. Philadelphia: University of Pennsylvania Press.

Burrus, Virginia (2006) 'Life after Death: The Martyrdom of Gorgonia and the Birth of Female Hagiography', in J. Børtnes and T. Hägg, eds, *Gregory of Nazianzus: Images and Reflections*, 153–70. Copenhagen, Denmark: Museum Tusculanum Press.

Burton, Philip (2001) *Augustine: The Confessions*. London: Everyman.

Burton, Philip (2005) 'The Vocabulary of the Liberal Arts in Augustine's *Confessions*', in K. Pollmann and M. Vessey, eds, *Augustine and the Disciplines: From Cassiciacum to Confessions*, 141–64. Oxford: Oxford University Press.

Burton, Philip (2007) *Language in the Confessions of Augustine*. Oxford: Oxford University Press.

Charles-Picard, Gilbert, ed. (1990) *La civilisation de l'Afrique romaine*. 2nd ed. Paris: Etudes Augustiniennes.

Cain, Andrew (2009) 'Rethinking Jerome's Portraits of Holy Women', in A. Cain and J. Lössl, eds, *Jerome of Stridon: His Life, Writings and Legacy*, 47–57. Farnham, UK: Ashgate.

Cain, Andrew (2013) *Jerome's Epitaph on Paula*. Oxford: Oxford University Press.

Cain, Andrew, and Lössl, Josef, eds (2009) *Jerome of Stridon: His Life, Writings and Legacy*. Farnham, UK: Ashgate.

Cameron, Averil (1993) *The Later Roman Empire, AD 284–430*. Cambridge, MA: Harvard University Press.

Cameron, Averil, and Garnsey, Peter, eds (1997) *The Cambridge Ancient History XII: The Late Empire, AD 337–425*. Cambridge, UK: Cambridge University Press.

Capps, Donald (1985) 'Augustine As Narcissist: Comments on Paul Rigby's "Paul Ricoeur, Freudianism, and Augustine's *Confessions*"', *Journal of the American Academy of Religion* 53.1:115–28.

Carrié, J.-M. (2004) 'Vitalité de l'industrie textile à la fin de l'antiquité', in *Antiquité Tardive* 12:13–43.

Carucci, Margherita (2007) *The Romano-African Domus: Studies in Space, Decoration, and Function*. Oxford: Archaeopress.

Clark, Elizabeth A. (1984) *The Life of Melania the Younger: Introduction, Translation, Commentary*. New York: Edwin Mellen.

Clark, Elizabeth A. (1998) 'The Lady Vanishes: Dilemmas of a Feminist Historian after the "Linguistic Turn"', *Church History* 67.1:1–31.

Clark, Elizabeth A. (1998) 'Holy Women, Holy Words: Early Christian Women, Social History, and The "Linguistic Turn"', *Journal of Early Christian Studies* 6.3:413–30.

Clark, Elizabeth A. (1999) 'Rewriting Early Christian History: Augustine's Representation of Monica', in J. Drijvers and J. Watt, eds (1999) *Portraits of Spiritual Authority*, 3–23. Leiden, The Netherlands: Brill.

Clark, Gillian (1993) *Women in Late Antiquity: Pagan and Christian Lifestyles*. Oxford: Oxford University Press.

Clark, Gillian (1994) 'The Fathers and the Children', in Diana Wood, ed. (1994) *The Church and Childhood. Papers read at the 1993 Summer Meeting and the 1994 Winter Meeting of the Ecclesiastical History Society.* Studies in Church History 31, 1–27. Oxford: Blackwell.

Clark, Gillian (1995) *Augustine: Confessions Books I–IV.* Cambridge, UK: Cambridge University Press.

Clark, Gillian (2004) *Christianity and Roman Society.* Cambridge, UK: Cambridge University Press.

Clark, Gillian (2007) 'Do Try This At Home: The Domestic Philosopher in Late Antiquity', in H. Amirav and B. H. Romeny, eds, *From Rome to Constantinople: Studies In Honour of Averil Cameron,* 153–72. Leuven, Belgium: Peeters. Reprinted in Clark 2011b.

Clark, Gillian (2008) 'Can We Talk? Augustine and the Possibility of Dialogue', in S. Goldhill, ed., *The End of Dialogue in Antiquity,* 117–34. Cambridge: Cambridge University Press.

Clark, Gillian (2011) *Late Antiquity: A Very Short Introduction.* Oxford: Oxford University Press.

Clark, Gillian (2011b) *Body and Gender, Soul and Reason in Late Antiquity.* Farnham, UK: Ashgate.

Clark, Gillian (2012) 'Philosopher: Augustine in Retirement', in M. Vessey, ed., *A Companion to Augustine,* 257–69. Chichester, UK: Wiley-Blackwell.

Clark, Gillian (2012b) 'The Ant of God: Augustine, Scripture, and Cultural Frontiers', in D. Brakke, D. Deliyannis, and E. Watts, eds, *Shifting Cultural Frontiers in Late Antiquity,* 151–63. Farnham, UK: Ashgate.

Clark, Gillian and Rajak, Tessa, eds (2002) *Philosophy and Power in the Graeco-Roman World: Essays in Honour of Miriam Griffin.* Oxford: Oxford University Press.

Clark, Patricia (1998) 'Women, Slaves and the Hierarchy of Domestic Violence', in S. Joshel and S. Murnaghan, eds, *Women and Slaves in Greco-Roman Culture,* 109–29. London: Routledge.

Clarke, Peter, and Claydon, Tony, eds (2011) *Saints and Sanctity.* Studies in Church History 47. Woodbridge, UK: Boydell and Brewer.

Conybeare, Catherine (2006) *The Irrational Augustine.* Oxford: Oxford University Press.

Cooper, Kate (2012) 'Love and Belonging, Loss and Betrayal in the *Confessions*', in M. Vessey, ed., *A Companion to Augustine,* 69–86. Chichester, UK: Wiley-Blackwell.

Courcelle, Jeanne, and Courcelle, Pierre (1965–1991) 5 vols. *Iconographie de Saint Augustin.* Paris: Institut des Études Augustiniennes.

Courcelle, Pierre (1963) *Les Confessions de Saint Augustin dans la tradition littéraire.* Paris: Institut des Études Augustiniennes.

Cox, Patricia (1983) *Biography in Late Antiquity: A Quest for the Holy Man.* Berkeley: University of California Press.

Cribiore, Raffaella (2001) *Gymnastics of the Mind*. Princeton, NJ: Princeton University Press.

Croom, Alexandra (2010) *Roman Clothing and Fashion*. 2nd ed. Stroud, UK: Amberley.

Croom, Alexandra (2011) *Running the Roman Home*. Stroud, UK: The History Press.

Daley, Brian (2006) *Gregory of Nazianzus*. London: Routledge.

Dal Santo, Matthew (2012) *Debating the Saints' Cult in the Age of Gregory the Great*. Oxford: Oxford University Press.

Davis, Stephen (2001) *The Cult of St Thecla: A Tradition of Women's Piety in Late Antiquity*. Oxford: Oxford University Press.

De Bruyn, Theodore (1999) 'Flogging a Son: The Emergence of the *pater flagellans* in Latin Christian Discourse', *Journal of Early Christian Studies* 7.2:264–73.

De Bruyn, Theodore, and Dijkstra, Jitse (2011) 'Greek Amulets and Formularies from Egypt Containing Christian Elements: A Checklist of Papyri, Parchments, Ostraka and Tablets', *Bulletin of the American Society of Papyrologists* 48:163–216.

De Ligt, Luuk (1993) *Fairs and Markets in the Roman Empire*. Amsterdam: J. C. Gieben.

Dickey, Eleanor (2002) *Latin Forms of Address: from Plautus to Apuleius*. Oxford: Oxford University Press.

Dixon, Suzanne (1988) *The Roman Mother*. London: Routledge.

Dodaro, Robert, and Lawless, George, eds (2000) *Augustine and his Critics: Essays In Honour of Gerald Bonner*. London and New York: Routledge.

Dossey, Leslie (2008) 'Wife-Beating and Manliness in Late Antiquity', *Past and Present* 199.1: 3–40.

Dossey, Leslie (2010) *Peasant and Empire in Christian North Africa*. Berkeley: University of California Press.

Dossey, Leslie (2012) 'Sleeping Arrangements and Private Space: A Cultural Approach to the Subdivision of Late Antique Houses', in D. Brakke, D. Deliyannis and D. Watts, eds, *Shifting Cultural Frontiers in Late Antiquity*, 181–97. Farnham, UK: Ashgate.

Drake, H. A., ed. (2006) *Violence in Late Antiquity: Perceptions and Practices*. Farnham, UK: Ashgate.

Drijvers, Jan and Watt, John, eds (1999) *Portraits of Spiritual Authority*. Leiden, The Netherlands: Brill.

Elm, Susanna (1994) *Virgins of God: The Making of Asceticism in Late Antiquity*. Oxford: Oxford University Press.

Elm, Susanna (2006) 'Gregory's Women: Creating a Philosopher's Family', in J. Børtnes and T. Hägg, eds, *Gregory of Nazianzus: Images and Reflections*, 171–91. Copenhagen, Denmark: Museum Tusculanum Press.

Elm, Susanna (2009) 'Family Men: Masculinity and Philosophy in Late Antiquity', in P. Rousseau and E. Papoutsakis, eds, *Transformations of Late Antiquity*, 279–301. Farnham, UK: Ashgate.

Evans Grubbs, Judith (1995) *Law and Family in Late Antiquity: The Emperor Constantine's Marriage Legislation*. Oxford: Clarendon.

Fagan, Garrett (1999) *Bathing in Public in the Roman World*. Ann Arbor: University of Michigan Press.

Fentress, Elizabeth (1999) 'Romanizing the Berbers', *Past and Present* 190:3–33.

Finn, Richard (2009) *Asceticism in the Graeco-Roman World*. Cambridge, UK: Cambridge University Press.

Fitzgerald, Allan, ed. (1999) *Augustine Through the Ages: An Encyclopedia*. Grand Rapids, MI: Eerdmans.

Fögen, Thorsten, ed. (2009) *Tears in the Graeco-Roman World*. Berlin: De Gruyter.

Fowden, Garth (1997) 'Polytheist Religion and Philosophy', in A. Cameron and P. Garnsey, eds, *The Cambridge Ancient History XII: The Late Empire*, AD 337–425, 538–60. Cambridge, UK: Cambridge University Press.

Foxhall, Lin (2013) *Studying Gender in Classical Antiquity*. Cambridge, UK: Cambridge University Press.

Frend, W.H.C. (1952) *The Donatist Church*. Oxford: Clarendon.

Garnsey, Peter (1970) *Social Status and Legal Privilege in the Roman Empire*. Oxford: Oxford University Press.

Garnsey, Peter (1997) *Ideas of Slavery from Aristotle to Augustine*. Cambridge, UK: Cambridge University Press.

Garnsey, Peter (1997) 'Sons, Slaves—and Christians', in B. Rawson and P. Weaver, eds, *The Roman Family: Status, Sentiment, Space*, 101–21. Oxford: Clarendon.

Gill, Meredith J. (1999) 'Remember Me at the Altar of the Lord: Saint Monica's Gift to Rome', in J. Schnaubelt and F. Van Fleteren, eds, *Augustine in Iconography: History And Legend*, 550–76. New York: Peter Lang.

Gill, Meredith J. (2005) *Augustine in the Italian Renaissance*. Cambridge, UK: Cambridge University Press.

Gillette, Gertrude (2013) 'Anger and Community in the *Rule* of Augustine', in M. Vinzent, ed., *Studia Patristica* LXX: 'St. Augustine and His Opponents', 591–600. Leuven, Belgium: Peeters.

Gillis, C. and Nosch, M.-L., eds (2007) *Ancient Textiles: Production, Craft and Society*. Oxford: Oxbow.

Goldhill, Simon, ed. (2008) *The End of Dialogue in Antiquity*. Cambridge, UK: Cambridge University Press.

Green, Roger (1995) 'Proba's Cento: Its Date, Purpose and Reception', *Classical Quarterly* 45.2:551–63.

Guédon, Stéphanie (2010) *Le voyage dans l'Afrique romaine*. Pessac, France: Ausonius.

Hägg, Tomas (2006) 'Playing with Expectations: Gregory's Funeral Orations on His Brother, Sister and Father', in J. Børtnes and T. Hägg, eds, *Gregory of Nazianzus: Images and Reflections*, 133–51. Copenhagen: Museum Tusculanum Press.

Hägg, Tomas (2012) *The Art of Biography in Antiquity*. Cambridge, UK: Cambridge University Press.

Hägg, Tomas, and Rousseau, Philip, eds (2000) *Greek Biography and Panegyric in Late Antiquity*. Berkeley: University of California Press.

Halperin, David (1990) *One Hundred Years of Homosexuality*. London: Routledge.

Harlow, Mary, ed. (2012) *Dress and Identity*. Oxford: Archaeopress.

Harmless, William (1999), 'Baptism', in Fitzgerald, ed., *Augustine Through the Ages: An Encyclopedia*, 84–91. Grand Rapids, MI: Eerdmans.

Harries, Jill (1999) *Law and Empire in Late Antiquity*. Cambridge: Cambridge University Press.

Harris, W.V. (2004) *Restraining Rage: The Ideology of Anger Control in Classical Antiquity*. Cambridge, MA: Harvard University Press.

Harrison, Carol (2000) *Augustine: Christian Truth and Fractured Humanity*. Oxford: Oxford University Press.

Head, Thomas (2001) *Medieval Hagiography. An Anthology*. New York: Routledge.

Hemelrijk, Emily (2012) 'Public Roles for Women in the Cities of the Latin West', in S. James and S. Dillon, eds, *A Companion to Women in the Ancient World*, 478–90. Malden, MA: Wiley-Blackwell.

Hermanowicz, Erika (2008) *Possidius of Calama: A Study of the North African Episcopate*. Oxford: Oxford University Press.

Hobson, Barry (2009) Latrinae et foricae: *Toilets in the Roman World*. London: Duckworth.

Howard-Johnston, James, and Hayward, Paul Antony, eds (1999) *The Cult of Saints in Late Antiquity and the Early Middle Ages*. Oxford: Oxford University Press.

Howard-Johnston, James (1999) 'Introduction', in J. Howard-Johnston and P. Hayward, ibid., 1–24.

Humfress, Caroline (2006) 'Poverty and Roman Law', in E.M. Atkins and R. Osborne, eds, *Poverty in the Roman World*, 183–203. Cambridge, UK: Cambridge University Press.

Humfress, Caroline (2012) 'Controversialist: Augustine in Combat', in M. Vessey, ed., *A Companion to Augustine*, 323–35. Chichester, UK: Wiley-Blackwell.

Hunter, David (2003) 'Augustine and the Making of Marriage in Roman North Africa', *Journal of Early Christian Studies* 11.1:63–85.

Hunter, David (2007) *Marriage, Celibacy and Heresy in Ancient Christianity*. Oxford: Oxford University Press.

James, Sharon and Dillon, Sheila. eds (2012) *A Companion to Women in the Ancient World*. Malden, MA: Wiley-Blackwell.

Jensen, Robin (2013) 'Christianity in Roman Africa', in M. Salzman, M. Sweeney, and W. Adler, eds, *The Cambridge History of Religions in the Ancient World*, Vol. 2, 264–91. Cambridge, UK: Cambridge University Press.

Jones, A.H.M. (1964) *The Later Roman Empire 284–602*. 3 vols. Oxford: Blackwell.

Joshel, Sandra and Murnaghan, Sheila, eds (1998) *Women and Slaves in Greco-Roman Culture*. London: Routledge.

Kaster, Robert (1988) *Guardians of Language: The Grammarian and Society in Late Antiquity.*

Kelly, Christopher (2012) 'Political History: The Later Roman Empire', in M. Vessey, ed., *A Companion to Augustine*, 11–23. Chichester, UK: Wiley-Blackwell.

Kenney, John Peter (2005) *The Mysticism of Saint Augustine: Rereading the Confessions.* New York: Routledge.

Klingshirn, William E. (2007) 'Comer y beber con los muertos: Mónnica de Tagaste y la adivinación de los sueños bereber', *Augustinus* 52.4:127–31.

Klingshirn, William E. (2012) 'Cultural Geography: Roman North Africa', in M. Vessey, ed., *A Companion to Augustine*, 11–23. Chichester, UK: Wiley-Blackwell.

König, Jason (2008) 'Sympotic Dialogue in the First to Fifth Centuries CE', in S. Goldhill ed., *The End of Dialogue in Antiquity*, 85–113. Cambridge, UK: Cambridge University Press.

Lancel, Serge, translation by Antonia Nevill (2002) *St. Augustine*. London: SCM.

Lawless, George (1987) *Augustine of Hippo and His Monastic Rule*. Oxford: Oxford University Press.

Lefkowitz, Mary and Fant, Maureen, eds (2005) *Women's Life in Greece and Rome*. 3rd ed. London: Duckworth.

LeMoine, Fannie (1996) 'Jerome's Gift to Women Readers', in R. Mathisen and H. Sivan, eds, *Shifting Frontiers in Late Antiquity*, 230–41. Aldershot, UK: Ashgate.

Lepelley, Claude (1978) *Les cités de l'Afrique romaine au bas-empire*. 2 vols. Paris: Etudes Augustiniennes.

Levick, Barbara (2002) 'Women, Power and Philosophy at Rome and Beyond', in G. Clark and T. Rajak, eds, *Philosophy and Power in the Graeco-Roman World: Essays in Honour of Miriam Griffin*, 133–55. Oxford: Oxford University Press.

Liebeschuetz, J.H.W.G. (2005) *Ambrose of Milan: Political Letters and Speeches.* Liverpool: Liverpool University Press.

Liebeschuetz, J.H.W.G. (2011) *Ambrose and John Chrysostom: Clerics between Desert and Empire*. Oxford: Oxford University Press.

Lindsay, Hugh (2004) 'The *laudatio Murdiae*: Its Content and Significance', *Latomus* 63:88–97.

Long, Alex (2008) 'Plato's Dialogues and a Common Rationale for Dialogue Form', in S. Goldhill, ed., *The End of Dialogue in Antiquity*, 45–59. Cambridge, UK: Cambridge University Press.

Louth, Andrew (2011), 'Holiness and Sanctity in the Early Church'. in P. Clarke and T. Claydon, eds, *Saints and Sanctity*, 1–18. Studies in Church History 47. Woodbridge, UK: Boydell and Brewer.

Lovén, Lena Larsson (2007), 'Wool Work as a Gender Symbol in Ancient Rome', in C. Gillis and M.-L. Nosch, eds, *Ancient Textiles: Production, Craft and Society*, 229–36. Oxford: Oxbow.

Ludlow, Morwenna (2007) *Gregory of Nyssa: Ancient and (Post)modern*. Oxford: Oxford University Press.

MacCormack, Sabine (1998) *The Shadows of Poetry: Vergil in the Mind of Augustine*. Berkeley: University of California Press.

Maguire, Henry (1999) 'The Good Life', in G. Bowersock, P. Brown, and O. Grabar, eds, *Late Antiquity: A Guide to the Postclassical World*, 238–57. Cambridge, MA: Harvard University Press.

Maraval, Pierre (1971) *Grégoire de Nysse: Vie de Sainte Macrine*. Sources Chrétiennes 178. Paris: Editions du Cerf.

Martin, Elena (2011), 'Commemoration, Representation and Interpretation: Augustine of Hippo's Depictions of the Martyrs', in P. Clarke and T. Claydon, eds, *Saints and Sanctity*, 29–40. Studies in Church History 47. Woodbridge, UK: Boydell and Brewer..

Mathisen, Ralph, and Sivan, Hagith, eds (1996) *Shifting Frontiers in Late Antiquity*. Aldershot, UK: Ashgate.

Matter, E. Ann (2000) 'Christ, God and Woman in the Thought of St Augustine', in R. Dodaro and G. Lawless, eds, *Augustine and his Critics: Essays In Honour of Gerald Bonner*, 164–75. London and New York: Routledge

Mattingly, David, and Hitchner, Bruce (1995) 'Roman Africa: An Archaeological Review', *Journal of Roman Studies* 85:165–213.

Mattingly, David, and Salmon, John, eds (2001) *Economies beyond Agriculture in the Classical World*. London: Routledge.

McAuslan, Ian, and Walcot, Peter, eds (1996) *Women in Antiquity: Greece and Rome Studies III*. Oxford: Oxford University Press.

McLynn, Neil (1994) *Ambrose of Milan: Church and Court in a Christian Capital*. Berkeley: University of California Press.

McLynn, Neil (2005) '*Genere Hispanus*: Theodosius, Spain, and Nicene Orthodoxy', in K. Bowes and M. Kulikowski, eds, *Hispania in Late Antiquity: Current Perspectives*, 77–120. Leiden, The Netherlands: Brill.

McLynn, Neil (2012) 'Administrator: Augustine in His Diocese', in M. Vessey, ed., *A Companion to Augustine*, 310–22. Chichester, UK: Wiley-Blackwell.

McWilliam, Joanne (1990) 'The Cassiciacum Autobiography', *Studia Patristica* 18.4:14–43.

Millar, Fergus (1968) 'Local Cultures in the Roman Empire: Libyan, Punic and Latin in Roman Africa', *Journal of Roman Studies* 58.1–2:126–34.

Miller, Judith (2007) 'To Remember Self, To Remember God', in J. C. Stark, , ed., *Feminist Interpretations of Augustine*, 243–79. University Park, PA: Penn State University Press.

Miller, Patricia Cox (2000) 'Strategies of Representation in Collective Biography: Constructing the Subject as Holy', in T. Hägg and P. Rousseau, eds, *Greek Biography and Panegyric in Late Antiquity*, 209–54. Berkeley: University of California Press.

Mitchell, Stephen and Van Nuffelen, Peter, eds (2010) *One God: Pagan Monotheism in the Roman Empire*. Cambridge, UK: Cambridge University Press.

Mitchell, Stephen (2010) 'Further Thoughts on the Cult of Theos Hypsistos', in S. Mitchell and P. Van Nuffelen, ibid., 167–208.

Nevett, Lisa (2010) *Domestic Space in Classical Antiquity*. Cambridge, UK: Cambridge University Press.

O'Daly, Gerard (1999) *Augustine's City of God: A Reader's Guide*. Oxford: Oxford University Press.

O'Donnell, James (1992) *Augustine: Confessions.* 3 vols. Oxford: Oxford University Press.

O'Donnell, James (2005) *Augustine, Sinner And Saint: a New Biography.* London: Profile Books.

Olson, Linda and Kerby-Fulton, Kathryn, eds (2005) *Voices in Dialogue: Reading Women in the Middle Ages*. Notre Dame, IN: University of Notre Dame Press.

Pelling, Christopher, ed. (1990) *Characterization and Individuality in Greek Literature*. Oxford: Clarendon.

Pelling, Christopher (1990) 'Childhood and Personality in Greek Biography', in C. Pelling, ibid., 213–44.

Parkes, M.B. (1992) *Pause and Effect: An Introduction to the History of Punctuation in the West*. Aldershot, UK: Scolar Press.

Perler, Othmar (1969) *Les Voyages de Saint Augustin*. Paris: Institut des Etudes Augustiniennes.

Pollmann, Karla (2004) 'Sex and Salvation in the Virgilian Cento of the Fourth Century', in Roger Rees, ed., *Romane Memento. Virgil in the Fourth Century*, 79–96. London: Duckworth.

Pollmann, Karla, and Vessey, Mark, eds (2005) *Augustine and the Disciplines: From Cassiciacum to Confessions*. Oxford: Oxford University Press.

Pollmann, Karla, and Otten, Willemien, eds (2013) *Oxford Guide to the Historical Reception of Augustine*. 3 vols. Oxford: Oxford University Press.

Poque, Suzanne (1984) *Le langage symbolique dans la prédication d'Augustin d'Hippone: Images héroïques*. 2 vols. Paris: Etudes Augustiniennes.

Poulsen, Birte (2012) 'Patrons and Viewers: Reading Mosaics In Late Antiquity', in S. Birk and B. Poulsen, eds, *Patrons and Viewers in Late Antiquity*, 167–87. Aarhus, Denmark: Aarhus University Press.

Power, Kim (1996) *Veiled Desire: Augustine's Writings on Women*. New York: Continuum.

Ramelli, Ilaria, translated by David Konstan. (2009) *Hierocles the Stoic: Elements of Ethics, Fragments, and Excerpts*. Atlanta: Society of Biblical Literature.

Rapp, Claudia (2005) *Holy Bishops in Late Antiquity*. Berkeley: University of California Press.

Rawson, Beryl, and Weaver, Paul, eds (1997) *The Roman Family: Status, Sentiment, Space*. Oxford: Clarendon Press.

Rebillard, Eric (1999), 'Punic', in G. Bowersock, P. Brown and O. Grabar, eds, *Late Antiquity: A Guide to the Postclassical World*, 656–7. Cambridge, MA: Harvard University Press.

Rebillard, Eric, translated by Elizabeth Trapnell Rawlings and Jeanne Routier-Pucci (2009) *The Care of the Dead in Late Antiquity*. Ithaca, NY: Cornell University Press.

Rebillard, Eric (2012) 'Religious Sociology: Being Christian', in M. Vessey, ed., *A Companion to Augustine*, 40–53. Chichester, UK: Wiley-Blackwell.

Rebillard, Eric (2013) 'William Hugh Clifford Frend (1916–2005): The Legacy of *The Donatist Church*', in M. Vinzent, ed., *Studia Patristica* LIII: 'Former Directors', 55–71. Leuven, Belgium: Peeters.

Rees, Roger, ed. (2004) *Romane Memento: Virgil in the Fourth Century*. London: Duckworth.

Rigby, Paul (1985) 'Paul Ricoeur, Freudianism, and Augustine's *Confessions*', *Journal of the American Academy of Religion* 53.1: 93–114.

Riggs, David (2001) 'The Continuity of Paganism between the Cities and Countryside of Late Roman Africa', in T. Burns and J. Eadie, eds, *Urban Centers and Rural Contexts in Late Antiquity*, 285–300. East Lansing: Michigan State University Press.

Riggs, David (2006) 'Christianizing the Rural Communities of Late Roman Africa,' in H.A. Drake, ed., *Violence in Late Antiquity: Perceptions and Practices*, 297–308. Farnham, UK: Ashgate.

Rousseau, Philip, and Papoutsakis, Emanuel, eds (2009) *Transformations of Late Antiquity*. Farnham, UK: Ashgate.

Rubenson, Samuel (2000), 'Philosophy and Simplicity: The Problem of Classical Education in Early Christian Biography', in T. Hägg and P. Rousseau, eds, *Greek Biography and Panegyric in Late Antiquity*, 110–39. Berkeley: University of California Press.

Saak, E. L. (2012a) *Creating Augustine*. Oxford: Oxford University Press.

Saak, E. L. (2012b) 'Augustine in the Western Middle Ages to the Reformation', in M. Vessey, ed., *A Companion to Augustine*, 465–77. Chichester, UK: Wiley-Blackwell.

Salzman, Michele, Sweeney, Marvin, and Adler, William, eds (2013) *The Cambridge History of Religions in the Ancient World*. 2 vols. Cambridge: Cambridge University Press.

Schnaubelt, Joseph, and Van Fleteren, Frederick, eds (1999) *Augustine in Iconography: History And Legend*. New York: Peter Lang.

Schofield, Malcolm (2008) 'Ciceronian Dialogue', in S. Goldhill, ed., *The End of Dialogue in Antiquity*, 63–84. Cambridge, UK: Cambridge University Press.

Schrodt, Paul (1999) 'Saints', in A. Fitzgerald, ed., *Augustine Through the Ages: An Encyclopedia*, 747–9. Grand Rapids, MI: Eerdmans.

Schroeder, Joy (2004) 'John Chrysostom's Critique of Spousal Violence', *Journal of Early Christian Studies* 12.4: 413–42.

Shanzer, Danuta (2002) '*Avulsa a latere meo*: Augustine's Spare Rib—Augustine, *Confessions* 6.15.25', *Journal of Roman Studies* 92:157–76.

Shaw, Brent D. (1984) 'Latin Funerary Epigraphy and Family Life in the Later Roman Empire', *Historia* 33.4:457–97.

Shaw, Brent D. (1987) 'The Family in Late Antiquity: The Experience of Augustine', *Past & Present* 115:3–51.

Shaw, Brent D. (1987b) 'The Age of Roman Girls At Marriage: Some Reconsiderations', *Journal of Roman Studies* 77:30–46.

Shaw, Brent D. (1993) 'Perpetua's Passion', *Past and Present* 139:3–45.

Shaw, Brent D. (2011) *Sacred Violence: African Christians and Sectarian Hatred in the Age of Augustine*. Cambridge, UK: Cambridge University Press.

Shaw, Brent D. (2013) 'Cult and Belief in Punic and Roman Africa', in M. Salzman, M. Sweeney, and W. Adler, eds, *The Cambridge History of Religions in the Ancient World*, 235–63. 2 vols. Cambridge: Cambridge University Press

Silvas, Anna (2005) *The Asketikon of St Basil the Great*. Oxford: Oxford University Press.

Stark, Judith Chelius, ed. (2007) *Feminist Interpretations of Augustine*. University Park, PA: Penn State University Press.

Thébert, Yvon (1987), 'Private Life and Domestic Architecture in Roman Africa', in P. Veyne, ed., *A History of Private Life I: From Pagan Rome to Byzantium*, 319–409. Cambridge, MA: Belknap.

Thébert, Yvon (2005) *Thermes romains de l'Afrique du Nord*. Rome: EFR.

Tougher, Shaun (2007) *Julian the Apostate*. Edinburgh: Edinburgh University Press.

Trout, Dennis (1999) *Paulinus of Nola: Life, Letters and Poems*. Berkeley: University of California Press.

Trout, Dennis (2013) '*Fecit ad astra viam*: Daughters, Wives, and the Metrical Epitaphs of Late Ancient Rome', *Journal of Early Christian Studies* 21:1–25.

Van Dam, Raymond (2003) *Families and Friends in Late Roman Cappadocia*. Philadelphia: University of Pennsylvania Press.

Van Fleteren, Frederick (1999) 'Babylon', in Fitzgerald, ed., *Augustine Through the Ages: An Encyclopedia*, 83–4. Grand Rapids, MI: Eerdmans.

Van Fleteren, Frederick (1999b) 'Jerusalem', in A. Fitzgerald, ibid., 462–3.

Van der Meer, F. (English translation, 1961) *Augustine the Bishop: The Life and Work of a Father of the Church*. London and New York: Sheed and Ward:.

Van Oort, Johannes (2012) 'Augustine and the Books of the Manichaeans', in M. Vessey, ed., *A Companion to Augustine*, 188–99. Chichester, UK: Wiley-Blackwell.

Vessey, Mark (2005) 'Response to Catherine Conybeare: Women Of Letters?', in L. Olson and K. Kerby-Fulton, eds, *Voices in Dialogue: Reading Women in the Middle Ages*, 73–96. Notre Dame, IN: University of Notre Dame Press.

Vessey, Mark, ed. (2012) *A Companion to Augustine*. Chichester, UK: Wiley-Blackwell.

Veyne, Paul, ed. (1987) *A History of Private Life I: From Pagan Rome to Byzantium*. Cambridge, MA: Belknap.

Vinzent, Markus, ed. (2013a) *Studia Patristica* LIII: 'Former Directors'. *Papers presented at the Sixteenth International Conference on Patristic Studies held in Oxford 2011*. Leuven, Belgium: Peeters.

Vinzent, Markus, ed. (2013b) *Studia Patristica* LXX: '*St. Augustine and His Opponents*'. *Vol. 18. Papers presented at the Sixteenth International Conference on Patristic Studies held in Oxford 2011* Leuven, Belgium: Peeters.

Vössing, Konrad and Stone, Harold (2013) 'Cult of Augustine', in K. Pollmann and W. Otten, eds, *Oxford Guide to the Historical Reception of Augustine*, Vol. 2, 846–9. Oxford: Oxford University Press..

Walcot, Peter (1987, reprinted 1996) 'Plato's Mother and Other Terrible Women', in I. McAuslan and P. Walcot, eds, *Women in Antiquity: Greece and Rome Studies III*, 114–33. Oxford: Oxford University Press.

Wallis, Faith (1988, reprinted with corrections 2004) *Bede: The Reckoning of Time. Translated with Introduction, Notes and Commentary*. Liverpool: Liverpool University Press.

Watts, Edward (2006) *City and School in Late Antique Athens and Alexandria*. Berkeley: University of California Press.

Webb, Diana (1980) 'Eloquence and Education: A Humanist Approach to Hagiography', *Journal of Ecclesiastical History* 31.1:19–39.

West, Rebecca (1933) *St. Augustine*. London: P. Davies.

White, Carolinne (2005) *Gregory of Nazianzus: Autobiographical Poems*. Cambridge, UK: Cambridge University Press.

White, Carolinne (2010) *Lives of Roman Christian Women*. New York: Penguin.

Whittaker, C.R. (1999) 'Berber', in G. Bowersock, P. Brown, and O. Grabar, eds, *Late Antiquity: A Guide to the Postclassical World*, 340–1. Cambridge, MA: Harvard University Press.

Wilkinson, John (1971) *Egeria's Travels*. London: S.P.C.K.

Wilkinson, Kevin (2012a) 'The Elder Melania's Missing Decade', *Journal of Late Antiquity* 5.1:166–84.

Wilkinson, Kevin (2012b) 'Dedicated Widows in *Codex Theodosianus* 9.25?', *Journal of Early Christian Studies* 20.1:141–66.

Williams, Rowan (2000) 'Insubstantial Evil', in R. Dodaro and G. Lawless, eds, *Augustine and his Critics: Essays in Honour of Gerald Bonner*, 105–23. London and New York: Routledge.

Williams, Rowan, and Chittister, Joan (2010) *For All That Has Been, Thanks: Growing a Sense of Gratitude*. London: Canterbury Press Norwich.

Wills, Garry (2011) *Augustine's Confessions: A Biography*. Princeton: Princeton University Press.

Wilson, Andrew (2001) 'Timgad and Textile Production' in D. Mattingly and J. Salmon, eds, *Economies beyond Agriculture in the Classical World*, 271–96. London: Routledge.

Wimbush, Vincent, and Valantasis, Richard (1990) *Ascetic Behavior in Greco-Roman Antiquity: A Sourcebook.* Minneapolis, MN: Fortress.

Wood, Diana, ed. (1994) *The Church and Childhood. Papers read at the 1993 Summer Meeting and the 1994 Winter Meeting of the Ecclesiastical History Society.* Studies in Church History 31. Oxford: Blackwell.

Index

Nicaea, council of 19 n. 53, 119
Nonna, mother of Gregory of
    Nazianzus 154–5, 159

original sin 174–5
Ostia, in civil war 17
    inscription commemorates
        Monica 164–5
    mystical experience at 113–4

pagan, meaning of 122–3
Patricius, father of Augustine 8–9, 43,
    46–8, 121, 172, 175–6
Paula, ascetic widow 90, 159–60
    Jerome on 155
Paulinus, bishop of Nola 28, 147
pauper, meaning of 45
Pavia, tomb of Augustine at 166–7
Perpetua, martyr 9, 84–5
Plato, model for philosophical
    dialogues 87–8
Plotinus, philosopher 115
Porphyry, philosopher
    his wife Marcella 92
    on union with divine 115
Possidius, author of *Life of Augustine*
    9, 17
pregnancy 64–5, 174–5
property
    Monica's 11–12, 48
    renunciation of 45–6
prostitutes 61–2, 173
psychological interpretations of
    Monica 14, 170–5
Punic language 127

relics 148
    of Monica 165, 168–9
rhetoric, taught by Augustine 16–17, 97
    can be learned informally 84
Romanianus, benefactor of
    Augustine 11, 37, 48, 87
Rusticus, cousin of Augustine 87,
    97–9, 102

sacrifice to gods of Rome 121–4
saint, definition 151–2
    saints intercede for the living 147–8

sea travel 15, 28
sisters, not mentioned 9–10
slave, wife as 58–9, 67–72, 75–6
slaves, as sexual partners 62, 173–4
    tasks in household 24–5, 49, 70
Sosipatra, philosopher 94–5
soul after death 149–52
space, domestic 42–45
speech, women's 84–6
subordination
    in household 66
    of women to men 72–3
Symmachus, prefect of Rome
    on religion 141
    on weaving 54

taxation 45–6
tears, cultural significance 14–15
    Monica's 29, 169–70
temples to gods of Rome
    as artistic heritage 124
    as meeting places 42, 125
textiles 50–4
Thagaste, Monica's home town 36–7
theatre, danger to Christians 124–5, 132
Theodorus, dedicatee of *de beata vita* 96–7
Theodosian Code 120
Theodosius I, emperor 17, 119–20, 122
Timgad, market town 36, 53
tombs, offerings at 26, 128
transport 38
Trygetius, student of Augustine 87, 99,
    101–2, 104–7

violence, domestic 59–61, 79
Virgil
    Augustine reads with students 96
    Augustine's allusions to 8, 28–30
    school text 88
"vulgar" Latin 89

water supply 41
widows
    clothing of 56–7
    as legal guardians 12
    need help 12
wool-work. *See* textiles
writings by women 84–5